The Power of Projections: How Maps Reflect Global Politics and History

ARTHUR JAY KLINGHOFFER

Foreword by Harvey Sicherman

Westport, Connecticut
London

Library of Congress Cataloging-in-Publication Data

Klinghoffer, Arthur Jay, 1941–
    The power of projections : how maps reflect global politics and history/
Arthur Jay Klinghoffer.
        p.   cm.
    Includes bibliographical references and index.
    ISBN 0–275–99135–0
    1. Cartography—History.   I. Title.
    GA201.K54   2006
    912—dc22   2006001247

British Library Cataloguing in Publication Data is available.

Library of Congress Catalog Card Number: 2006001247
ISBN: 0–275–99135–0

First published in 2006

Praeger Publishers, 88 Post Road West, Westport, CT 06881
An imprint of Greenwood Publishing Group, Inc.
www.praeger.com

Printed in the United States of America

The paper used in this book complies with the
Permanent Paper Standard issued by the National
Information Standards Organization (Z39.48–1984).

10 9 8 7 6 5 4 3 2 1

Dedicated to my late parents, Sidney and Libby, for introducing me to the world, and for telling me that if I continued digging with my plastic shovel I would eventually reach China.

Contents

THE CARTOGRAPHICAL REVOLUTION

Maps

Acknowledgments

The author would like to thank Michael Siegel and the Rutgers Cartography Laboratory for preparing the maps for this book, and the Rutgers Research Council for funding this project.

Foreword

In June of 2001, it was my privilege to deliver the Robert Strausz-Hupé Lecture of the Foreign Policy Research Institute, named in honor of its founder. I titled it, "Does Geography Still Matter?" Strausz-Hupé, then ninety-eight, was pleased to hear again of the verities he had sought to inculcate in Americans a half-century earlier when he pioneered the academic study of geopolitics.

That was the year when the U.S. Naval War College, home to Admiral Mahan, the great 19th Century American advocate of geopolitical thinking, ran a conference called, "The Revival of Geopolitics." And only a few months later, on September 11, 2001, Americans were violently reintroduced into a world they thought had been superseded by the end of the Cold War. Before long, we would become more familiar than we cared to be with the rugged features of the Afghan landscape and then not much later, the contours of Iraq, ancient Mesopotamia.

The teaching of geography as a prerequisite to understanding our world is so sensible that the neglect of it in American schools and society can only be described as stupefying. Yet, as Strausz-Hupé wrote me, thinking about the subject is still foreign to the American experience. Much of this can be traced to the intellectual origins of geopolitics, or geography applied to international relations.

Geography, a supposedly scientific study, got tangled up in the 19th Century with two sets of ideas, neither liked by Americans. The first, the European school, harnessed geography to the service of racial politics that justified imperial expansion. It culminated in the Haushofer school that, exploited by Hitler and Mussolini, rationalized the overturning of the European Balance of Power to favor Nazi and Fascist ambitions.

The second, the Anglo-Saxon school, found in Admiral Mahan, Sir Halford Mackinder, and Professors Nicholas Spykman and Robert Strausz-Hupé, analyzed geography to defend the Balance of Power. This school's most influential practitioners were Theodore Roosevelt and Franklin Roosevelt, the latter going so far as to install his own map room in the White House. Balance of Power geopolitics justified American naval expansion and a permanent role for the United States in sustaining a world order favorable to the democracies.

Neither of these schools, however, suited American popular tastes. We did not like so-called "power politics." America was better than that, so President Wilson reminded us, and justified U.S. entry into World War I by promising a new international order that would be free of the amoral tactics of the old, failed balance of power. In 1945, the U.N. was established by FDR partly on the same grounds. Thus, Americans saw geopolitics and the study of geography as doctrines for bad times and the darker side of humanity.

While the Cold War sustained some interest in the topic, American schools gradually abandoned geography (and geopolitics) at the college level. Predictably, when the Cold War ended, interest in geography almost vanished. The reigning ideas of the nineties all proclaimed geopolitics to be obsolete. Globalization transcended borders while technology overcame limits. American foreign policy and international relations were taught at leading universities without reference to maps. Theory and transcendent concepts were the preferred tools to understand the new era.

Events even during the nineties, however, revived the importance of geographical study. Conflicts in the Balkans and the Middle East could not be understood without it. Asia's economic crisis in 1997 demonstrated that even international capital had a preferred geography, namely, those places where investments were less at risk. Finally, the war on terrorism could hardly be followed much less conducted without reference to geography and history. The very concept of a "Caliphate" advocated by the Jihadis such as Osama bin Laden, for example, had specific geographical references, including, among other places, the Iberian Peninsula (medieval Andalusia, modern-day Spain).

The study of geography has therefore reemerged as a critical tool not only for popular understanding but also statecraft itself. This is all for the better. The task now is to convert new interest into a permanent habit of study.

In doing so, friends of geography must avoid excessive claims. Geography offers crucial insights but not the only insights. And the study of geography, certainly as reflected in maps and geopolitical theories, can be fraught with dogma and propaganda.

Even classic geopoliticians were not immune from these dangers. Admiral Mahan, for example, drew most of his lessons about sea power from the age of sail, not steam. Sir Halford Mackinder's "heartland" had to be adjusted steadily westward lest his pivot of history become the largely barren steppes of Central Asia. FDR's attempt on the eve of World War II to incorporate Greenland and Iceland into the Western Hemisphere, hence protected by the Monroe Doctrine, makes comic reading.

The use of geography for propaganda purposes is equally instructive. 19th Century British Prime Minister Lord Salisbury, so the story goes, was constantly beset by British MPs proving—by use of Mercator projection maps—that the Suez Canal was just a thumb's length from the Straits at Istanbul, the better to justify British opposition to Russian pressure on the Ottoman Empire in the Balkans. And in our times, a mere glance at the variety of images available to depict the Arab-Israeli conflict over the much promised—and very much over mapped—Holy Land, will establish the point.

Precisely because of the importance of geography to international relations and the pitfalls in studying it, Professor Arthur Klinghoffer's book is to be applauded. The reader will find here a real passion for the subject tempered by a broad understanding of how, and how not to use it. He covers the classics; explains the scientific changes in cartography; and has a keen eye for propaganda. In short, the reader will find the book an indispensable guide to the geographical analysis of international politics. Although still foreign to our thinking, unless "we do the map," we shall not succeed in securing our liberty and prosperity in the 21st Century.

Harvey Sicherman
President of the Foreign Policy Research Institute

Introduction

It's time to start our journey into the world of maps, a virtual odyssey through the contours of terrestrial space. All we need to bring along is our curiosity as we expand our minds and spur our creativity by noticing relationships that we had never considered previously.[1] There will certainly be a visual component, and a conceptual one will also be evident since mapping is a schema that may be applied to the brain, genome, emotions, literature or cyberspace in addition to continents, mountains, and coastlines.

Maps inspire adventure and appeal to the heart as well as the mind. They are exotic and mystical, arousing the imagination, so children are understandably entranced by maps of amazing places accompanying the texts in *Treasure Island* and *Winnie the Pooh*. Joseph Conrad's introspective adventurer in equatorial Africa, Charlie Marlow, recounted his youthful fascination with the "blank spaces" in maps that beckoned with "delightful mystery."[2] The unknown is hypnotic, whereas the known becomes mundane. What is most alluring is that which is not revealed on the map, as this absence triggers inventiveness in accordance with Jonathan Swift's ditty: "So geographers in Afric maps, With savage pictures fill their gaps; And o'er unhabitable downs, Place elephants for want of towns."[3]

Maps must obviously be accurate if used as guides for reaching a particular destination, but making them too exact stultifies the spirit and has been parodied by Lewis Carroll, who was actually an Oxford don named Charles Lutwidge Dodgson. Renowned for his zany *Alice's Adventures in Wonderland*, Carroll displayed his spatial inquisitiveness and wit again in *Sylvie and Bruno, Concluded*. The issue was how do you represent the world, and a suggestion was made that you should make maps with increasingly larger scales until the maps are equal in size to the areas they literally cover. Carroll playfully pointed out that a country would not receive any sunlight in such a situation so, instead of employing a map, the country itself could be its own map.[4]

Argentine post-realist writer Jorge Luis Borges later returned to this theme of overintellectualization, spoofing the application of "exactitude," which fails to leave room for dreams and originality. Borges, like Carroll, described precise cartography in which the map scale was equal to reality and the kingdom in question was completely obscured. The map became the same as the territory, thereby precluding any symbolic interpretation, and its great detail served no purpose as it only replicated the kingdom. The map was therefore a substitute for reality, eliminating any flight of fancy by the viewer.[5] Maps should arouse some emotional reaction from the observer, and "exactitude" is to be avoided as it renders the ocular experience a hollow exercise.[6]

Maps clearly have a geometric dimension linking them to the sciences, but they also are undoubtedly associated with the arts. Peter Turchi, an author of fiction enamored with cartography, compares maps to creative writing. In both, the stimulated producer applies subjectivity through the making of choices, and the consumer becomes a participant by responding to what he sees or reads. Turchi also points out that writers "map" their works, and that a story is "a kind of map." Fiction and mapmaking share a common approach to the specificity of presentation. Some information must be included in order to communicate, but too much constricts the imagination of the beholder.[7]

The fluid and inventive nature of maps also makes them comparable to the human condition. English poet John Donne evoked geographical imagery when he mused "no man is an island, entire of itself; every man is a piece of the continent, a part of the main." [8] Similarly, *Brave New World* author Aldous Huxley referred to "the essential otherness of the mind's far continents." He also perceived "an Old World of personal consciousness and, beyond, a dividing sea, a series of new Worlds."[9] American poet Oliver Wendell Holmes expounded upon maps as metaphors for life, pieces that must be put together to complete the whole. Fragments gradually replace blank areas, like a jigsaw puzzle assembled for a child.[10]

Before we embark upon our own cartographical journey, let's determine what type of wanderers we will be. Not tourists, for their peregrinations are brief, their interpretations superficial, and they soon return home. Not explorers either, because they have preconceived agenda. They know what they are looking for, and their scrutiny is conditioned by their expectations. No, we will go as travelers—aware of possibilities and open to new ideas. There is a limit, however, for we will not be "knights-errant" like Don Quixote and will remain balanced rather than unhinged. Windmills will not be confused with giants.[11]

We will be careful about letting any ingrained conceits influence our sensual perceptions. As sixteenth-century Spanish missionary Bartolome de las Casas sagely warned: "It is a wonder to see how, when a man greatly desires something and strongly attaches himself to it in his imagination, he has the impression at every moment that whatever he hears and sees argues in favor of that thing."[12] In the same vein, Aldous Huxley cautioned that "our perceptions of the external world are habitually clouded by the verbal notions in terms of which we do our thinking. We are forever attempting to convert things into signs for the more intelligible abstractions of our own invention."[13] Our views are shaded by subjectivity, with observations thus becoming expressions of ourselves. Prior convictions may therefore mistakenly validate what we think we see.[14]

A related problem is that people tend to seek out the familiar, or assess quite unusual images in such a context. What you find generally resembles what you already know. British novelist Graham Greene, while traveling in Liberia, described his "pleasure in a sight so vaguely, so remotely English," and he had a sense that "every step was towards home."[15] For those geographically cut off from their own milieu, even the absence of fellow human beings has a powerful impact. German environmental geographer Alexander von Humboldt, exploring the Orinoco region of South America at the turn of the nineteenth century, noted that it was "strange and sad" that men were not essential to the natural order there. Donald Thomson, an Australian anthropologist researching in Arnhem Land in 1935, likewise expressed his exultation after eight lonely days spying at other "human beings": "It was as if they were old friends from whom we had been parted only a few hours."[16]

Realize along our journey that seeing something does not necessarily make it true. Mark Twain's fictional Tom Sawyer wisely, if inelegantly, queried: "There used to be forty thousand million people that seen the sun move from one side of the sky to the other every day. Did that prove that the sun *done* it?"[17] Even worse than misinterpreting one's observations is to lie about them due to boastfulness, anticipated financial reward, or an intent to mislead rivals. Tellingly, Jonathan Swift's narrator Gulliver, surely a font of tall tales, nevertheless claimed that he was sticking to the truth. He also recommended a prepublication veracity oath for travelers since "the credulity of mankind" is "so impudently abused."[18]

Enough with the admonitions! Let's set off on our virtual quest for geographical knowledge! Let's expose our senses to new impressions! Let's experience the joys of discovery! Let's keep our itinerary flexible, for imagine what Moses would have missed had he taken the direct route to the Promised Land instead of acquiring prophetic insights from wandering for forty years! Remember that mapping is partly a process of inquiry and revelation, and not just a methodology of classification and depiction.

CHAPTER 1

The Cartographer's Mirror

Imagine that a large chunk of ice has just broken loose from an Antarctic glacier and has started to drift aimlessly out to sea. It has become a giant iceberg, but perhaps it is more—an island. Such an interpretation may seem to be stretching credulity, but few people pause to consider the ramifications of their oft-reflexive geographical concepts. Can an island float, or must it be anchored to the seabed? Can it change locations with the currents? Can it be underwater most of the time, only to crack the surface at low tide? China lays claim to many submerged rock formations in the South China Sea and, when they start to jut above the waterline, sends units of its navy clambering up these slippery crags to plant the flag. Of course, their mission is not just to assert the definition of an island. Under international law, possession of an island endows its owner with a two-hundred-mile exclusive economic zone in all directions—and this means control over offshore oil and mineral rights. Geography is much more than physical description; it is a critical attribute enhancing a country's power and wealth.

What constitutes an island is debatable, as is stipulating the nature of a continent. As our sheet of ice separates from Antarctica, does this mean that Antarctica has just become a smaller continent? Should the floating ice still be considered part of Antarctica? Actually, what is the difference between an island and a continent? Australia was traditionally described as an island prior to the twentieth century, but it now has the status of a continent. The combination of Europe, Asia, and Africa could indeed be interpreted as a huge island, as could that of North and South America. But, wait! What about the Suez and Panama Canals? Must these man-made alterations of geography be taken into account?[1] If so, then Africa, North America and South America have become island continents.

It is readily apparent that there is no objective natural geography upon which all can agree. Maps superimpose concepts such as continents and a prime meridian that reflect the mapmaker's experiences, values, aesthetics, and politics. Cartographers certainly apply scientific principles, but it is obvious that they produce different maps of the same regions. Maps are not reality, but interpretations of it. They are made for a purpose, and they incorporate a great amount of human subjectivity. In his novel about a very real and renowned Venetian cartographer from the Renaissance period, author James Cowan's protagonist Fra Mauro acutely analyzes his latest creation by observing: "Gazing at the map, I begin to see a portrait of myself."[2]

THE MIND'S EYE

Maps are projections. Everyone is familiar with light passing through a film or transparency in order to produce an image on a screen. Maps are formed the same way. Let's visualize a lit bulb that is placed within a see-through globe. The features on this globe are then reflected upon a paper wrapping that may afterward be flattened. The spherical globe is therefore used to create a map on a two-dimensional surface, with the nature of the projection varying as a consequence of the paper being arranged cylindrically or conically.[3] Such projections may be manipulated to suit the cartographer's agenda, and are thus critical to ideological and geopolitical debates.

Secondly, a mapmaker superimposes his own vision upon the world so that his cartography is conditioned by the classical psychological function of projection. What he presents may seemingly appear objective, but it is to a considerable extent a product of his own cultural and political proclivities—and even of his imagination. As in the above example, there is an internal activation of the external as one's psyche is projected as an image. This image represents what the mapmaker is unwilling to admit overtly, and is frequently generated subconsciously. The cartographer's projection of the outer world is therefore dependent on his own inner psychological state as his maps are based on an "act of seeing" rather than on "what was seen."[4]

When a child draws a map of his neighborhood, he egocentrically tends to place his own home near its center. Early man acted similarly when viewing the sun, stars, and the horizon as he incorporated what he saw with his spiritual and cosmological perspectives to arrive at some understanding of his own place in the universe.[5] He as the observer remained fundamental to his mental picture, and so did his physical location. Once drawn maps started to appear about the seventh century B.C., ethnocentric values (societal composites of individual egocentrism) came to determine what was depicted at the center. In a like manner, most civilizations developed a belief that the sun and planets revolved around the earth.[6]

Geographical maps reflect perceptions of space that are socially conditioned, and they are basically mental. They are "mediators" between a person's inner world and the physical world, and they "construct" the world rather than "reproduce" it. People tend to see what they describe, rather than vice versa, and they formulate an image more than they develop a means of wayfaring.[7] Conceptual categories, such as continents or oceans, emanate from the cartographer's intellect and are then applied to his maps just as constellations are formulated to provide a systematic vision of the skies. There is now a field of psychogeography, which is based on understanding how projections deriving from "the topography of the mind" underlie one's perceptions of "natural and social reality" and precipitate action in the world.[8] More extreme and questionable is the process of "remote viewing," which is used by intelligence agencies in an effort to locate hostages or enemy personnel. The "viewer" visualizes distant places without any exposure to their physical reality. In fact, cartographers have for centuries prepared maps of areas they have never seen. However, they have relied on the experiences and descriptions of others, so there has been at least some grounding in on-the-spot reality. Nevertheless, caution is required prior to acceptance of the findings of travelers, adventurers, "discoverers," and their kind. Their accounts may be precipitated by ulterior motives but, more importantly, one tends to see what one expects to see.[9] Columbus' narratives about the "Indies" in "Asia" are a case in point.

Maps are often exhibited as decorations. They may be hung on walls, or even painted on them as in Renaissance Italy. They also could be in the form of tapestries (as was common in England and Flanders), screens (as in sixteenth-century Japan), landscape paintings (as in seventeenth-century Netherlands), or mosaics (as in ancient Rome). They additionally have their own aesthetic qualities in terms of design, craftsmanship, and pictorial representation. Many cartographers have been artists as well, and their creative proclivities have often trumped their practicality and objectivity as technicians.[10]

Christian maps from the Middle Ages were not accurate geographically, and woe be to any navigator who tried to rely on them. That is why portolan charts of coastal regions were produced in Europe starting in the late twelfth century. Japanese maps were elegant and attractive, with little regard for precision, perhaps because of the country's insularity, stress on secrecy, and limited involvement in exploration.[11]

Also undercutting objectivity were imagination and fantasy. Cartographers often had inadequate information, and some parts of the world were completely beyond their knowledge. There was thus a considerable expanse of *terrae incognitae* on maps, which the cartographers filled with monsters, giants, fierce animals, deformed humans, and other representatives of the feared unknown.[12] There were also imaginary Atlantic islands such as Antillia, St. Ursula, Frisland, and the Islands of Brendan. When exploration demonstrated that they were not at their supposed locations, they were not discarded but rather moved further west.[13]

REALITY CHECK

Like most peoples in ancient times, the Greeks at first believed in a flat earth. However, by the time of Pythagoras in the sixth century B.C., the evolution of geometry had led to the concept of sphericity, and this perspective was adopted by Aristotle two centuries later. The Greeks, using mathematics and astronomical observation, surely laid the foundation for cartography even though their aim was to understand the cosmos rather than seek practical applications.[14] In the third century B.C., Eratosthenes calculated the circumference of the earth, and Aristarchus stipulated that the earth revolved around the sun. Eratosthenes also created a predecessor of the grid system, which led to the latitude and longitude measurements of Hipparchus in the following century.[15] Claudius Ptolemy, living in Alexandria in the second century A.D., then adapted the Greek scientific principles to cartography and produced maps of the known world. Ptolemy divided the earth into 360 degrees of longitude and refined the grid (known as the graticule), but he went astray in asserting that the earth was the center of our "solar" system.

Determining location was essential for rigorous mapmaking. The Chinese actually devised a grid system by the first century B.C., but they were unaware of the earth's sphericity or circumference, did not apply astronomical calculations, and did not take the earth's curvature into account. Chinese grids, unlike those developed by the Greeks, therefore did not evolve into a comprehensive framework of latitude and longitude within which locations could be specified by coordinates.

Quadrants, cross staffs, astrolabes, and *kamals* gradually became useful instruments for computing latitude, but measuring longitude accurately for long proved insolvable despite the invention of sextants and chronometers, since the earth's rotation affected the gauging of time. This complication was not overcome until precision clocks were effectively applied to the task in the late eighteenth century.[16]

Designating direction was also critical for cartography, particularly to serve navigators. One could get some guidance from the sun and stars, but cloudy skies and storms would obviate such efforts. Depth soundings were helpful, but much of the Mediterranean and other waterways were too deep for utilizing this method. Winds could aid in determining direction, but there were obviously periods of lassitude. A magnetic compass was the solution, but it took many years to recognize its importance. The Chinese probably had such a device by the first century A.D., based on the magnetic properties of lodestone, but they used it for feng shui determinations of placement and harmony rather than for navigation or cartography. It wasn't until the early twelfth century that the Chinese compass was adopted for these purposes, mainly by Arab and Persian seamen. This was prior to the 1302 date cited by the Italian town of Amalfi, which claims that the navigational compass was invented there.[17]

Science has been applied to cartography for thousands of years. Surveying instruments, printing technologies, satellite imagery, and computers have surely left their mark—but cartography itself is still not quite science. Even if satellite photos are employed as the basis of maps, there is nevertheless some lack of scientific objectivity, since the range, angle, scale, and other factors may be chosen to achieve a desired purpose. Clearly, the colors used on maps are not those existing in reality. Maps can illustrate only a version of the reality they purport to represent due to the limitations of scale and inaccuracies produced by the psychological projection of the mapmaker. Nevertheless, maps appear to be definitive because they do not provide caveats or indicate speculation as do written texts.[18] The reality of the portrayal may thus be closer to the essence of the cartographer's mind than to that of the world depicted. Maps, to a degree, therefore replace physical reality and serve as a substitute for it.

Maps, as "data-storage systems" for geographers, additionally can be no more scientific than the information upon which they are based.[19] Cartographers are like statisticians, and what appear in their output to be facts should be subjected to an evaluation of their sampling and margin of error. Data is also changeable. A photographer may take photos of the same tree at each hour of the day, but they all come out differently due to the time factor. Although less perceptible, maps are also affected by time as geography is impermanent.

Maps and pictures are two-dimensional representations of a three-dimensional reality, and both contain an altered perspective even if there is an effort to conceal it.[20] Actually, maps are a tertiary portrayal of reality. They are derivatives of spherical globes, which themselves represent the earth inaccurately as they fail to take into account the flattening of the earth's poles and the equatorial bulge, thus distorting features such as distance and angles. Maps additionally mislead the viewer as to contiguity since the far left and far right portions of rectangular world maps are in fact adjacent to each other geographically. The human eye cannot see more than half of a globe at one time, so the cartographer must adjust his perspective. His conception of mapmaking is therefore as critical as his production technique.[21]

The earth, like an organism, evolves. It is dynamic, not static, and geography is in part the study of change within space.[22] About 250 million years ago, there was one land mass now known as Pangaea. It broke up around fifty million years later, creating separate territories such as Gondwanaland, which itself fragmented approximately seventy million years afterward. Such impermanence has impacted Western minds for millennia through the legend of Atlantis, an island destroyed by a volcanic eruption, and through the continental drift theory developed by German meteorologist Alfred Lothar Wegener in the early twentieth century. Both have contributed to our notions of perpetual earthly transformations, and recent studies of plate tectonics have served to reinforce such perceptions.

South America and Africa are no longer connected. Neither are North America and Asia, which had a land bridge until at least 20,000 B.C. What was once the South Pole is now in Africa. Towns formerly on the mainland of India and Turkey are presently under the sea, and some areas of settlement that were once on the shore have effectively shifted inland due to silting. Look at where Ur, the birthplace of Abraham, is today! Lakes are drying up, and new islands are rising from beneath the ocean. An extensive Lake Bonneville has been reduced to a considerably smaller Great Salt Lake, and the 1963 birth of Surtsey off the coast of Iceland has been a media sensation. If global warming takes place, coastlines will recede and island nations such as Kiribati and the Maldives may disappear. Even now, the configuration of shores along the littoral changes daily with high and low tides.

Geographical tinkering through landfills and man-made lakes has altered our topography, and name changes have helped to keep mapmakers in business. There may be valid historical and cultural reasons why Gold Coast became Ghana, or East Pakistan became Bangladesh, but there is also a frivolous side to geography. In 1950, Hot Springs, New Mexico, hoped to attract tourists by adopting the title of the popular radio show "Truth or Consequences." Chile likewise in 1966 renamed one of the Juan Fernandez Islands "Robinson Crusoe Island" because Alexander Selkirk, the inspiration for Daniel Defoe, spent 52 months there in isolation. Bermuda similarly in 1960 came up with "Paradise Island" as a replacement for Hog Island.

River courses frequently shift, creating political controversy if they happen to be international boundaries. Delineating the exact boundary along the 1,200-mile-long Rio Grande has for long embroiled the United States and Mexico, as has the issue of using the river's water. Many new treaties have had to be renegotiated, ranging from terms agreed upon in 1848 to those adopted in 1944, and there is now relative tranquility due to the work of the International Boundary and Water Commission. Problems have been much more serious along the Ussuri on the Russian-Chinese border. The 1860 Treaty of Peking (Beijing) set forth terms of agreement, but the Ussuri freezes during the winter and floods its banks during the spring. The navigational channel therefore fluctuates, and there are several arms of the river that make it difficult to calculate its thalweg, or middle shipping line, through the main channel. Compounding this confusion is that islands in the river change location as the waters shift, and that these islands are not mentioned in the Treaty of Peking.[23] It is therefore not surprising that competing claims led to the dramatic military clash between Soviet and Chinese troops in March 1969, and that the two sides used different names (Damansky or Chenpao—now more commonly written Zhen Bao) to describe their island battleground.

POLITICAL IMPACT

When a child, I loved to study the world atlas and I copied maps of countries in the belief that I was somehow attuned to the facts and certainty of life on earth. When my family bought its first car, I was always in charge of the AAA "TripTik" so we could keep to the "correct" route. Gradually, I started to discern the underlying assumptions. My teachers, unfortunately, had to put up with me as I badgered them with questions about how explorers such as Columbus could "discover" places where others already lived—or how a river or waterfall could be "discovered" when those residing nearby obviously knew where they were. I came to understand why Greenland was so large on maps, but not on the globe, and that people in the Southern Hemisphere did not walk upside down. All inhabitants of the earth had their heads toward the sky, but why was Australia always at the bottom of the map?

When the Korean War broke out in 1950, I happened to be the "current events" reporter that very day in my third-grade class, and I informed my classmates about the hostilities. I then followed the war meticulously on maps in the *New York Times*, and it became evident that their arrows and lines were connected to military tactics and politics as much as to what I conceived as geography. I later became a political scientist specializing in international relations, but my fascination with maps remained, and I came to view them as the visual representation of world politics.

Maps have an agenda and are part of what is now fashionably known as the "discourse." They are never completely neutral or objective, and it is not accidental that cartography tends to emphasize territory and boundaries rather than mountains or plains. Maps are redrawn for political reasons; witness the changes brought about by the Versailles Conference just after World War I. New states were created in the Middle East, and Austria-Hungary was broken into fragments. Maps may also influence events, not just reflect them. This became apparent in regard to strategies applied during World War II and the Cold War when the type of projection used was closely entwined with policymaking.

Maps may even assume personae and become actors in their own dramas. In May 1999, American aircraft fired a missile into the Chinese embassy in Belgrade, Yugoslavia, killing four people inside. This unsurprisingly fomented a diplomatic row, so the U.S. government tried to blame a map instead of the military and intelligence personnel responsible.[24] Even if we assume that the attack was accidental, a map certainly did not choose the target. The official explanation was that targeting was based on an outdated map that did not show the embassy at that location. Perhaps true, but the embassy had moved there three years earlier, in 1996. This new location appeared on tourist maps of Belgrade, and had even been visited by American diplomats. Someone in command should have recognized this when selecting a map that would provide the basis for targeting. In addition, the American government explained that the real target was a military procurement center for the Serbs. Was this building on the old map? No! Then why were targeting coordinates so far off? Again, the map was blamed. The address of the procurement center was on that street, but the building did not appear on the map. Therefore, using addresses on a parallel street on a different map, the location was extrapolated—but, clearly incorrectly. What is interesting about this whole affair is that maps have a sense of authority and power, so they were invoked to back up the American contention that the attack was accidental. The maps were also portrayed as capable of accepting responsibility.

As this examination of maps unfolds, it will become apparent that the reader will have to unlearn what he or she assumed to be factual. Cartographical objectivity is really a myth, as the mapmaker's viewpoint affects scale, centering, orientation, naming of locations, and many other factors such as what is included on the map itself. Subjective perceptions are inherent in maps, so an aim of this book is to delve beneath the images on the surface to comprehend how they developed as projections of the cartographer. Furthermore, it must be stressed that one's outlook on the world reflects historical and political circumstances—and that it is culturally bound. The mapmaker's focus therefore evolved from presenting the relationship between the earth and its people to the larger universe, to depicting humankind's theological connection to deities or supernatural forces. It then shifted to providing a product serving coastal trading and, later, oceanic commerce and exploration. Afterward there were the military dimensions of land and sea power and, presently, the interdependency of globalization and the ramifications of rising cultural tensions. Discerning the cartographer's vision is therefore the key to analyzing maps.

Cartographers have frequently been inaccurate in their depiction of the external world in terms of location, direction, distance, size, and shape. Notwithstanding, their maps are critical to an understanding of the motivations and reasoning processes employed, since such visual representations are microcosms of the cartographers' operational frameworks derived from the societal milieu. Technical aspects of mapmaking may be fascinating in regard to mathematics and craftsmanship, but cartography is really much more—the intellectualization of space across time.

Instruments of Power

CHAPTER 2

Cultural Factors

Maps have been called "mirrors of culture and civilization" and "cultural texts." They do more than describe the areas of habitation, as they locate humans "in a cultural and psychological sense as well."[1] Maps reflect the spiritual qualities of people's mores, and serve as an eye on the social order of a given period and place. Some maps, such as those representing journeys, which used to be drawn by Indians in Mexico and the North American plains, have an inherent time dimension. History may also be portrayed effectively through patterns evident in a sequence of several maps.[2] Cartography is most assuredly linked directly to history. The ancient Chinese often accompanied their maps with texts, and military maps function in this manner as well.[3]

Spatial knowledge may be presented in the cognitive form of drawn maps, but many people do not realize that there is also "performance cartography" involving rituals, dance, songs, and poetry. Vikings and southern Indian navigators memorized rhymes about their routes. The Inuit had songs with travel itineraries and supplemented them with stone markers known as *inuksuit*.[4] Distance was frequently an important consideration. The Romans carefully applied linear measurements to their road system, but many societies instead saw space allocation as indicative of travel time. In the early nineteenth century, Thais measured distances on the basis of time as an aid to troop movements in a military conflict. Europeans during the Baroque period (1550–1750) also stressed travel time and paid little consideration to surface area. Caroline Islanders east of the Philippines have traditionally laid out stones as maps. They place numbers between the stones to signify the days required to complete a trip by sea, and numbers on them for the days needed to circumnavigate each island by boat.[5] The Asante in what is now Ghana envisioned the town of Kumasi as the center of their kingdom, which was considered to be a circle forty days in diameter. Beyond this frontier, distances were also determined by days. Such a mental map had a practical political function, since one could figure out how long it would take couriers to deliver decisions made in Kumasi to outlying areas.[6]

As geographical distance increased, maps of nonmodernized peoples became more supernatural and dependent on astrological concepts. Maps thus functioned as the "interface" between the secular and the spiritual, and as a medium for "spiritual wayfinding."[7] They had a decidedly sacred dimension, and often included a religious depiction of negative forces and a netherworld. A survey of Australian Aborigines revealed that, if asked for directions to distant places, their responses were much more accurate if the site was deemed sacred. Myths, not geometry, conditioned their spatial perceptions.[8]

Maps incorporated the celestial and terrestrial and cosmologically placed humankind within the universe. The Fon in Benin had the image of a calabash in which the sun, moon, and sky were in the upper part, and the earth floated in a lower part filled with water. The earliest known pictorial map of more than local concern, drawn in Babylonia in the sixth century B.C., similarly viewed the earth as a disc surrounded by water. This was a common motif, but various cultures depicted the earth as an egg, tortoise, human body, bowl, wheel, sphere, tetrahedron, square, or a series of interconnected squares.

The Gumatj clan of Australian Aborigines has developed maps that are simultaneously paintings and religious icons, and they are completely understandable only to those initiated into the clan's secrets. For the Gumatj, connections between places are interpreted as tracks made by ancestral beings, and land is given to humans by these beings. Their particular clan has the crocodile as such an ancestor so maps are drawn in the shape of a crocodile, and the parts of his body are presented as corresponding to geographical locations.[9]

WHICH WAY IS UP?

Projecting their ethnocentrism, Aristotle and Ptolemy positioned the earth at the center of the universe. Similarly, the Temple of Tenochtitlan appeared at the heart of Aztec maps and Jerusalem was at the center of the Madaba mosaic. This Byzantine map from about 565 A.D., which is in Jordan, presents Jerusalem as ten times too large due to intentional distortion of the scale. When the most prominent Islamic cartographer of the Medieval period, Mohammed al-Idrisi of Ceuta, was commissioned by King Roger II of Sicily to produce a world map, he put Mecca and the Arabian peninsula at the visual focal point of his 1154 masterwork.

They were there again in his map of 1161. Al-Idrisi abetted his geographical placement by orienting his maps toward the south, thereby putting Arabia at the prime location near the top above Europe.[10]

The Chinese believed, according to the concept of *tienxia*, that there was an order under heaven that located China at its center. A fifth-century B.C. map was therefore composed of concentric rectangles, with the inner one being the royal palace. Then appeared the capital, the lands of feudal princes, the pacified zone, the barbarian zone, and the "lands of uncivilized savages."[11] There was no standardized scale, as each area going outward from the royal palace was made increasingly undersized. Such a diminution of moral value as the focus moves away from the center, the "self," may be interpreted as evidence of "egocentrism."[12] This Sinocentric approach was fostered by Confucianism, but then undercut by the first century due to inroads made by Buddhism. As a consequence of the Indian cultural influence, the Buddhists' sacred Mt. Meru (also revered by the Hindus) was often depicted at the core of Chinese maps. Other maps had their centers at Kunlun Shan in western China. This Chinese cartographical outlook was similar to that of many Southeast Asian societies, as states were defined by their centers, not their boundaries. Outlying areas were assessed by their relationship to the center, and government authority became weaker when the distance from the center increased. The status of territories was thus hierarchical rather than egalitarian.[13]

In the late sixteenth century, China started to call itself *Zhongguo*, the "middle kingdom" or "central state." This term dated back to ancient times, but had not been in general usage. Sinocentrism returned and, ironically, was backed by the Italian Jesuit priest Matteo Ricci, who arrived in China in 1583. Ricci hoped to convert the Chinese to Christianity and thought that revealing European cartographical skills would enhance Chinese attraction to his proselytizing. Ricci, who was committed to not denigrating Chinese cultural values, then unintentionally proceeded to offend his Chinese hosts when he showed them a European map of the world on which China was located at the eastern edge. He quickly made amends in 1584 by producing a new map centered horizontally in the Pacific at what we now consider to be 170 degrees east longitude. China was thus displayed prominently. Ricci additionally catered to the Chinese tradition that texts reveal truth by providing a commentary for his map.[14]

In the mid-nineteenth century, Governor Hsu Chi-yu of Fukien (Fujian) province reacted to China's defeat in the 1839–42 Opium War by trying to understand its Western enemies. He considered cartography to be significant, especially the fact that Westerners had actually seen most of the places they had mapped. Hsu adopted Western cartographical techniques, and his perspective has been incisively summarized by Fred

Drake, an expert on Chinese concepts in the humanities. According to Drake: "He had realized that the Confucian image of China as a supreme power in the center of a moral order was no longer accurate. China now competed for survival in a world of states which looked not to morality or virtue for legitimacy, but rather to industrial and military power."[15] Such an analytic breakthrough proved to be both profound and strategic, but it did not really alter the cartographical tendency to center world maps in the Pacific, thereby accentuating China's position. This remains the case today in regard to Chinese maps, as the Atlantic Ocean is marginalized and sometimes not even depicted with its full width.

The Japanese adopted Buddhism in the sixth century and were soon making maps focused on Mt. Meru.[16] Religious culture thus trumped national pride, but the introduction of Eurocentric maps in the sixteenth century engendered a chauvinistic backlash, and Japan was then moved toward the center. Historically, Japanese cartography was rather parochial, since Japanese did not travel extensively. Maps therefore concentrated on Japan itself, with neighboring countries relegated to the fringe. Furthermore, Japan was a grouping of islands, so the importance of water transport was shown by exaggerating rivers and coastal peninsulas.[17] European influence then led to the production of more world maps, many derived from Ricci's.

Japan was largely closed to foreigners during the period 1636–1854, except for some Dutch and Chinese traders based in Nagasaki. A six-panel folding screen, labeled in Chinese but including smaller notations in Japanese, dates from the seventeenth or eighteenth century and places its center in the Pacific. Europe, not surprisingly, is relegated to the upper left edge.[18] In the early nineteenth century, an atmosphere of seclusion and xenophobia led to many maps being centered on the emperor's place of residence—Kyoto. This signified a rejection of the feudal Tokugawa government headquartered in Edo (Tokyo).[19] Traditionally, all distances in Japan had been measured from the same point in Edo, the Nihonbashi Bridge, which had been constructed by the Shogun Tokugawa Ieyasu in 1603. Delineation of latitude and longitude, and the uniformity of scale, were later developed on the basis of European cartographical practices, and northern orientation became the norm. Previously, many maps had been oriented toward the west.

There is still no standardization of maps in terms of their longitudinal center, even though a zero prime meridian running through Greenwich, England, has been established. Europeans are likely to deploy the prime meridian down the middle of their maps, but the Chinese prefer the international dateline in the Pacific, and Americans have generally portrayed the United States as the hub, with protective oceans on either side and Europe and Asia off at the peripheries. Consequently, Eurasia is often bifurcated. Realize that maps of regions may also feature different centers

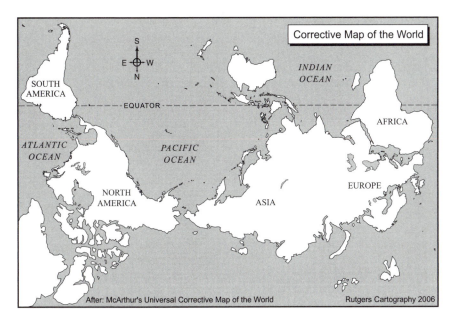

Corrective Map of the World

in order to express cultural attitudes. For example, noted British historian Norman Davies maintains that Poland's importance in European history has not received significant recognition. His books therefore feature maps of Europe that have their axis twisted toward a western orientation so as to produce a Polish-centric continent.[20]

The orientation of maps is arbitrary. There is no scientific reason why north should be at the top, and why Americans should go "up north" or "down south." Cultural tradition dictates cartographical design just as it determines whether writing should be from left to right, right to left, or top to bottom. Actually, less-modernized societies do not always standardize direction. It can vary based on the perspective of a person approaching a location, or the use of a meandering river as a fixed reference. Drawn maps, however, generally conform to a pattern, and the northern orientation goes back to the ancient Greeks. The maps produced by Ptolemy were particularly influential in this regard.

Why the Greeks chose north to be at the top of maps is not known, but many cultures believed that placement there implied a stronger connection to ethics.[21] This was similar to the concepts of sacred mountains and of God being in heaven. Indian maps often incorporated this ethical image into an eastern orientation, as did medieval Christians. East is the direction of the rising sun and, for Christians, it additionally represents Paradise.[22] In fact, the word "orientation" implies eastward. A map of Britain produced about 1250 by Matthew Paris, an English monk and historian, was oriented northward, but such deployment did not become common in Europe until the fifteenth century. Such usage seems to have been prompted by the rediscovery of Ptolemaic maps and widespread employment of the compass.[23]

Prior to Ricci's impact, Chinese cartography was predominantly oriented southward. Two Hunan maps from the early second century B.C. exemplify this custom, perhaps developed because the apogee of the sun at the summer solstice was visible in the southern part of the sky.[24] South was also the royal direction, and Chinese compasses pointed toward magnetic south. Emperors sat with their backs to the north, and their palaces faced south from their location north of the capital's east-west axis. Islamic mapmaking, which was influenced by the Chinese, also featured a southern orientation. This is evident in the twelfth-century works of al-Idrisi.

Contemporary maps throughout the world are almost always oriented northward, but there is an important exception: Stuart McArthur's Universal Corrective Map of the World. Published in Australia in 1979, it has a southern orientation and is longitudinally centered on Canberra, Australia. This means that Europe is at the lower right corner, and the United States at the lower left. According to a commentary on the map, it is aimed at raising Australia from the "gloomy depths of anonymity in the world power struggle," and proclaims: "No longer will the South wallow in a pit of insignificance, carrying the North on its shoulders for little or no recognition of her efforts. Finally South emerges on top. . . . LONG LIVE AUSTRALIA—RULER OF THE UNIVERSE!"[25]

THE CROSS AND THE CRESCENT

Cartographers project their religious values onto their maps. Ancient Indians paid little attention to mathematics or scale, as the holiest sites were portrayed as unrealistically large, and pilgrimage routes were given prominence. Observation as a means of gathering geographical information was subordinated to the Hindu belief that sensory perceptions were illusory.[26] Christian maps from roughly the sixth through fifteenth centuries were based on similar assumptions. St. Augustine, the renowned fourth- and fifth-century North African theologian, had also minimized knowledge of the material world gathered by the senses, for he believed that human intellect was supplied by God and that the earth was the fulfillment of God's promise through scripture. It was His creation.[27] The empirical and geometric foundations of cartography, developed by the Greeks, were eschewed in Europe as mapmaking became less practical and more theological. Efficient causes were replaced by final causes and God's plan; purpose and revelation moved the emphasis from what is to what ought to be.[28] Medieval world maps (*mappaemundi*) thus were didactic representations of man's relationship to God. The thirteenth-century Ebstorf map from Germany stressed the world as Christ's embodiment, with his head appearing at the top, his feet at the bottom, and his hands at the sides. Jerusalem, notably at the center, was therefore a symbolic navel.[29] Some maps presented the twelve apostles presiding over geographical regions. Cartography served the faithful, so the sixth-century Madaba map featured roads to religious sites and a very detailed depiction of Jerusalem. Sites not associated with Christianity were either left out entirely or displayed less conspicuously.

The Islamic tradition included legends such as utilization of the astrolabe prior to Noah, or the discovery by David of the magnetic properties of lodestone—which then led to the compass. There was also an interpretation that the rock that killed Goliath was lodestone.[30] Nevertheless, the *Quran* did not provide much guidance for a cosmological image of the world, and most Islamic cartography was less theological than that of the Christians. Muslims derived mapmaking concepts from the more scientific Chinese and the works of Ptolemy. While medieval Europeans were generally ignorant of this Alexandrian intellectual dynamo, the Muslims had based much of their cartography on Ptolemy since the beginning of the ninth century when the Abbasid Caliph Mamun of Baghdad acquired his geographical writings during a military victory at Ankara.[31] Ptolemy's books were quickly translated into Arabic, and his charts of latitude and longitude were widely distributed. Maps, such as those produced by al-Idrisi in the twelfth century, were made to scale, but no grids were drawn until the fourteenth century.

Although not basically theological, Islamic maps performed an important religious function. Muslims face Mecca while engaged in prayer, and a wall niche in mosques (the *mihrab*) orients worshipers in that direction. Determining the *qibla*, the sacred direction to Mecca, was therefore crucial, so the preparation of *qibla* maps became widespread during the period from 1000 to 1800. Introduction of the magnetic compass in the twelfth century contributed to this process, as did the astronomical observations of navigators and the Ptolemaic location tables. Ahmad bin Majid al-Najdi, the eminent fifteenth-century expert on Islamic nautical knowledge, interestingly commented on the "science for the determination of the *Qibla*, and people who make religious decisions will find a need for it."[32] Science and religion were therefore fused, rather than counterpoised.

CHRISTIAN GEOGRAPHY

European cartography during the Middle Ages was mainly developed by monks who applied scripture to geography and who used their maps as metaphors for theology.[33] Their preference for an eastern orientation derived from Genesis 2:8, which states: "And the Lord God planted a

Garden eastward, in Eden." Consequently, Adam and Eve were often included in the eastern portion of maps.[34]

Genesis 2:10–14 refers to four rivers flowing out of Eden, and they were depicted as the Tigris, Euphrates, Indus, and Ganges.[35] The continents were related to Noah's sons Ham, Shem and Japhet in accordance with the Genesis 10:1–32 passage about the division of nations. Ham represented Africa; Shem, Asia; and Japhet, Europe.[36] In the northern section of maps were the lands of Gog and Magog—the latter described in Genesis 10:2 as a son of Japhet. These nefarious dwellers in the geographical margin were seen as barbarians planning to attack the civilized world at the end of days. According to Ezekiel 38:15–16, the assault by an army on horseback would come from the north and would take over Israel "as a cloud to cover the land." Jeremiah 4:6 quotes the Lord as warning: "Out of the north the evil shall break forth upon all the inhabitants of the land." Revelation 20:7–8 asserts that Gog and Magog were incited by Satan.

Another scriptural reference influencing cartography was the centrality of Jerusalem, based on the declaration in Ezekiel 5:5: "Thus saith the Lord God: This is Jerusalem! I have set her in the midst of the natives, and countries are round about her."[37] Even more critical was the concept of an earth that was mostly land. In the words of Esdras (Ezra) II 6:42, a book in the Apocrypha: "On the third day you commanded the nations to be gathered together in the seventh part of the earth, but six parts you dried up and kept them so that some of them might be planted and cultivated and serve before you." This image of an earth that was one-seventh oceans not only pervaded Christian cartography but, as we will see later, impacted dramatically on the race between the Spanish and Portuguese to reach the Indies.

Folklore that Christians believed the earth to be flat, and that they mocked Columbus with warnings that he would fall off its end, bears no historical validity. In fact, European kings during the Middle Ages were frequently portrayed holding an orb, symbolizing the earth. The cross atop the orb indicated Christ's sovereignty over it.[38] The issue of flatness vs. sphericity did not really concern key theologians such as Sts. Augustine and Thomas Aquinas, and Christian scientists overwhelmingly endorsed sphericity prior to Columbus' voyage to America. On the other hand, flat-earthers did have some Biblical support. Isaiah 40:22 refers to "He that sitteth above the circle of the earth," as it could certainly be flat and circular. More directly, Job 38:13 mentions "the ends of the earth"—an allusion without meaning if it was spherical. There is also the observation by Paul in Hebrews 8:5 that "Moses was admonished of God when he was about to make the tabernacle: for, See, saith he, that thou make all things according to the pattern showed to thee in the mount." This could imply that the earth must have the same shape as the tabernacle—which was the tent protecting the Ark of the Covenant and the Holy of Holies. Exodus

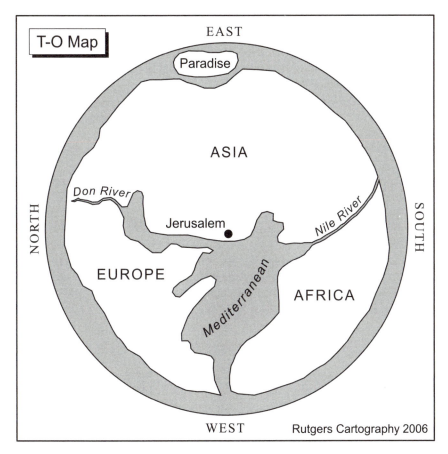

T-O Map

25–27 does describe the tabernacle as a rectangular prism, and certainly not as a sphere. It was reportedly 30 cubits long, 10 wide, and 10 high and situated in a courtyard measuring 100 by 50 cubits. The tabernacle was surely three dimensional, but its rectangular shape accorded more closely to a flat map than to a spherical globe.

The sphericity concept had another complication cited by the flat-earthers. Drawing upon Aristotle's belief that there was an equatorial hot zone that prevented human transit, and adding to it the Biblical explanation that all humans were descended from Adam and the three sons of Noah who populated the continents, then how could humans exist beyond the hot zone? Such an interpretation led cartographers to the position that there was no southern continent inhabited by humans. Of course, Australia had yet to be "discovered" by Christian Europeans. Additionally pertinent was the idea of *antipodes*, beings whose feet were assumed to face opposite those of Europeans. Not only would they be walking upside down if the earth was spherical—and possibly fall off of it—but they could also not have been, according to the hot zone hypothesis, human. This issue about *antipodes* obviously bedeviled the advocates of sphericity.

So-called "T-O maps" were common from the eighth through the fifteenth centuries. They were round ("O"), and had a horizontal diameter perpendicular to a lower vertical radius ("T"). The circular earth related back to Isaiah, and it was covered mostly with land as cited in Esdras II. Water frequently was situated around the circumference, forming a border. The "T" was in the form of a cross known as the *tau*, and clearly represented the Crucifixion. Jerusalem was at the center, and the three continents depicted implied the Trinity. "T-O maps" had an eastward orientation, with the lines of the "T" delineating waterways. The Mediterranean Sea was thus the vertical part of the "T," and the Nile and Don (sometimes the Danube) combined made up the crossbar.[39] This synthesis of scripture and "sacred" geography amply demonstrated the psychological projection of the cartographers and the importance of culture in interpreting a not- so-objective "reality."

CHAPTER 3

The Political Jigsaw

Maps represent power, and are not just schematic devises. In ancient China, a defeated state would present its maps to the victor as a sign of submission and acceptance of territorial dismemberment. The same was true in Java, where a vanquished leader in 1293 turned over a map and census records to a Chinese military commander. Also a Chinese state seeking alliance with a stronger one would yield its maps in an act demonstrating secondary status, and outlying areas would provide maps to the emperor as tribute. During the first three centuries B.C., the Chinese ruler had an adviser on cartography, and maps were customarily buried in the tombs of high officials as symbols of their authority that would ease passage to an afterlife.[1]

When the Red Army occupied part of Finnish Karelia in 1940, approximately sixteen million maps of the region were confiscated in conjunction with annexation by the Soviet Union. Then, at the end of World War II, U.S. military intelligence searched through the area that was to become the Soviet sector of Germany for maps of Central Asia produced by Swedish cartographer Sven Hedin, who had worked on behalf of Germany in the course of the war. They were located at two sites and transferred to the National Aeronautics and Space Center in Maryland before the Soviets had the opportunity to acquire them.[2]

Maps therefore may be an accomplice to force as cartography can buttress territorial claims, recognize the renaming of locations, diagram the journeys of "explorers," and basically propagate the concept that power can be exercised over space. Thus, when Alonso de Santa Cruz served as royal cosmographer to Philip II of Spain from 1555 to 1567, the maps he prepared increasingly included territory in conjunction with the expansion of Spain's empire in the New World.[3] Mapmaking was therefore consonant with state power projection.

UNDER CONTROL

Maps serve political ends and are submitted as evidence in litigation over land ownership, boundaries, and laws of the sea.[4] Surveying often goes along with military operations, and British technicians proficient in measurement were linked to the development of the Empire as they accompanied James Cook on his eighteenth-century voyages. They also mapped India in the nineteenth century. As noted British geographer J. B. Harley observed, "To catalog the world is to appropriate it."[5] This statement is a bit hyperbolic, but it is surely true that those who make and collect maps have a power advantage over those who do not. Cultures devoid of a cartographical tradition, as was the case in Amazonia, have witnessed extensive encroachments on their lands, and those that did generate but not preserve maps are similarly afflicted. Asians, unlike Europeans, generally did not assemble atlases, and some Asian societies looked upon maps as impermanent. Thais periodically discarded their map archives, and Tibetans wiped away their mandalas created from sand.[6]

There is an account of an Inuit elder in the Arctic who drew many maps but then threw them away because he saw them not as material objects but rather as a record of environmental features. The importance was in constructing them, and this act brought prestige within his Inuit community, since mimicry of the environment was viewed as strengthening attachment to the land.[7] There is also the situation of the Nisga'a people in Canada's British Columbia. They did not make maps, but were affected by the Supreme Court's 1996 decision that oral traditions could be accepted legally as the basis for territorial claims. The Nisga'a quickly began to draw maps to back their land claims. In the past, other American Indian groups had often referred to "lost maps" supportive of their legal rights. One may have been prepared by Nez Perce Chief Joseph, or his brother Ollokot, but the absence of cartographical evidence certainly made such map claims difficult to substantiate.[8] Also recognize that Indian nations such as the Zuni tended to see territory in a multifaceted manner with political boundaries not coinciding with those delineated for other purposes. There were distinct areas for agriculture, grazing, hunting, plant collection, mineral collection, and religious use.[9]

Mapmakers give voice to authority due to the fact that they frequently serve powerful patrons. This connection tends to be masked, but maps are commonly commissioned by the government or military, and the services of cartographers are in greatest demand during wartime. When Japan felt that there was a Russian threat from the north in the late eighteenth century, the emperors started to map Hokkaido and Sakhalin.[10] In the United States, the largest share of the intelligence budget goes to the National Reconnaissance Office (established during the Cold War to deal with satellite photography) and the National Geospatial-Intelligence Agency (founded in 1996 as the National Imagery and Mapping Agency to analyze satellite imagery). As is well known, high officials consider knowledge of cartography to be an asset to their authority, so rulers and generals are often portrayed poring over maps or globes. Queen Elizabeth I was frequently depicted in this manner (as in the "Ditchley Portrait" and the "Armada Portrait"), a symbol of the security of Britain and the strength of the Empire. Early seventeenth-century Mughal Emperor Jahangir is shown in paintings holding a globe, standing on one, and using one as a footstool. In sixteenth-century Spain, King Philip II spent considerable time perusing his map collection—possibly an exercise in vicarious control of an empire by a monarch who was unable to see most of it personally.[11]

Maps may portray state authority in many ways. Boundaries with other countries are provided, administrative subdivisions delineated, and capitals labeled prominently. The Japanese traditionally stressed authority on their maps, with one from the Momoyama period (1573–1615) using visually striking red lines to demonstrate the linkages between the provinces and the capital. The Chinese often placed administrative centers in the middle of their regions, even if they were not actually located there. Also notable was a route strip map of Britain published by the printer John Ogilby in 1675. He had supported the pro-monarchical forces during the Civil War and praised the restoration that brought Charles II to the throne. His map therefore included royal crests along the roads and an accompanying text stressing loyalty to the crown.[12]

Maps are habitually kept secret for national security and commercial reasons. In ancient Egypt, they were stored in a sacred depository presided over by a priestly caste known as the "Learned Men of the Magic Library." These maps had cosmological importance and were not revealed publicly.[13] In 1504 Portugal issued a royal edict imposing a death penalty for the transfer of maps or logs to other countries, as well as a ban on the export of cartographical instruments. All maps were examined for sensitive information, some were destroyed, and those retained were placed in a royal chart room under governmental control.[14] Spain maintained secrecy in regard to charts and sailing directions used by trading vessels, and insisted on their return along with the log upon completion of the voyages. Notwithstanding, the Spanish were generally more open than the Portuguese in regard to maps, as they sent copies to allies and even appointed a Portuguese, Diogo Ribeiro, as royal "Pilot Major" in 1523.[15]

Portugal's security arrangements pertaining to maps were closely related to the great maritime competition with Spain, but the timing points specifically to the race to Asia to obtain spices. Vasco da Gama reached India in 1498, and details of this voyage and ensuing expeditions to Asia during the first half of the sixteenth century then came under a veil of silence on critical details. Also pertinent was the 1502 publication in Italy of the so-called "Cantino map." Alberto Cantino had been detailed to Portugal by the Duke of Ferrara to gather material on Portuguese explorations. He turned out to be a highly efficient spy, since he apparently managed to coax some unnamed Portuguese mapmaker to draw for him a map of the known world. This significant cartographical effort included information from Portuguese expeditions to Brazil and Greenland in 1500 and to Newfoundland in 1501. This "Cantino map," not drawn by Cantino himself, caused a scandal in Portugal and evidently served as the triggering event behind the royal edict of 1504.

The 1578 account of a British effort to locate a Northwest Passage through North America was censored in advance of publication and its preface indicated that information had been excluded in reference to latitude, longitude, distance, true position, and compass variations.[16] Later, in negotiating the Treaty of Paris following the American independence struggle, the British based their positions on a 1755 map that designated earlier boundary arrangements along the Canadian border with red lines. Once the treaty settlement turned out more favorably than the British had imagined, they kept their 1755 map secret.[17] In the Soviet Union, a 1939 atlas featuring maps of the country was published prior to World War II, but later withdrawn due to security concerns.[18] Even now, China is unwilling to release some eighteenth-century maps from the Qing dynasty.[19]

The Japanese tradition of not making maps very precise was related, in part, to a concern that enemies could glean vital geographical information. Maps were not to fall into foreign hands, as gruesomely emphasized by the story of geographer Takahashi Kageyasu, who supervised the Japanese government's explorations and was the designer in 1810 of an influential world map. In 1826, he met Philipp Franz von Siebold, a German doctor who had been dispatched to Japan by the Netherlands three years earlier to report on Japanese scientific knowledge and the prospects for Dutch-Japanese trade. Takahashi wanted to acquire some of Siebold's European books, but Siebold asked for Japanese maps in return. Takahashi risked the death penalty by shipping them to Siebold in Nagasaki, and a sudden typhoon in 1828 then led to his downfall as Takahashi's cache of maps was confiscated from the wreckage by Japanese authorities. There is some dispute as to whether the ship in question was on its way to Nagasaki, or whether Siebold had already received Takahashi's materials and had loaded them onto a different ship for delivery to the Dutch government.

In any case, the Siebold-Takahashi relationship had been compromised with fatal consequences for Takahashi. He was arrested, and he died in prison in 1829 before the investigation of his case had been completed. His body was then immersed in brine for the purpose of preservation until the verdict. In 1830, Takahashi was found guilty and his corpse was subjected to the sentence of beheading post mortem.

Siebold, who was well respected by the imperial court for his scientific expertise, had raised suspicions due to his surveying—including altitude measurements of sacred Mt. Fuji. He had also performed depth soundings in Japanese waters. Once Takahashi's maps were found to include coverage of northern Japanese areas coveted by Russia, Siebold was placed under house arrest for thirteen months, found guilty in 1829 of possessing maps illegally, and then expelled in 1830 rather than imprisoned. He was forced to relinquish the maps in his possession but had already made duplicates, which he managed to take with him upon his departure because a Dutch-Japanese agreement permitted the inspection only of incoming ships. In 1853, Siebold used his map collection to advise the Russian monarchy on Japan, and American Commodore Matthew Calbraith Perry was aided that same year by some of Siebold's maps in entering the Bay of Edo on his mission to open up Japan to more extensive foreign trade. Nevertheless, Japan withdrew the expulsion order against Siebold in 1855 and he returned in 1859 to spend three more years there engaged in scientific interchange. In a strange twist, he was even presented with a sword of honor by the Japanese government.[20]

Misleading foes on the location of potential military targets has a long history throughout the world. During the Cold War, maps of Moscow did not include the site of K.G.B. headquarters. The sixties witnessed American efforts to hide the C.I.A. complex in Langley, Virginia. Turnoff signs on the George Washington Memorial Parkway referred only to "B.P.R.," which was the Bureau of Public Roads. This organization did indeed have facilities in Langley, but there was no additional routing to the C.I.A.

Beginning in the late 1930s, the Soviet Union went to great lengths to distort its maps. The aims were to fool foreign intelligence agencies and prevent accurate bomb attacks. Map scales were not provided, so precise distances could not be determined. Coastlines were altered, and latitudes and longitudes were routinely represented incorrectly. Rivers, railroad hubs, and bridges were moved slightly—and the area around Leningrad had "rotational and linear displacement." Some river towns were depicted on the wrong bank. In 1988, the chief Soviet cartographer admitted the distortions and declared that they were made on instructions from the K.G.B. By then, advances in satellite photography had undercut most advantages sought through false cartography.[21]

GEOGRAPHY AND POLITICS

Early maps were usually cosmological, with religious concepts out-weighing any delineation of political units in the form of "countries." Territory was acquired by conquest, but there was no notion of "discovery" in which large swatches of land could be claimed. When Marco Polo and Abu Abdallah ibn Battuta traveled extensively in the thirteenth and fourteenth centuries respectively, no territory was gained for their homelands Venice and Morocco. The late fifteenth century then initiated an age of "discovery" by Europeans, and the fragmentation of the world into states began to take shape. Assigning place names signified control and cultural influence as countries such as Spain engendered many new "Trinidads," "Salvadors," and locations christened after saints.[22] Maps in the sixteenth and seventeenth centuries stressed authority and sovereignty, with politics becoming the basis of cartographical representation. This is still the case, as maps supply data on economic performance, life expectancy, and so forth in reference to political units—countries. Even weather maps have been politicized, focusing more on forecasts for countries and regions within them than on meteorological phenomena that cut across borders.

Americans call Deutschland "Germany," Chinese refer to the United States as "Meiguo," and Israelis call Spain "Sfarad." There are historical and cultural reasons for such usage, and the intent is not political. It does make sense that maps made for speakers of a particular language should indicate locations in an understandable manner. However, competing names for geographical locations evolve due to rankled national sensibilities. The "Persian Gulf" vs. "Arabian Gulf" controversy has led to the politically correct, but vague, term "the Gulf."[23] The British and French go their own ways in labeling the waterway between them, which the British call the "English Channel" and the French refer to as "La Manche" (The Sleeve). Magyars who see the Transylvania area of Romania as part of a greater Hungary insist on town names such as "Temesvar" and "Nagyvarad" as opposed to the Romanian "Timisoara" and "Oradea." Many militant Islamists are now alluding to sections of the "Indian Ocean" as the "Islamic Ocean." A highly provocative act of gamesmanship took place during the Sino-Soviet conflict when Beijing renamed the street outside the Soviet embassy "Down With Revisionism Lane."[24]

Both Koreas object to the term "Sea of Japan," preferring the "East Sea." Korea and China had used the latter name historically, but there had been other variations such as "Sea of Korea," "Oriental Sea," and "Sea of Whales." A study of eighteenth-century maps at the British National Library reveals that of the 80 labeling this body of water, 62 used the designation "Sea of Korea," 7 "East Sea," 2 used both of these expressions, 6 "Sea of Japan," and 3 "Sea of China." As Japanese military strength grew in the late nineteenth century, and Japanese maps started to be published in English editions, "Sea of Korea" became less common and "Sea of Japan" became predominant. Japan's annexation of Korea in 1910 solidified this trend. In 1929, the International Hydrographic Organization accepted this usage.

Once Korea emerged from Japanese control after World War II, Koreans gradually seized upon the name issue as a matter of national pride. South Koreans began pressuring for reform in the sixties, arguing that "Sea of Japan" was a remnant of colonialism. It favored "East Sea," and did not seek to revert to "Sea of Korea." Since joining the United Nations in 1991, South Korea has sought support from the U.N. Conference on the Standardization of Geographic Names—but Japan has rejected any compromise. The 7th U.N. Conference in 1998 recommended that there be dual labeling, "Sea of Japan" and "East Sea," pending resolution of the dispute. Many atlases and organizations have adopted this usage, but U.N. agencies and CNN have come up with another approach—no labeling of this sea at all.[25]

A fascinating feud over names involves Macedonia. A map war initially led by geographers has embroiled Greece, Bulgaria, and Serbia since the late nineteenth century. In the course of the Balkan Wars of 1912–13, Greece annexed an area in Thrace that it considered to be Macedonian.[26] After World War I, Yugoslavia was created, and it later established a federal republic of Macedonia. For Greeks, Macedonia (although in a more westerly location) was the land of Alexander the Great and was clearly Greek culturally. For Slavs in the Macedonian republic of Yugoslavia, the context was Slavic since a language known as Macedonian is indeed Slavic and related to Bulgarian, not Greek. Eventually, in the early nineties, Yugoslavia disintegrated and its republic of Macedonia became independent. When it attempted to join the United Nations under the name "Republic of Macedonia," Greece strongly objected and imposed trade sanctions. The brouhaha was resolved in March 1993 when the two countries agreed to the usage "Former Republic of Macedonia," and the new state entered the United Nations under that moniker.

The sensibilities of minority nationalities within countries also create some naming controversies. The English-French bilingual debate in Canada's province of Quebec arose out of the minority status of French Canadians, but the imposition of Francophone reforms over the past 30 years has caused consternation among Quebec's minority Anglophones. In Belgium, Flemings and Walloons have different names for many towns, but highway signs signify only one depending on whether you are in Flanders or Wallonia. Passing from one region to another is very confusing. Upon entering Wallonia, for example, Leuven becomes Louvain. This isn't too problematic but, when crossing the opposite way, Anvers is replaced by Antwerpen. Finland maintains bilingual signs in Finnish and

Swedish for major locations and, if secondary ones have a sizable ethnic minority, notation is made in two languages as well.

Name differences also come into play when there are conflicting legal claims. What are the Falklands for the British are the Malvinas for the Argentines. Japan and China are at odds over the Senkaku or Diaoyu Islands. The five islands and three reefs were taken by Japan in 1895, administered by the United States after World War II, and later returned to Japan in 1972 as part of a deal over Okinawa. The problem is whether they are geographically a part of the Ryukyu chain or are within the waters historically associated with Taiwan. Since China considers Taiwan to be an integral component of its territory, China has since 1971 been claiming the Diaoyu Islands. Potentially, oil and fishing rights are at stake in this controversy.

Another issue is sequential name changes. British Honduras became Belize upon independence, and Rhodesia turned into Zimbabwe. These alterations were not contentious because colonial labels were discarded by liberated peoples. So too with the breakup of the Soviet Union when names were changed minimally in an assertion of identity. Thus Moldavia became Moldova, Byelorussia emerged as Belarus, and the capital of Ukraine switched from Kiev to Kiiv. On the other hand, some substitutions have led to political altercations. Burma renamed itself Myanmar in 1989, but the United States still refuses to accept the new appellation as a means of protesting the country's policies. The Soviet city of Stalingrad (previously known as Tsaritsyn) was changed into Volgograd in 1961 during Khrushchev's anti-Stalin campaign, while St. Petersburg went through a cycle of being Petrograd and Leningrad before reverting to the name designated in 1703 by Peter the Great. The 1914 switch to Petrograd took place in the course of World War I as St. Petersburg was deemed too Germanic in sound at a time when Russia was battling the Kaiser's troops. Leningrad came next after the 1924 death of the Soviet leader, but it fell out of favor in the declining years of communism and was replaced by St. Petersburg in 1991.

Sometimes a clash of geographical concepts, instead of names, causes political friction. The 1945 Yalta agreement permitted the Soviet Union to occupy the Kurile Islands, which were Japanese. The Red Army then proceeded to seize the Kuriles, plus four additional islands off the coast of Hokkaido. Moscow claimed that they were part of the Kurile chain, while Tokyo maintained to the contrary that they were "northern territories" of Japan. This dispute has yet to be resolved.

The Shatt al-Arab is a waterway delineating 50 miles of the Iran-Iraq border. There is disagreement over whether it is a tidal river or an estuary of the Gulf, but the main bones of contention have always been where to draw the boundary line and what navigational rights would thus be in force. Efforts to reach accommodation go back almost two centuries, but contemporary difficulties developed during the British mandate following World War I when London backed Iraq's position setting the border on the waterway's Iranian bank. Iran was given permission to engage in limited navigation to the port of Khorramshahr and the Abadan refinery, yet Iraq exercised complete sovereignty over the Shatt al-Arab. In the 1975 Algiers agreement, the two countries concurred that the thalweg principle would be applied so as to split the waterway down its deepest navigational channel. This favored Iran, but was balanced by Teheran's commitment to end all assistance to Iraqi Kurds fighting against their Baathist government. Iraq abrogated this agreement when it invaded Iran in 1980, and the end of the Iran-Iraq war eight years later then reinstated the accord reached in Algeria.

Norway and the Soviet Union had a lengthy rivalry over competing claims in the Barents Sea. The Norwegians wanted to apply the equidistance principle based on determining the median line between islands owned by the two countries. It was a recognized component of international law, but many governments—including the Soviet Union's—backed the sector principle, which would serve to the advantage of states with lengthy Arctic coastlines. A pie-shaped wedge would be drawn from the most easterly and westerly Arctic shore points of the Soviet Union, and would extend all the way to the North Pole. Naturally, Oslo would have secured more of the Barents Sea if relying on the equidistance principle, and Moscow by adherence to the sector principle. Offshore oil rights were the prize.

The same sector principle has been applied in the Antarctic region. Although land claims to Antarctica are frozen for 50 years under a 1991 treaty signed by 24 countries, control over sectors could still provide rights at sea in a region that may be rich in oil deposits. Britain's claim is grounded on the extension of a sector southward from the Falklands. If Argentina had managed to secure the islands in 1982, its own sector would have expanded considerably, with the northern base of its wedge running from Cape Horn in the west to the South Sandwich Islands (which were officially part of the Falklands) in the east—a line known as the "Arc of the Southern Antilles."[27] The sector principle also played a major role in the Beagle Channel dispute between Argentina and Chile. Both countries supported this principle, but they clashed over ownership of islands in the Beagle Channel and Chilean access to the Atlantic coast that would be determinants in the definition of the two sectors. Mediation by Pope John Paul II in 1984 produced a compromise between these two predominantly Catholic rivals.

Disputes over territory may be flamboyantly displayed on postage stamps, which are government produced. There have been stamp wars between Bolivia and Paraguay, Guyana and Venezuela, Belize and Guatemala, and over Argentine and Chilean claims in Antarctica.

Not surprisingly, the Falklands and Argentina have issued competitive stamps depicting controversial maps. In 1922, when the Irish Free State was established, stamps were printed showing no border with Northern Ireland (Ulster)—a component of the United Kingdom. Implications of territorial ambition were also apparent when Romania produced a commemorative sheet in 1993 that featured a greater Romania that had existed after World War I. It included lands that had been incorporated into contemporary Bulgaria and Moldova. Protests against excessive nationalism led to the termination of sales after only 28 days.[28]

Geographical claims may appear in flags, which are symbols of authority over territory. The flag of Somalia displays a five-pointed star representing the Somali people in former Italian, French, and British Somalilands plus those within Kenya and Ethiopia. These latter two locations indicate territorial claims on neighboring states. The flag of the Comoros has four stars to indicate its islands, but Mayotte is actually independent and Anjouan and Moheli are autonomous. The flag of the Greek-controlled Republic of Cyprus sports within itself a flag of the entire island of Cyprus prior to the Greek-Turkish partition.

MIDDLE EAST CAULDRON

The Arab-Israeli conflict has wrought continued violence over land, boundaries, and national self-determination. It likewise has provided a telling example of how maps may be used selectively as instruments of politics. The boundaries set forth in the 1947 U.N. partition plan for Palestine were rejected by all Arab states because they legitimized the creation of Israel. They were then superseded by the 1949 armistice lines drawn following the first Arab-Israeli war, which included a larger Israel, no Palestinian Arab state, and new statuses for Jerusalem, the West Bank, and Gaza. Jerusalem, under the U.N. plan, was to be administered as a "special international regime," but West Jerusalem came to be annexed by Israel and East Jerusalem by Trans-Jordan. The latter also added considerable land west of the Jordan River, which was then deemed the "West Bank." Trans-Jordan thus extended westward beyond the river and concurrently changed its name to Jordan. Gaza was militarily occupied by Egypt, but not incorporated.

Many intriguing cartographical issues arose from these developments. Israeli maps portrayed the country's de facto armistice line boundaries, and Jordanian and Egyptian control over the West Bank and Gaza. Almost all world maps also depicted the West Bank as Jordanian even though only two countries, Britain and Pakistan, recognized this annexation de jure. Arab maps varied. Some adhered to the de facto situation, but many refused to portray Israel as a regional state. Its area was labeled "Palestine," and radical Arabs additionally included the West Bank and

Gaza under this designation. Other Arab maps demonstrated acceptance of Israel, but only within the partition boundaries, so they followed the guidelines of the 1947 U.N. map. This was ironic as, at the time it was issued, the Arabs had opposed partition as a solution.

Jerusalem was problematic. Israel established its capital there in 1950, although the U.N. plan had not placed Jerusalem in either Israel or the Palestinian state that was authorized by the General Assembly but never created by the Arabs. Most countries therefore located their embassies in Tel Aviv, a legal signal that they did not recognize Jerusalem as the capital and that the future status of the city was still negotiable. As a consequence, maps indicating Jerusalem as Israel's capital could basically be interpreted as correct in a de facto sense since the government of the Jewish state clearly operated from there. However, many maps with an anti-Israeli perspective designated Tel Aviv as the capital although it obviously wasn't. It was a case of politics and wishful thinking transcending facts on the ground.

The 1967 Arab-Israeli war further complicated matters as Israel asserted authority over the West Bank, Gaza, East Jerusalem, Syria's Golan Heights, and Egypt's Sinai. East Jerusalem was incorporated into Israel, as was some West Bank land that was annexed to Jerusalem. Cartographers therefore had many options, which tended to reveal their political proclivities. Those who were sympathetic to Israel labeled the West Bank, Gaza, the Golan Heights, and Sinai as "administered territories" and used the phrase "Judea and Samaria" for Jordan's former West Bank. They also included all of Jerusalem within Israeli territory. Mapmakers who were ideologically neutral generally referred to "occupied territory" and maintained the term "West Bank." Some pro-Jordanian maps still depicted the West Bank as part of Jordan, but that country's claim to the area was eventually renounced in 1988 in deference to Palestinian prospects for statehood. Arab cartographers portrayed East Jerusalem and the expanded section of Jerusalem as "occupied territory," and surely didn't recognize these places as components of Israel's capital despite the 1981 extension of the capital to all of Jerusalem. Israeli settlements in "occupied territories" were noted, but not usually identified. Presenting the Hebrew names of settlements could possibly lend legitimacy to the Israeli presence.

Numerous Arab maps indicated that the Golan Heights was annexed by Israel. This is an exaggeration as Israel did impose its laws there in 1981, but did not incorporate the territory. As for the most radical Arab interpretations, such maps displayed an entity described as "Palestine" that included Israel (plus Jerusalem), the West Bank, and Gaza. The most extreme Palestinian Arab maps also placed all of Jordan within "Palestine."

In the post-1993 period a Palestinian Authority has been established in the West Bank and Gaza, yet there is no actual independent state of

Palestine. Most international maps have stayed with the terms "West Bank" and "Gaza," but maps published by the Palestinian Authority describe these areas as "Palestine." Furthermore, Palestinian Authority maps usually leave out Israel and assign its territory to "Palestine," with the added designation that it is "occupied territory." Israeli towns that are historically Arab, such as Nazareth, Acre (Akko), and Jaffa (Yafo), are shown—but Tel Aviv is often left out because it was established by Zionist immigrants.

In 1995, Israel and the Palestinian Authority worked out a tentative deal over the future capital of a Palestinian state that demonstrates a great amount of creative map analysis. Israel maintains that all of Jerusalem is an inherent part of the Jewish state, while the Palestinians insist that their prospective capital must be in that city. What can emerge from such a quandary? Abu Dis. It is an Arab village that had been outside the Jerusalem boundary of the British mandate, inside the U.N. partition's Jerusalem, outside of Jordanian East Jerusalem during the period 1949–67, and straddling the line separating the post-June 1967 expanded Jerusalem from the West Bank. Most of it is in the West Bank, but it can be accurately asserted that a small part of Abu Dis is within Jerusalem. Therefore, Israel can agree to a Palestinian capital in the portion of Abu Dis that is outside of Jerusalem's current boundary, but the Palestinians may proclaim that their capital is within Jerusalem on the basis of the 1947 U.N. partition plan. In May 2000 the Israeli cabinet voted 15 to 6 to place the West Bank section of Abu Dis under direct Palestinian administration, and the legislature (Knesset) then concurred in a 56 to 48 tally. Nevertheless, the Israeli-Palestinian peace talks of 2000–2001 broke down without any agreement, and the status of Abu Dis, as well as that of Palestine itself, is in abeyance. Placing the issue of a Palestinian capital on the table again is still possible, but there is now the added complication, sure to come up in negotiations, of the Israeli barrier built between the two parts of Abu Dis.

Maps may clearly be manipulated, and the grab bag of tools available to the cartographer is extensive. How this intentional process operates will now be addressed as we come to understand the subjectivity of mapmaking techniques.

CHAPTER 4

Sleight of Hand

Advertisers attempt to sell their products, be they physical commodities or political candidates. Mapmakers do likewise as they describe, communicate, and organize information into simple patterns that are visually attractive, comprehensible, and convincing. They too have some subjective agendas, so it is instructive to know who commissioned the work and the cartographer's country, publisher, and audience.[1] Nazi Germany's skillful use of propaganda maps is well documented, and opinionated journalistic cartography boomed in the United States during the thirties. An expert at the Library of Congress maintains that such journalistic cartography demonstrated that maps could be "active," "dynamic," "suggestive," and "demonstrative"—clearly a far cry from scientific objectivity. He describes maps as "educational tools," an observation similar to that of a British geographer who notes "the hidden curriculum of maps."[2]

Customers for maps have their own professional needs, and this leads cartographers to accentuate varying features depending on their audience. Navigators obviously prefer a great amount of coastal detail, aviators look for the delineation of great circle arcs, government officials focus on location and boundaries, military planners are mainly concerned about logistics and terrain, and religious establishments seek accurate information about holy sites and pilgrimage routes. Maps are therefore geared toward representing selective portions of the total reality.

MAKING CHOICES

The mapping process is not quite "an intricately, controlled fiction," as is portrayed in a basic geography textbook, yet it does have tendencies toward manipulation.[3] At the time of the 1897 Klondike gold rush in the Yukon, maps sold to potential prospectors colored the territory yellow to imply the presence of gold. The label "gold field" was then super-imposed in a contrasting color throughout the Yukon, including areas where gold had not been found. Roads to the gold sites misleadingly showed easy accessibility, as such maps were distributed by equipment, outfitting, and transportation companies or by the trade boards of spe-cific towns. One outfitter in Seattle prepared a yellow map of the Yukon and listed its items for sale on the rear. Vancouver and Victoria in Canada were then competing with Seattle and San Francisco in the United States as jumping-off points. The Klondike was exclusively within Canada, but one American map moved the Alaskan border 70 kilometers eastward so that many gold fields would appear to be in the United States. A map distributed by Canadian entrepreneurs along the Lake Bennett route depicted it in red and claimed that the trip from the Victoria-Vancouver area took only 12 days. Alternative routes, presented via an unusual projection that made them look longer than they really were, were listed as taking 42 and 25 days. It was true that the Lake Bennett route was shorter, but one could not tell from the map that it was more difficult to traverse, included hiking through a mountain pass, and was more expensive than alternative routes because it required traveling part of the way by steamer. Such cartographical shenanigans encouraged 100,000 adventurers to set out for the Yukon, but only 40,000 made it there. The number lucky enough to find gold was a paltry 4,000.[4]

Often, exclusions from a map are more indicative of the cartographer's agenda than what is actually incorporated. Such "political silences" are especially pertinent when they are by design and not attributable to defi-cient data or ignorance.[5] Maps, unlike globes, may be "framed" so that what is included implies a sense of unity, with extraneous factors being left out. Interconnections between areas are not evident, as they are when represented spherically.[6]

Technical aspects of mapmaking may be treated with smoke and mirrors by the cartographer. If he doesn't want to illustrate certain details, then he can apply a smaller scale. One geographer complained that such a proce-dure was often employed on ethnic maps to disregard minority groups.[7] The selection of a projection technique is critical. Projections are based on using mathematics to create a flat map of a nearly spherical earth. This is essential to practicality as it is not feasible to assemble a collection of globes instead of an atlas. Projections are related to printing technology in the sense that they are generally produced rectangularly to conform to the shape of books.[8] Projections serve an extremely useful function, but they all represent compromises regarding size, shape, direction, or distance as all cannot be presented accurately in two dimensions simultaneously.

As will be seen in later discussions of World War II, and when examining the late twentieth-century leftist assaults on traditional cartography, the method of projection is based on choices that may be strongly motivated politically. In addition, orientation and placement may be juggled so as to serve a preconceived purpose. Countries may be put in proximity on a flat map, or at countering ends of the earth. Cartographers favoring an alliance between the United States and Western Europe can consequently place these areas near each other by employing a polar projection, whereas those opposed can use a map with the equator as an east-west axis and locate the center longitudinally in the Pacific. This serves to separate the United States and Europe, contributing to an image of a weak relationship.

Graphic elements have political implications. For example, coloring Chechnya differently from the rest of Russia would buttress that region's declaration of independence. Advocacy of Taiwanese independence would be advanced by a hue distinct from that used for China. What color should be applied for the "Northern Territories" (or southern Kuriles) now incorporated into Russia, but claimed by Japan? When an apartheid government controlled South Africa, would it have been appropriate to portray the four supposedly independent black homelands in an alternative color? What about the color of the U.S. commonwealth of Puerto Rico, or of France's overseas departments? Prior to Algerian independence in 1962, should this area have been colored the same as France, which maintained that Algeria was part of the metropole and not a colony?

Labeling, captions, and text are also controlled by the mapmaker. Are places given their indigenous appellations or those supplied by former colonial powers? Describing a country or region as "liberated" would be expressing a value judgment. Should there be any special notation for Hong Kong, which is officially within China but operates in accordance with the principle of "one country, two systems"? Some usage may be technically accurate, but misleading. Birobidjan in the Soviet Union was established under the rubric of being the "Jewish autonomous region" (*oblast*), but no more than 30,000 Jews lived there out of the Soviet Union's more than two million. Diego Garcia, an island in the Indian Ocean, may be labeled as British but it is in practice an American military base.

Symbols, arrows, and data may be biased. Maps of Medieval Europe that display either castles or cathedrals project the cartographer's attitude toward the secular-religious debate. Dots delineating the distribution of ethnic groups, or major weapons, can enhance the visibility of certain factors via bright coloring. Arrows pointing outward, or lines around areas of deployment, can make military formations appear either offensive or defensive. Rather interesting is the story of a British map issued early in World War II. It indicated Soviet and German advances into Poland through the use of arrows. When reprinted in China, only arrows of Soviet movements were included.[9]

The compilation of maps leaves considerable room for ideological juggling. A study of approximately two hundred maps of Macedonia from the nineteenth and twentieth centuries reveals how rival political movements produced sequences depicting ethnic distribution to fan jingoistic claims.[10] "Combination" maps placing images of different time periods side by side may be used, as in Nazi Germany, to illustrate a country's shrinking size—an affective spur to revanchism and *lebensraum*. Look also at atlases. They naturally devote more space to the country of publication, but their coverage of the rest of the world features clear preferential treatment. Let's assume that an American atlas presents maps of the United States first, but Europe is almost always second. Not only that, but there are more maps of Europe than of other continents such as Africa and South America, and many of them have a large scale to accentuate details. Going further, maps of Great Britain, France, and Germany are frequently given considerable space on a page, while those of Scandinavia or the Balkans get lesser attention. Atlases additionally display the cultural biases of their editors in regard to which cities deserve inset maps. Usually New York, London, and Paris—but rarely Shanghai or Mexico City.[11]

LINE DANCE

Land boundaries, which are political lines of separation without any area, were not well developed until the seventeenth century—with the 1648 Treaty of Westphalia playing a noteworthy role within the European context. Previously there had been frontiers based on geographical features as well as historical and cultural traditions, but they had little legal specificity as to location. In fact, government administrative centers frequently moved. Boundaries, often delineated in treaties, were then reinforced by surveying and mapping and established as a "centripetal force" reversing the previous "centrifugal force" of the frontier. Whereas frontiers tended to integrate disparate peoples, boundaries separated them and accentuated political division. It is therefore not surprising that when the first British jigsaw puzzle maps were produced in the eighteenth century, the pieces represented political units.[12]

The boundary between Morocco and the Spanish (Western) Sahara provided a clear divide until 1975 when Spain announced its intention to decolonize. Morocco then mobilized hundreds of thousands of its citizens for a November 1975 "Green March" across the boundary, which served its purpose in February 1976 when Spanish troops withdrew and Morocco annexed about two-thirds of Spanish (Western) Sahara's territory. Mauritania acquired the other third, but this land was transferred to Moroccan control in 1979. Further complicating the matter was that indigenous forces determined to establish an independent state declared the constitution in 1976 of a Saharan Arab Democratic Republic that was recognized by most members of the Organization of African Unity and by the U.N. General Assembly. These organizations were striking a blow against colonialism and annexation, but were additionally advancing the concept that existing boundaries should be maintained.

Efforts to re-designate boundaries are often buttressed, and possibly legitimized, by citing maps. During the 1959 Sino-Indian conflict, premiers Zhou Enlai and Jawaharlal Nehru frequently referred to atlases in their exchanges. Ironically, in terms of ideological perception, the boundary lines to which they alluded had been drawn up many years earlier by either the British colonial authorities who ruled India until 1947 or by the independent state of Tibet, which existed from 1911 to 1951.[13]

One problem with cartographical portrayals of state boundaries is that they generally don't distinguish between those that are de jure (legally recognized) and those that are de facto (borders in practice only).[14] Further variations would be former boundaries, disputed boundaries, or ceasefire lines. An interesting 1925 Chinese map distinguishes between the "present frontier" and the "legitimate frontier." Not surprisingly, the latter includes extensive claims to Mongolia, Malaya, Indo-China, Thailand, the Diaoyu Islands, and part of the Soviet Union. A 1954 Chinese map is similar, and has a label for "Chinese territories taken by imperialism."[15]

A suggestion for clarity and standardization would be to draw a boundary differently depending on whether it is de jure or de facto. Two distinct colors could be utilized, or one type of boundary could be indicated by a solid line and the other by an interrupted one.[16] Variations, or perhaps chicanery, among cartographers would be reduced—but there are other forces at work. A Swedish participant at a 1964 London geographical conference presciently declared: "I must say as a map maker and atlas maker we have not only to take into consideration what the governmental authorities have to say but also what the publishers want and what the school authorities say. . . . Don't always blame the cartographers."[17] Beware the hidden hand of patrons.

War can produce boundary changes, but there are many other scenarios. Consider the breakups of the Soviet Union and Yugoslavia, or the 1990 merger of the two Yemens. Also relevant is that lines pertaining to military occupation zones in Germany were turned into the borders of East Germany and West Germany. Kashmir is divided between India and Pakistan by a "line of control," and the border between China and India is deemed a "line of actual control."[18] There is indubitably great leeway for the cartographer in presenting these distinctions.

Many countries, including India and then Pakistan itself, have been partitioned for the purpose of ethnic separation. Cyprus was divided between Greeks and Turks in 1974, and the existence of the ensuing "green line" has been perpetuated by the Greek Cypriot rejection of reunification proposed in the April 2004 referendum. Germany and Korea were split by Cold War politics. The former was reunified in 1990, and the latter may eventually take a similar path. Palestine's 1948 partition has undergone many de facto boundary changes, with a permanent solution now entwined with the issue of the Israeli barrier currently under construction. It will establish a new de facto arrangement between Israel and the West Bank, and is called a "fence" by Israeli proponents and a "wall" by Arab protesters.[19]

Vietnam was reunified in 1975, but it presented an intriguing analytical conundrum along the way. Just what is an armistice line, and what is a state border? The 1954 Geneva Conference established a "military demarcation line" at the seventeenth parallel, with the final declaration asserting that it is "provisional and should not in any way be interpreted as constituting a political or territorial boundary." There was to be a July 1956 election for the country as a whole, but it never took place. Did the demarcation line become moot, for separate governments were set up in the north and south—the Democratic Republic of Vietnam and the Republic of Vietnam? North Vietnam, backed by the Soviet Union, maintained that there was no state boundary between the zones and that the war taking place in the area was therefore civil. South Vietnam, supported by the United States, viewed the demarcation line as a new border, so it interpreted the war as one of state aggression by North Vietnam. The American "White Paper" of February 1965 concurred, accusing North Vietnam of attempting "to conquer a sovereign people in a neighboring state." Decisions made by mapmakers during the years 1954–75 thus were closely entwined with their politics. Those indicating a "provisional military demarcation line" were not sympathetic to American policy toward Vietnam, while those placing a boundary between North and South Vietnam justified U.S. intervention in defense of a state considered sovereign by Washington. One must look carefully at maps from this period as minor differences over a short border are ideologically telling. The reunification of Vietnam, engendered by South Vietnam's military defeat, then removed this rather large bone of contention.

CHAPTER 5

In the Eye of the Beholder

Psychological projection provides the basis for geographical concepts as the interpreter establishes a vision from his own point of reference. Saharan Tuaregs designate directions from the relationship between their own location and the Islamic holy city of Mecca, so north is known as "the left," south as "the right," east as "the country in front," and west as "the country behind."[1] In Asia, the Chinese, Koreans, and Japanese all labeled bodies of water to their east as the "East Sea." Koreans not surprisingly used to refer to the "West Sea" separating Korea from China, the same place deemed to be the "East Sea" by the Chinese.[2] The Chinese saw India as "the West," looked upon the "Indian Ocean" as the "Southern Ocean" or "Lesser Western Ocean," and ascribed the term "Large Western Ocean" to the "Atlantic."[3]

Europeans, from their global position, delineated the "Eastern" and "Western" Hemispheres, and described the "East" as the "Orient." Many European perceptions became standardized in maps because of their continent's domination of cartography for the past four centuries, but a backlash against "Eurocentrism" toward the end of the twentieth century has made modest inroads into the geographical vocabulary. "West Asia" is making strides as a rough replacement for the "Middle East," but no renaming of the "West Indies" is in sight. The word "Oriental" has become "politically incorrect" in reference to people, because it is predicated on defining them in the context of a European interpretation of direction rather than in terms of a self-definition of place or cultural heritage.

CONFIGURATIONS

The concept of continents has always been arbitrary. The ancient Greeks, and later the Chinese, recognized a contiguous land mass incorporating what we describe as the continents of Europe, Asia, and Africa. Frozen seas at its northern reaches for long blocked successful circumnavigation, which would have proven that there was a "world-island," but it was basically perceived that way and the Greeks even thought that there must have been a southern land mass to balance it. This was long before the European "discoveries" of Australia and Antarctica.[4]

The Greeks gave names to the three regions we now consider to be continents, but no boundaries were described, and the visualization of continents did not really become significant geographically until the fifteenth century. Cardinal Pierre d'Ailly maintained in 1460 that there must be land to the east of Asia to act as its balancer and, indeed, "America" was soon "discovered."[5] The 1519–22 voyage of Ferdinand Magellan's (Fernao Magalhaes') fleet demonstrated that South America was not part of Asia, and this separation between continents was then noted in a 1538 world map prepared by the prestigious Flemish cartographer Gerardus Mercator (Gerard Kremer). It was not proven, however, until the eighteenth century that North America was distinct from Asia.

America at first was recognized as one continent, but shortly thereafter as two. Eighteenth-century European "discoveries" in the South Pacific then led to another continent known as "Oceania" or "Australia/Oceania." In the twentieth century, Australia was promoted to continental status—in part because of its contribution to the Allied military effort in World War II. So was Antarctica, which had become a center for scientific research. There are currently seven continents, but it is conceivable that "Oceania" may become one in its own right.

The boundary between Asia and Africa shifted from the Nile to the Suez Canal, but Egypt's Sinai Peninsula remains in Asia. Africa and Europe were closely linked until the Renaissance by the Mediterranean Sea, but Africa then developed a completely separate identity. The distinction between Europe and Asia is quite amorphous. Russia extends across both continents. Turkey is mostly in Asia, but may eventually enter the European Union. According to Foreign Minister Ismail Cem, "We consider ourselves both European (since seven centuries) and Asian, and view this diversity to be an asset."[6] Israel is surely in Asia, yet it is ostracized by its neighbors. It is kept out of the Asian Games and basically has to function as a European state. Israeli teams play in European basketball and soccer leagues, and an Israeli song is represented in each year's Eurovision contest. At the U.N. Security Council, where rotating seats are filled on the basis of geographical region, Israel has been placed (as a temporary member) in an eclectic group with Western Europe, the U.S., Canada, Australia, and New Zealand.

CHRISTENDOM

Europe was an indeterminate area north of the Mediterranean Sea. It was recognized on medieval "T-O" maps, but its underlying conceptual foundation was religious more than geographical. Especially after the rise of Islam in the seventh century, Europe became a counterweight and developed an attitude of "spiritual superiority," which, in the view of cultural historian Gerard Delanty, disavowed the core of European identity in the "Orient." The Biblical tradition, both Old and New, grew out of events in an area that had become primarily Islamic. The evolution of religious zones thus led Europe to adopt the term "Christendom" in the ninth century, and to move its regional focus northwestward.[7] At the same time, Islam also had a religious interpretation of geography that separated the *dar al-Islam* (abode of peace) from the infidels' *dar al-harb* (abode of war).

The Crusades to free Jerusalem from the Saracens (Muslims) began in 1095 and lasted for nearly two hundred years. European Christians did control the city from 1099 to 1187, but it then reverted to Islamic authority. The Ottoman Empire occupied the Balkans in the fifteenth century, bringing Islamic forces into Europe just when the Moors were about to be expelled from Spain. Turkey's foreign minister correctly points out that Christian Europeans viewed the Muslims as the "Other," but he additionally explains that the Islamic perspective was quite similar. The Ottomans did not consider race to be an important component of identity, but they believed that "social and political differentiation" were determined by who was Muslim or non-Muslim.[8]

Thrown into this religious confrontation was the amazing legend of Prester John. It had a strong impact on Christendom, and Prester John frequently appeared on European maps beginning in 1307.[9] He was considered to be a presbyter, a church elder and priest who led a congregation, and he was brought to the attention of Europeans in 1145 when Bishop Hugh of Jabala, Syria (but now within Lebanon), met with a representative of Pope Eugenius III. Edessa, a town in Turkey near the Syrian border, had fallen to the Muslims the previous year and Bishop Hugh was then dispatched to Rome by Prince Raymond of Antioch, who was allied with the papacy against the Byzantines. Bishop Hugh described Prester John as a likely descendent of one of the three "wise men," and as a powerful Nestorian Christian leader living east of Armenia and Persia.[10] Nestorius, a fifth-century Bishop of Constantinople, had drawn distinctions between the human and divine aspects of Christ, and his followers were active in Asia all the way to China.

Bishop Hugh probably didn't invent Prester John, but he certainly transmitted his legend to Europe. He told the Pope that Prester John wanted to support the Crusades, and that he had sent an army to defend Jerusalem. Unfortunately, his troops had not been able to cross the Tigris en route, so Bishop Hugh was seeking more European help for the religious war against the Muslims. He was successful, as the Pope called for a Second Crusade, and German and French fighters departed for the Holy Land in 1147.[11]

Sometime between 1156 and 1165, a letter supposedly sent by Prester John was received by Byzantine Emperor Manuel I Comnenus and a copy was forwarded to Holy Roman Emperor Frederick Barbarossa. The mysterious presbyter maintained that he lived in India, ruled a rich kingdom, and was anxious to participate in the Crusades. Many Christians at that time believed that St. Thomas had gone to India in the first century, and that a Christian community existed there. There was therefore a golden opportunity to forge an alliance with a Christian leader who could strike against the Muslims from their rear. Consequently, Pope Alexander III addressed a letter to Prester John in 1177 offering to provide an instructor in Catholicism. Of course, no contact was made. Then, in 1245, Pope Innocent IV dispatched a Franciscan monk named Giovanni da Pian del Carpini to look for Prester John in Mongolia. Another intention was to develop cooperation with the Mongols to confront the Muslims since Mongol strength was evident as a result of their expansion into Europe.[12] Missionaries were also sent to Mongol-controlled areas in an effort to enlist support against the Muslims.

The myth of Prester John was soon furthered by Marco Polo in the late thirteenth century, as the Venetian explorer claimed that Prester John had lived among the Mongols, but had been killed earlier that century by Genghiz Khan. Marco Polo thus conformed to the legendary account that Prester John was in the East, but he did not emphasize Prester John's potential role as a Christian ally in a confrontation with the Muslims.

The Reformation divided Christianity. "Christendom" was no longer a unifying concept, so usage of the term "Europe" became increasingly common. "Europe" stood in contrast to the Ottoman Empire, but also to the lands "discovered" by the Spanish and Portuguese in America and Africa. The spread of Christianity then undercut Europe's sole claim to preservation of the faith, and the secularizing tendencies of the Renaissance and Reformation also served to reduce the salience of religion as Europe's defining characteristic.[13]

The status of Russia was highly problematic. Although Christian, it was considered to be on the frontier and only its most western portion was considered to be an integral component of Europe. This outlook had been evident previously in the "T-O" maps that depicted the Don River as Europe's eastern boundary, and Russia itself produced few printed maps until the seventeenth century. In 1697–98, Tsar Peter the Great commissioned (in Amsterdam) the first modern Russian map. It was published at first with Russian labeling, and then for a broader audience in 1699 with Latin. In 1715, Peter began an institutionalized cartographical program under the aegis of the Naval Academy, and a seven-year survey of Russia was completed in 1727, after Peter's death. Based upon these developments, detailed geographical knowledge about Russia was extended eastward and the Ural Mountains came to be depicted as the boundary of Europe. This revision of geography was reflected in a 1730 map produced by a Swedish military officer imprisoned by the Russians, and in a 1745 atlas prepared by the Russian Academy of Sciences. Russia's first atlas had been published in 1737.[14]

The Ottoman presence continued to rankle Europeans as an alien, "Asian" intrusion. Therefore, in the late nineteenth century, they coined the expression "Near East," which was to be applied to the region between Europe and the "Far East." The aim was to detach cognitively the Ottoman Empire from Europe, so the "Near East" consequently included the Balkans, which clearly were located in Europe geographically. After the demise of the Ottomans in World War I, "Near East" was no longer applied to the former Ottoman territories in Europe, and the term "Middle East" was introduced for Turkey and other countries in western Asia.[15] The geography of Europe thus was influenced by political and cultural considerations, demonstrating that the definition of a continent goes beyond mere physical features.

The Europeans not only developed their own continental identity, but that of Asia as well. Asia was delineated by the ancient Greeks, but its relationship to Europe was not really clarified until the eighteenth and nineteenth centuries when the Europeans contrasted themselves to the inhabitants of a continent ostensibly featuring agrarianism, a low level of development, and political despotism. The distinction between Europe and Asia was deemed civilizational as well as geographical as the Europeans invented their own vision of the identity of the "other." Basically, the peoples of Asia did not perceive of themselves as "Asians" until the Europeans classified them that way.[16]

SELF-CENTERED

Longitude is a crucial geographical concept, but it is evidently a projection from the human mind rather than a physiographical feature of the earth's surface. We can, nevertheless, rather easily accept that a spherical earth has 360 degrees of circumference, even though this figure was arbitrarily set, and that numbered meridians apply some sense of order and standardization to the world. More controversial is determining where zero degrees of longitude, the prime meridian, should be located since it can be placed anywhere without any mathematical consequences. The path toward adoption of a Greenwich prime meridian therefore did not include rancor over geometry, but was fascinating politically due to its great power rivalries and machinations.

Ptolemy drew the prime meridian through the Canary (Fortunate) Islands, the westernmost spot in the world known to the Greeks. Islamic cartographers, who relied extensively on the writings of Ptolemy, generally went along with his prime meridian but sometimes positioned it instead on the West African coast.[17] Indians tended to have it running through Ceylon (Sri Lanka), while Europeans used many locations such as Greenwich, Lisbon, Paris, and Cadiz. Americans preferred Washington, D.C., New York, or Philadelphia.

Beginning in the late eighteenth century, the British pressed for universal recognition of Greenwich. After all, they produced most of the sea charts used by navigators plus they had historically been marginalized visually by European maps concentrating on the Mediterranean. The 1871 International Geographical Congress in Antwerp accepted Greenwich as far as the sea was concerned, but stipulated that coastal harbor charts could be based on any prime meridian. France agreed, and this system was supposed to become obligatory after fifteen years. Then, at the 1875 IGC congress in Rome, France backtracked and maintained that its approval of Greenwich had been conditional upon British adoption of the metric system. The 1883 Seventh International Geodesic Conference in Rome, attended by scientists, recommended Greenwich, but the battle was really political and a solution could not be found until diplomats assembled in Washington in 1884 for an International Meridian Conference.[18]

In August 1882, U.S. President Chester Arthur had proposed such a conference—and he then secured support through a Congressional resolution. In October 1883, the railroad industries of the U.S. and Canada adopted a General Time Convention for North America that was based on Greenwich Mean Time. Britain had established this time synchronization for itself in 1843, but its extension to North America was the brainchild of Sandford Fleming, who had moved from Britain to Canada in 1845. Fleming was a railroad surveyor who recognized that scheduling of trains had to be coordinated in a logical manner. Localities were using different time systems, causing bedlam, so he recommended in 1878 that the world should be divided into 24 time zones. Each zone would therefore cover 15 degrees of longitude, and Greenwich would be the hub for calculations. No zonal line would actually run through Greenwich as this would divide Britain into two zones. Instead, there would be one zone with Greenwich along its central axis. It would stretch 7 1/2 degrees both eastward and westward. Fleming's time zone concept was approved in the General Time Convention, thereby establishing five time zones for North America.

This system was non-governmental, but time zones would inevitably have to be related to the prime meridian issue. This acceptance of Greenwich Mean Time was thus a boon to Britain's prospects for placement of the prime meridian through Greenwich.[19]

Forty-one delegates from 25 countries convened at the International Meridian Conference. All were European or American, except for representatives from Japan, Turkey, Liberia, and Hawaii. The United States backed Britain and proposed a Greenwich meridian drawn through the Old Royal Observatory, which dated from 1675. France knew that it didn't have sufficient support for selecting Paris, so it protested that the conference should only decide whether a prime meridian was necessary, not where it should be located. This gambit failed, so it then called for "absolute neutrality." This meant that the meridian should not intersect any European or American state. The United States and Britain responded that, to the contrary, it must be aligned with a major astronomical observatory and this limited the choice to Greenwich, Washington, Paris, or Berlin. A Canadian delegate then explained why Greenwich was preferable: The shipping industry relied on maps with a Greenwich meridian. France sensed potential defeat and therefore tried to link the prime meridian issue to the metric system. An American delegate argued that it was actually a French system of measurement, not a neutral one, but Britain agreed to endorse an international metric convention as long as it was not compulsory in application. France, recognizing that practicality and commercial considerations favored the British position on the prime meridian, had tried to appear above the political fray by stressing science and rationality. This approach eventually failed.

By a vote of 22-1-2, the Greenwich meridian was adopted. San Domingo voted "no" as a sign of support for France. France and Brazil abstained. France, displeased that its rival Britain had been victorious, then played havoc with the delineation of time zones. The conference had not standardized them, so France in 1891 went on Paris Mean Time rather than Greenwich Mean Time. This caused confusion in the boundaries of time zones, so France in 1896 accepted the mean at Greenwich but continued to refer to "Paris Mean Time." This maneuver was accomplished by moving Paris Mean Time westward by 9 minutes and 21 seconds to conform to the Greenwich meridian.[20]

Political friction was evident at the conference. France was in competition with Britain, and the United States backed its former colonial ruler. The United States even presented the resolution advocating a Greenwich meridian. Washington's stance seems have been influenced by a desire to preserve Anglophone unity and help establish a worldwide bloc composed of Britain, its Empire, and the United States. Together, they could dominate shipping and communications, as well as represent an impressive grouping in terms of population and wealth.[21]

There was some foot-dragging by both France and the United States in switching over from reliance on Paris or Washington meridians respectively. Britain did not go metric. On the other hand, there was definitely cartographical sense in choosing Greenwich. Whereas the conference had not attempted to formalize an international dateline, it was assumed that it would be 180 degrees around the world from the prime meridian. This meant having it run through the Bering Strait and the Pacific, intersecting very little land. The location was therefore very practical, and it was made universal in 1893. So as not to have it divide any countries, the line was bent in some areas.[22]

Worldviews

CHAPTER 6

Completing the Circle

The "Age of Discovery" began in the fifteenth century and featured exploration by European countries—particularly Portugal and Spain. European influence was extended outward through the establishment of colonies and the spread of Christianity, with sea power the driving force furthering this geographical diffusion. This imperial ambition was reflected in the development of maps, which also acted on a quasi-legal basis as substantiation for overseas territorial claims. Maps proliferated in Europe at this time due to Johannes Gutenberg's invention of movable type, but the first printed maps were actually made in China in the twelfth century.

European advances in seafaring were related to the revival of Ptolemaic cartography, which was indirectly reintroduced by the Muslims. They had relied on Ptolemaic concepts of latitude, longitude, and sphericity since the ninth century, but it was not until 1400 that Ptolemy's works published in Arabic reached Florence, to be translated into Latin by 1407.[1] Portolan charts, which had originated in the thirteenth century, were also vital to the European cartographical renaissance. Their emphasis on scale and accurate depiction of coastlines was based on empirical observation (including use of the compass), a process quite distinct from Christian cartography prevalent at that time in Europe.[2] This combination of Ptolemaic mapmaking and portolan charts spelled the death knell of the religious framework of analysis, while exploration simultaneously undermined many of its precepts. Whereas the *mappaemundi* portrayed a land-based world of three interconnected continents, room had to be made for much more spacious oceans, and for America.[3] Portuguese voyages toward the Cape of Good Hope also dispelled notions of an impassable "hot zone," or the presence of non-human Antipodeans in the southern reaches. "Discovery" thus proved to be cognitive as well as geographical.

Christopher Columbus exemplified the bridge between theologically grounded projections superimposed on the world and cartography's spirit of evolving personal examination and verification. He also attuned mapmaking to the prospects of empire, linking it to diplomacy and commerce. Columbus' vision was constrained by invalid cultural assumptions, but he was still a great navigator who extended European geographical knowledge by challenging conventional wisdom and setting forth in a new direction.

CONTRASTING IMAGES

Spurred by Marco Polo's tales about the riches of the Orient, the Spanish and Portuguese became engaged in a race to Asia to secure spices—with the former heading eastward and the latter westward. Both assumed the sphericity of the earth, so disregard any distorted notions about the supposed aims of Columbus and Magellan. The critical point was that the two competing powers differed in their calculations of the distance to the "Indies." One factor was that Portugal was more advanced in cartography due to its employment of Jewish and Muslim mapmakers, many of them coming from Majorca and Barcelona. The Jewish role in Portuguese cartography was so extensive that many charts and logs used Hebrew letters as a cipher corresponding to numbers. This provided a security system effective against spies and pirates.[4] Furthermore, Jews and Muslims were not influenced by Christian cartography and recognized that large oceans could lie to the west en route to Asia. Portugal also employed Martin Behaim, the German geographer who produced a path-breaking terrestrial globe in 1492. It caught the essence of the age as far as Europe was concerned as traveling either east or west to arrive at the same place could best be visualized on a globe.

Prince Henry the Navigator (Dom Henriques) set Portugal on an eastward course in the mid-fifteenth century, in part because the goal was to trade with India rather than China. Constantinople had fallen to the Ottomans in 1453, thereby blocking the overland route to Asia. Papal bulls in 1455 and 1456 granted Portugal exclusive exploration rights to the south and east, an arrangement solidified in the 1479 Treaty of Alcacovas and in another bull of 1481. Portuguese seamen then navigated down the West African coast, and King Joao II approved funding for the 1487–88 voyage of Bartolomeu Dias for his expedition around the southern tip of Africa.[5] At the time, maps tended to compress Africa latitudinally, so the Portuguese voyages extended the perception of Africa vertically and helped alter the more horizontal view of the world that had prevailed in the European imagination.[6]

The Spanish adhered more to the Esdras II concept of the earth being composed primarily of land, and they did not anticipate the existence of a large Pacific Ocean. This assumption, linked to an underestimated computation of the distance to Asia, led them to believe that the shortest route to the Orient's spices was westward. Part of the problem was determining how many degrees of longitude were taken up by the Mediterranean Sea. Ptolemy had incorrectly calculated the distance from Alexandria to Tangier at 54 degrees, when it was actually 35 degrees and thirty-nine minutes. Based partly on this error, he asserted that the width of the Mediterranean was 62 degrees when it was really only 44 degrees. Ptolemy's mistakes pertaining to latitude were later corrected through careful measurement, but such a scientific approach in regard to longitude was not yet available in the late fifteenth century.[7] Thus exaggerating the longitudinal width of the Mediterranean would naturally shorten the estimated distance westward to Asia. Underestimating the earth's circumference due to reliance on Marinus of Tyre (circa 100 A.D.) and Ptolemy would only compound such an error.

The Portuguese were not affected by this issue as they planned to go eastward and could rely on the observations of the Arabs and Chinese rather than on abstract mathematics. The Arabs and Chinese influenced each other cartographically. The former acquired knowledge of the grid system and compass, the latter of the Indian Ocean, African coastline, and the calculation of angles. Most significantly, the Arabs had figured out by the eleventh century that Ptolemy (and Hipparchus before him) was wrong in describing the Indian Ocean as a closed sea due to a land connection between southern Africa and Asia. If this was truly the case, Africa could not be rounded on the way to Asia and the Portuguese effort would be in vain.[8] The Arabs had sailed southward along the East African coast, and may also have been aware of Herodotus' contention that the Phoenicians had circumnavigated Africa clockwise starting from the Red Sea about 600 B.C.[9] This knowledge that one could travel around Africa to Asia was secured from the Muslims by the Venetian cartographer Fra Mauro of San Michele, who had been hired by Afonso V of Portugal to produce a world map. Fra Mauro's 1459 work, submitted to the Portuguese crown, depicted the sea passage to Asia and a rather accurate shape for Africa.[10] Portugal therefore had a distinct advantage over Spain, which did not possess this information. It protected this secret from other Europeans, but the Chinese clearly were well aware of African geography. Their maps from 1320, 1389, and 1402 all show that the Atlantic and Indian Oceans met at the Cape of Good Hope.[11]

When Bartolomeu Dias turned northward after passing the southern tip of Africa, he did not prove absolutely that the Indian Ocean wasn't an inland sea, since it was possible that Africa's reputed land link to East Asia started beyond the point along the shore that he had reached. However, it is likely that Dias had heard prior to his voyage that Asia could be accessed by sea, as Portugal had garnered such information from emissaries and spies sent to the Middle East and the northern portion of the East African coast.[12] In 1487, King Joao II had also dispatched Pero da Covilha to see if there was a sea route to India. He journeyed to Ethiopia and Somalia and then continued on to India by land and by sea. On his return trip in 1489–90, he traveled the East African coast from Somalia to Mozambique. Da Covilha concluded on the basis of information provided by Indian Ocean navigators that Africa could be circumnavigated, and that voyages from Europe to India were feasible.[13] Dias could not benefit from da Covilha's findings because he had left Portugal in 1487 and rounded the Cape of Good Hope in 1488.

WESTWARD HO!

Navigator and cartographer Christopher Columbus, who was possibly Genoese, wanted to sail westward to Asia. He first sought the financial backing of Portugal, but King Joao II turned him down in 1484 because he had underestimated the distance to Asia.[14] Columbus then approached Queen Isabella of Spain in 1486. She appointed a commission to evaluate his proposal, which recommended in 1490 that he be denied funding. His plan was deemed impractical, as a round-trip journey could take three years. Significantly, there was no criticism of Columbus' belief that the earth was spherical, since the sixth-century flat-earth theory of Cosmas Indicopleustes had little influence. However, once the Spanish defeated the Moors at Granada in January 1492, King Ferdinand and Queen Isabella were emboldened to establish an overseas empire. They consequently approved Columbus' expedition in April. Also influencing them was the desire to compete with the Portuguese in the race to Asia, for Dias had already reached the Cape of Good Hope.[15] In August, the intrepid navigator set sail for Asia—but, in October, he reached landfall in the Bahamas off the American coast.

Did Columbus have any prior knowledge of America's existence? There is no hard evidence that he did, but there are two main lines of speculation related to a possible visit to Iceland and to familiarity with Viking voyages garnered from Portuguese sources. Surely the Vikings had been to what later came to be called "America," most notable being the trips in 986 and 1001 by Bjarne Herjulfsson and Leif Ericson (Eiriksson) respectively. Could Columbus have learned about their findings during a reported stay in Iceland in 1477? In his papers, there is a reference to his having been at 73 degrees north latitude and far to the west. On the other hand, his diary entry for December 21, 1490, indicates that the furthest north he had been was to England. Adding to the confusion is that his son Ferdinand may have misinterpreted Columbus' notation about conceivably having traveled as far north as Iceland. Unfortunately, Ferdinand's claim appeared publicly only in Italian translation after his Spanish original was missing. Nevertheless, Columbus could have heard about Viking expeditions irrespective of any journey to Iceland. The British, sailing from Bristol, had been trading with Iceland since 1427, and Columbus may have acquired information about the Vikings from them. Furthermore, Columbus could not have known that the Vikings had been to a new continent rather than the northeast portion of Asia. European maps that took the Viking expeditions into account assumed that their destination had been Asia.[16]

Without ever having been to Iceland, Columbus still could have learned about the Vikings from the Portuguese. Here again, available evidence is inconclusive. There are reports that the Portuguese financed Scandinavian voyages to "America" (in the vicinity of Newfoundland) during the period 1471–81, and that navigator Joao Vaz Corte-Real even sailed with the Scandinavians. If so, Columbus may have relied on Portuguese narratives about the Vikings and "America" and his purported reference to having been to Iceland personally may actually have been based on Portuguese accounts.[17] Whatever may have transpired, Columbus kept any advance knowledge about "America" secret as he sought financial backing for an expedition. He probably did not want to be preempted, nor did he want to acknowledge earlier journeys that could lay the foundation for territorial claims.[18]

Columbus' optimism about reaching Asia by sailing westward was partly a result of his underestimation of the distance involved. He was influenced by Ptolemy's east-west exaggeration of the Mediterranean, and by Marco Polo's account of Asia extending an extra 30 degrees longitudinally. Columbus in addition relied heavily on Pierre d'Ailly's treatise of 1410 and Henricus Martellus' map of 1489, which also incorporated such errors. Pierre d'Ailly was a French cardinal and theologian, while Henricus Martellus (Heinrich Hammer) was a German cartographer resident in Florence. More controversial is the impact of the map prepared by Paolo dal Pozzo Toscanelli in 1474. Toscanelli was a Florentine astronomer, mathematician, and geographer whose miscalculation of the earth's circumference led him to favor a westward route to Asia rather than the Portuguese effort eastward. Toscanelli may have written to Columbus about his views, but no original copy of such a letter has been located.

There is no evidence that Columbus knew about Martin Behaim's 1492 globe prior to his departure from Spain, but he was familiar with world maps on which it was based. Behaim's work was commissioned by his birthplace Nuremberg's town council, which was composed of businessmen, and he himself was engaged in commerce. His globe therefore included many notations about trade and depicted a sea route passing by the Cape of Good Hope toward Asia. Behaim's measurement for the circumference of the earth, however, was 25 percent too small, and it therefore encouraged those who believed that Asia was not too distant if one sailed westward. In fact, China was about 230 degrees west of Portugal, yet Behaim's globe showed it only 130 degrees away. Of course, Behaim was as yet unaware that an entire New World separated Europe from Asia. Behaim's globe interestingly included the three kings in the area of the Indian Ocean, illustrations of Prester John in both Asia and Africa, and a reference to Gog and Magog, but Behaim did not accentuate the traditions of the Christian *mappaemundi* and did not mark off any Garden of Eden.[19]

Columbus' geographical perceptions were distorted due to his acceptance of some aspects of Christian cartography. Especially influencing him was Esdras II's notion of limited oceans. Columbus often cited Esdras II in his writings, and this incorrect depiction of land mass led him to minimize the breadth of the seas between Europe and Asia. Additionally affecting Columbus was Christian cartography's assumptions that all continents were connected, and that there were only three continents. He therefore could not imagine that he had actually sailed to a "new" continent.[20] Columbus was a religious Catholic who had an apocalyptic interpretation of the end of the world, expected the rise of an Antichrist, and saw himself as similar to Jesus as a "good shepherd" who would convert the heathens (as in John 10:11 and 16). Columbus even began to write a *Book of Prophesies* about his divine Christian mission. On his third voyage to the New World in 1498, he found fresh water in the sea off South America. It had come from a river that we now know as the Orinoco, but Columbus' Biblical frame of mind rendered it one of the rivers from Paradise described in Genesis. In such a manner, Columbus' "inner vision" engendered expectations that influenced his interpretation of what he had found, and this process became increasingly self-reinforcing as he made more discoveries in America[21]

In common with other navigators, Columbus could not just define new things that he saw without reference to conceptual categories already imprinted on his mind. His description of lands and peoples were therefore divorced from the reality of their existence. So firm was Columbus' reliance on his own conceit that he inaccurately projected his own illusions, and even managed not to see what he didn't want to know.[22]

As it became apparent that Columbus had "discovered" America and had not been to Asia, Christian theology was forced to deal with a new problem. If the sons of Noah settled in three continents, and if all humans descended through Noah's line, then how would American "Indians" fit into this scenario? Were they human? After controversy over this issue, Pope Julius II concluded in 1512 that "Indians" were human and were descendents of Adam and Eve. In his interpretation, they were originally Asians but had departed from Babylonia prior to the time of Noah and the flood.[23] This astute papal explanation thus reconciled theology with the evolving perception of world geography. It additionally provided a theoretical framework for proselytizing in the New World, as heathen souls could not be saved there unless the "Indians" were included within humankind.

In March 1493, Columbus stopped in Lisbon on his way back to Spain. He met with Joao II, who was worried that Columbus may have visited lands that should have belonged to Portugal under previous zonal arrangements such as the 1454 papal bull and a treaty with Castile, a region that had become part of a unified Spain in 1479. Basically, Portugal had the rights to lands south of the Canaries. Columbus, whose patron was Spain, refused to say anything that would put Spanish territorial claims in jeopardy.[24]

The Vikings had surely been to America before Columbus, but he was frequently credited with this "discovery" because his voyages symbolized Spain's westward quest for Asia. In reality, Columbus had failed to reach Asia as planned and did not provide gold for Spain's coffers. His reputation plummeted, and he was even arrested in 1500 for being an incompetent administrator of Spain's possessions in the New World. The current image of Columbus as a hero, who possibly proved that the world is round, is surely a case of posthumous rehabilitation. He was not lionized at his time and, as will be seen, Vasco da Gama and Portugal won the race for Asia's riches.[25]

BIFURCATION

Columbus' voyage to the New World accelerated Portuguese-Spanish competition over areas of exploration. Therefore, in May 1493, Pope Alexander VI agreed to mediate. Born Rodrigo Lancol y Borja (Borgia) in Spain, he had become Pope in 1492 with the support of Ferdinand and Isabella. His four bulls on the matter were favorable to Spain, as it was given rights to all of the New World. Basically, the Pope maintained that non-Christian lands would be divided between the two Catholic powers—with Portugal being entitled to territories north and east of a line running west of the Azores and Cape Verde, and Spain being granted control to the south and west. Assignment of zones at sea was not addressed.[26] This solution was mainly based on longitude, a mathematical formulation, and did not contain elements of Christian cartography.

Portugal was unhappy with the papal bulls, claiming that they included a miscalculation of the distance from the Azores to Columbus' landing point in the New World and that they did not leave adequate passage for their ships down the west coast of Africa. Spain strongly endorsed the bulls and sent Columbus westward on a second voyage of "discovery" only four

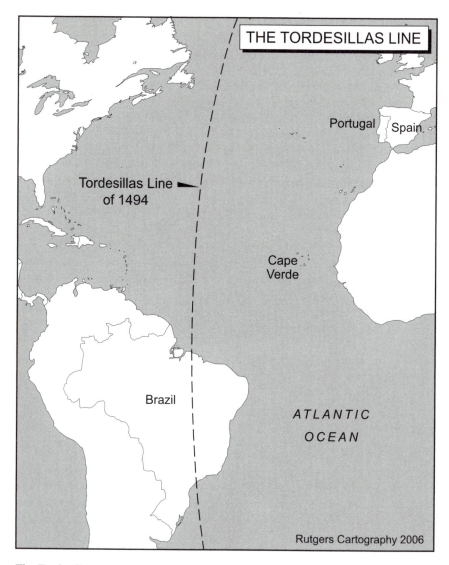

The Tordesillas Line

months later. Continuing differences were then reconciled in the June 1494 Treaty of Tordesillas. The dividing line was moved 14 degrees westward (more than six hundred miles) in order to satisfy Portugal, which may have coveted fishing rights east of Newfoundland. Spain was permitted to retain lands "discovered" prior to July 1494 in the area it was relinquishing. Columbus was still on his second voyage, but he in fact had not found new territories for Spain covered by this temporary waiver clause. Probably unbeknownst to both Spain and Portugal, part of what came to be Brazil lay within Portugal's zone. Actual landfall in Brazil most likely did not take place until 1500 when Portuguese navigator Pedro Alvares Cabral arrived there accidentally after being blown off course on his way to India.[27]

The Treaty of Tordesillas, based on maps rather than a globe, inferentially assigned lands throughout the world to Portugal and Spain. The zones extending from the partition line in the Atlantic had no limit, and theoretically would therefore meet again somewhere on the opposite side of the earth. However, the Pacific Ocean had not been explored by Europeans, and no line was established there 180 degrees from the one in the Atlantic. The two Catholic monarchies were granted the rights to empire, but they were later challenged by Protestant powers such as England and the Netherlands that didn't accept the provisions of Tordesillas.

Portugal's explorations eastward became involved with our erstwhile mythical figure, Prester John. After much of the Mongol Empire had become Islamic in the thirteenth century, the prospect of finding a Christian ruler in Asia was remote. No sizable Christian community had even been detected in India, where St. Thomas was believed to have established a Christian presence in the first century. The focus then shifted to Africa, with particular attention given to Ethiopia since Christian kings were believed to reign there. It was maintained that while Prester John was at one time associated with India, Ethiopia was really part of India. There was indeed a basis for such an assumption, with sources for almost four centuries referring to Ethiopia that way.[28] Maps from the early fifteenth century started to depict Prester John in Ethiopia, and Portuguese navigators going southward along the West African coast looked for a route to Ethiopia. At that time, many Europeans thought that a tributary of the Nile emptied into the Atlantic, so the Portuguese hoped to sail eastward along this tributary to the land of Prester John, and then return to Europe via a northward Nile route.[29] Furthermore, the Nile was correlated with the rivers from Paradise mentioned in Genesis—so why shouldn't Prester John live near the Nile? Later, it was demonstrated that the waters of Ethiopia were indeed a major source of the Nile.

In 1487, Joao II sent Afonso de Paiva and Pero da Covilha to Ethiopia via Egypt. Paiva disappeared, and Covilha detoured on his royal mission to India before arriving in Ethiopia in 1493. He met "Prester John," who was actually Emperor Eskender, and then ended up living there permanently. When he decided in 1520 to leave, he was denied permission.[30] In 1497, Vasco da Gama had set off for India in search of Prester John. He carried letters addressed to him, and he thought that he had found his man once he had reached India in 1498. In his log for May 28, 1498, da Gama relates that he told an Indian ruler that Portugal has dispatched him to establish contact with a Christian king such as himself. Da Gama was completely off the mark since the gentleman was actually a Hindu, and da Gama had mistaken Hindu temples for Christian churches.[31]

There were now two Prester Johns, one in Ethiopia and another in India. The Portuguese thus acknowledged that the Prester John story was a legend, but they also aligned in the early sixteenth century with the Emperor of Ethiopia against the Muslims. This paralleled the rationale for the original Prester John myth. Surely the same Prester John, who was supposedly alive in 1145, could not still have been around four hundred years later.[32] Yet the Flemish cartographer of German ancestry Ortelius (Abraham Ortels) did entitle a 1573 map "The Kingdom of Prester John," and this venerable Christian leader continued to appear on other maps throughout the late sixteenth century.[33]

The Spanish surge westward, exemplified first by Columbus' expeditions, was perpetuated by the Portuguese explorer Magellan. He approached his country's crown for support, arguing that the Treaty of Tordesillas had placed the spice-rich Moluccas in the Portuguese zone, but he was denied backing three times because of his westward focus. This fit in better with Spain's endeavors, and Magellan was consequently financed by Portugal's rival after claiming that the treaty really put the Moluccas in the Spanish zone. Significantly, he used a globe at his meeting with Charles I (who was also selected in 1519 as Holy Roman Emperor Charles V) to make his point. Magellan then worked out a deal in which the first five "Spice Islands" (Moluccas) "discovered" would belong to Spain, while the next two would be his property.[34] Magellan never made it. He left Spain, sailed westward via Cape Horn at the southern tip of South America, and then landed in the Philippines in 1521. He was killed in an attack on his party, although two of his ships did later reach the Moluccas.[35] After his death, Juan Sebastian d'Elcano assumed command of one of his vessels and sailed westward back to Spain. This circumnavigation of the earth, proving its sphericity, had never been Magellan's intention, but he has been indelibly linked to this interpretation in the public imagination.

Magellan's voyage engendered controversy over the status of the Moluccas, which the 1524 Badjoz-Elvas Conference failed to resolve. Agreement was then reached in the 1529 Treaty of Saragossa. Portugal was to pay Spain for rights to the Moluccas, and a new line was set in the Pacific to delineate spheres of influence. The Portuguese did not realize that the Moluccas had been within their zone under the Treaty of Tordesillas. Spain had already been unsuccessful in several attempts to develop a spice trade there as the ships that reached the Moluccas from Mexico and Peru failed to complete a return voyage. Asia was then basically left to the Portuguese, although Spain did claim the Philippines in 1542 and established a colony there in 1564. Portugal took control over Macao in 1553 and developed it into a way-station for trade with Japan.[36] Mapmaking had become a matter of politics and geometry, with no religious principles applied. The age of Christian cartography was over as European states moved in the direction of rationalism and empiricism—as well as global rivalry.

CHAPTER 7

New Directions

Columbus' voyages, predicated on going west to arrive east, coincided with the development of a global world image based on sphericity. What remained was to fill in unknown areas, with the Europeans seizing the lead in this endeavor. Using geometric projections, grids, and scale, they came to dominate cartography for centuries and were also careful to preserve their maps. Europeans explored, traded, and colonized as they replaced the blanks with boundaries and additional political units rather than with imaginary monsters. Maps went hand in hand with this evolution of political economy, helping to forge a discipline emphasizing the interconnectedness of regions. Consequently, a strong sense of international history began to emerge among the European imperial states.

Columbus' landfall to the west opened up new possibilities of reaching the Orient in that direction. Consequently, in 1496, King Henry VII of England authorized John Cabot (Giovanni Caboto, a Venetian born in Genoa) and his sons to sail westward to China. Henry believed that Columbus had actually been to Asia, and he wanted the Cabots to engage in the spice trade there. In the "letters of patent" given to them, Henry intentionally did not approve of voyages to the south—probably because he didn't want to provoke the Spanish and Portuguese within their spheres of control under the Treaty of Tordesillas. The expedition failed to find China or any other territory, but Newfoundland and Nova Scotia were reached on the second voyage in 1497. John Cabot, like Columbus, thought that he had actually been to Asia. He and his crew never returned from a third effort in 1498.[1]

Although it soon became apparent that Columbus had not been in the vicinity of India or China, this did not necessarily negate the idea that the areas he "discovered" were part of Asia. Only one land mass conceivably could have existed to the west, and such an interpretation would have been consistent with the ancient Greek theory of contiguous continents surrounded by water. Irrespective of the continental configuration, there was surely terra firma to the west that had to be transited along the route to the Orient. Finding a sea passage through it was thus deemed to be the key to acquiring Asian spices. Intellectual historian Loren Baritz effectively sums up the conceptual impact of the "discovery" of America this way: "For those like Columbus, to whom the east was a place while the west was a mere direction, the New World could not assume independent importance. For this mentality, long active, the New World was an obstacle to westward progress toward the east. The search for a southwest or northwest passage occupied men's attention for over four hundred years."[2] The quest for these anticipated passages lured European explorers to and fro across the seas as nothing less than the Orient's riches were the expected reward.

LINKAGE?

Juan de la Cosa, who had served as a pilot on Columbus' second voyage, produced a map in 1500 that did not place Cuba and other places they had visited on the East Asian mainland. Such questioning of the geographical context of Columbus' expeditions was common in Europe at a time when there was growing acceptance that, in reality, a New World lay to the west. It was distinct from East Asia, but this did not necessarily mean that it was not connected to the Asian continent. De la Cosa depicted the northern and southern regions of the New World (later to be known as North and South America) as attached, but he did not try to delineate the western portion of North America. Whether or not it extended to Asia was left unclear.[3]

Notwithstanding, the New World was quickly recognized as a continent in its own right. The Florentine navigator Amerigo Vespucci, sailing on behalf of Spain, made numerous journeys to the New World during the years 1497–1507 and was convinced that it was not Asia but rather "the fourth part of the earth." He referred to it as "Mundus Novus," but this did not negate the possibility that it was geographically linked to Asia just as Europe was. Venetian cartographer Giovanni Contarini on his 1506 world map, and German geographer Martin Waldseemuller on his 1507 map, treated the New World as a separate continent. Waldseemuller, in honor of Vespucci, thus coined the southern part of the New World "America"—from Vespucci's first name, Amerigo—and he included an ocean between the New World and Asia. He did not use the terms "Asia" or "India" for the northern part, but he did err in portraying a sea passage through what is now Central America.[4] Mercator's 1538 world map then applied the term "America" to both the northern and southern portions of the New World.

In 1513, the Spaniard Vasco Nunez de Balboa traversed the Isthmus of Panama and arrived at the "South Sea." Magellan soon crossed this "Pacific Ocean," proving that a great body of water separated America and Asia. Nevertheless, a northern land bridge between them was still possible, and this engendered speculation about the true relationship between Greenland and the Asian continent.[5] The northern expanse west of Greenland had not been explored by Europeans, so several prominent cartographers surmised that Greenland was an eastern extension of Asia. Such a depiction appeared on Contarini's 1506 map, and on those produced by Johannes Ruysch, a Fleming, in 1508 and by Francesco Rosselli, a Florentine, that same year. In addition, some believed that Greenland was a component of an Arctic land mass that connected to Asia further west. This rendering was evident on the 1537 globe of Flemish mathematician and astronomer Gemma Frisius (Gemma Reiner), who was Mercator's mentor. Norse maps from the seventeenth century exhibited a similar configuration.[6]

Mercator and Ortelius, in the sixteenth century, affirmed on their maps that a strait divided America and Asia. However, no evidence was presented until 1648 when Russian explorer Semyon Ivanovich Dezhnev provided a controversial account of his journey there. Peter the Great wanted conclusive proof, so he hired Danish navigator Vitus Bering and wrote instructions in January 1725 for him to follow the coast northward from Kamchatka to see whether it would join Asia to America. Peter then died, and his plan was transmitted to Bering by Empress Ekaterina. Bering explored the region in question, and reported that he had in August 1728 reached 67 degrees and 18 minutes north latitude. Bering wrote that "we had fulfilled the instructions given us by His Imperial Majesty of eternally blessed and deserving memory," and had found that the Asian coast did "not extend farther to the north" and there was "nothing beyond Chukatka on the eastern extremity." He therefore "turned back." Bering accordingly reasoned that a strait separated the continents, but he did not see the American coast. It was possible that Asia and America were attached further north. In 1732, Mikhail Gvozdev and Ivan Fyodorov looked upon the Alaskan shore—and a 1741 expedition led by Bering confirmed this observation.[7]

Russia kept Bering's observations secret because of Spanish claims under the Treaty of Tordesillas. The Spanish Empire was advancing northward from New Spain (Mexico) into what is now the United States, and it coveted territories as far north as the present British Columbia. Spanish wariness about Russian intentions in the area thus led to the 1773 expedition headed by Juan Perez (Juan Josef Perez Hernandez) who went to 54 degrees and 40 minutes north latitude, where British Columbia now meets the Alaskan panhandle.[8]

RICHES OF THE ORIENT

Beginning in the sixteenth century, the possible existence of a strait between Asia and America had major implications. A new sea route from Europe to Asia could potentially be established, bypassing the overland Silk Road controlled by the Muslims, and commercial states could forge trade relations without having to challenge Spanish and Portuguese dominance of the southern seas. The search for a Northwest Passage thus obsessed the European powers, especially England, the Netherlands, and France. Perhaps there was a channel around the Arctic expanse of North America that connected to another strait entering the Pacific Ocean? This concept would be viable only if Greenland was not attached to Asia. Alternatively, maybe a river system linked the Atlantic and Pacific Oceans via North America? In either case, there would be great financial rewards. Looking further south was not practical due to the Spanish and Portuguese presence, and the Southwest Passage "discovered" by Magellan was hazardous as well. Balboa had already determined that no waterway permitted transit through the Isthmus of Panama.

A Northwest Passage was anticipated as a balance to the Strait of Magellan, and as a means of egress for the westward-flowing north equatorial current. Optimism was also inspired by the expectation of eventual wealth derived from spices, and by the penchant of cartographers to depict the Passage in order to sell more maps. Gemma Frisius displayed the Northwest Passage on his 1544 world map, as did Mercator in 1569. Mercator's parallel meridians prevented him from presenting the Arctic accurately, so he provided an inset with a polar projection portraying Greenland as an island that could be bypassed by sea.[9] Ortelius followed suit in 1570. It is also important to note the cartography of Giacomo Gastaldi, a Venetian. Venice profited from overland trade with Asia, and looked askance at any new competitive sea route. Venetian mapmakers were therefore reluctant to admit that a Northwest Passage was plausible, as evidenced by Gastaldi's 1546 map that had Asia and America attached. However, his 1561 map placed a strait between the continents—an admission that a Northwest Passage was indeed feasible.[10]

France did not accept the Tordesillas line so, in 1533, it successfully lobbied Pope Clement VII to reinterpret its provisions. According to this revision, the line would apply only to Spanish and Portuguese lands, not to those that would be "discovered" by France. Consequently, France took the lead in the search for the Northwest Passage.[11] In 1523–24, Tuscan navigator Giovanni da Verrazano was dispatched westward, where he mistakenly thought that he had located the Passage west of the Outer Banks of what became North Carolina. Jacques Cartier made three voyages from 1534 to 1541, including passage down the St. Lawrence River, but no Passage was encountered. Seventeenth-century expeditions by Samuel de Champlain, Jacques Marquette, and Louis Jolliet, and by Robert Cavelier de La Salle also did not find a route connecting the Atlantic to the Pacific. Of course, we now know that such a river route does not exist. This was confirmed by later exploration in Western Canada by Alexander Mackenzie in 1789 and 1792–93, and by observations in the American Northwest by Meriwether Lewis and William Clark in 1804–06.[12]

The British concentrated on locating an Arctic Northwest Passage. Oriental spices were the main attraction, but furs, timber, and whales could also be profitable. Martin Frobisher was unsuccessful in three 1576–78 voyages, as was John Davis in three attempts in 1585–87. Henry Hudson, set adrift following a mutiny, lost his life in 1611 after "discovering" the bay that bears his name.[13] Michael Lok, a merchant who financed Frobisher's expeditions and served as their publicist, also produced a map in 1582 that included a Northwest Passage north of Canada. So did John Dee on his 1583 map. He was a geographer and mathematician, an aide to Queen Elizabeth I, and a rabid proponent of seeking the Passage. Such promotional cartography was common in regard to the prospective Northwest Passage, and it served to mislead the navigators who relied on such maps.[14]

Once Frobisher had failed to find the Northwest Passage by transiting it from the east, the British may have started to operate along a second track. Information on this matter is highly controversial (partly because Drake's journal and charts cannot be located), but Elizabeth I and John Dee may have asked Francis Drake to investigate prospects for a Northwest Passage by sailing east from the Pacific. According to Canadian maritime historian Samuel Bawlf, Drake's 1577–80 voyage to the Pacific included a mission to find the Northwest Passage. Drake clearly reached the coast of California, but Bawlf maintains that he actually got to 57 degrees north latitude in southern Alaska in 1579. Bawlf claims that Drake falsified maps to show that he had been further south, and agreed with Dee upon his return to England to keep secret his effort to find a Northwest Passage so as not to provoke Spanish complaints about intrusion into their zone.[15] Later, in 1778, British navigator James Cook certainly sailed into the Bering Strait from the south, but he was unable to proceed in search of the Passage due to icy conditions.

In addition to the Northwest Passage, a Northeast Passage from Europe eastward through the Arctic was also considered by the British and Dutch.[16] Of course, it was dependent on the existence of a strait between Asia and America. In 1553, Sebastian Cabot organized a British expedition commanded by Hugh Willoughby, who ended up freezing to death.

Willem Barents, a Dutchman, sailed there three times from 1594 to 1597. He died of starvation or scurvy after his ship was trapped in pack ice. Henry Hudson traveled the Northeast route in both 1607 and 1608 for the Netherlands. All of these journeys were in vain, and it was not until 1879 that Swedish navigator Nils Adolf Erik Nordenskjold managed to transit the Northeast Passage. In 1905, the Norwegian Roald Amundsen was the first to complete a voyage through the Northwest Passage. He had left on his expedition in 1903 as a citizen of greater Sweden, but returned home in 1906 to a newly independent Norway. Thus, after more than three centuries of efforts by France, Britain, and the Netherlands, both Passages were eventually transversed by Scandinavian navigators experienced in icy Arctic waters.

ANTIPODEAN IMAGES

Spain and Portugal dominated the seas, including access to the New World and the Orient. Britain, the Netherlands, and France challenged them by seeking Northwest and Northeast Passages, and also by leading the search for a potential southern continent that could serve as a rival sphere of influence. Indeed, the Passages and southern continent were related in the sense that a Passage would be a bypass around the Spanish and Portuguese. As noted, James Cook attempted to sail into a Northwest Passage from the Pacific and was the same person who headed British expeditions seeking this continent. Additionally, the Dutch explored near the tip of South America to see if a southern continent blocked their route westward to such a place.[17]

Pythagoras, in the sixth century B.C., emphasized universal harmony that included celestial spheres serving to balance the earth. The ancient Greeks then extended this interpretation to the terrestrial symmetry of both land and climate zones. Basically, they were aware of a large territorial mass in the Northern Hemisphere that was viewed as three interconnected continents. A southern counterweight was only hypothesized, and it was believed to have some connection to "Antarctica," an area balancing a territorial Arctic. Crates, in the second century B.C., even drew three southern continents.

In 43 A.D., Roman geographer Pomponius Mela produced a fascinating map portraying three attached continents in the Northern Hemisphere, the equator stretching across an engirding sea, and a southern region labeled *"Antichthones,"* the term used by Pythagoras for a non-earthly counterforce. Ptolemy, in the second century A.D., maintained that such a southern continent was linked to Africa and Asia—thereby creating an enclosed Indian Ocean. Christian geographers during the Medieval period then proclaimed the existence of the Antipodes, and the Ptolemaic revival in the fifteenth century strongly reinforced such thinking.[18]

Was the projected southern continent habitable? Aristotle thought that this was possible, but Christian theologians generally rejected the idea that the descendants of Noah could cross the burning tropics and settle in the Southern Hemisphere. A notable exception was Archbishop of Norway Einar Gunnarson who, in the mid-thirteenth century, endorsed the habitability of a southern temperate zone.[19] Basically, a southern continent represented the unknown, a place on which Europeans imposed their fantasies. Oddity and perversity prevailed, with basic principles of science applied in the Northern Hemisphere thrown by the wayside. The exotic predominated in the European imagination regarding ethnography, animals, and nature, with one satire written by a seventeenth-century Franciscan monk describing naked, red-fleshed, hermaphrodites about eight feet tall.[20]

Prior to its "discovery," America was not assumed by Europeans to exist. They were wedded to the tri-continental vision, and few argued on behalf of a Northern Hemisphere balancer. The southern continent was different perceptually as it was anticipated. The concept preceded the "discovery." Once America had been found, the need for a southern counterweight became even stronger in European minds. Although such a continent had not yet been verified by Europeans, Pope Clement VIII authorized a mission in 1601 to save souls there. He then dispatched Pedro Fernando de Quiros, a Portuguese employed by Spain, on a 1605 journey from Callao, Peru, but Quiros could not locate such a land and instead ended up in the New Hebrides Islands.[21]

The geographical nature of any southern continent was unknown, so areas such as Australia, New Zealand, and Antarctica were potentially included. Land linkages of this continent to Asia, Africa, and America were also theorized, but Portuguese trips eastward to the Moluccas, plus the voyages of Dias and Magellan, eliminated these possibilities. This projected continent was called *Terra Australis,* Latin for "southern land," and was frequently referred to as *Terra Australis Incognita* due to its non-"discovered" status. French cartographer and mathematician Oronce Fine (Orontius Fineus) displayed this hypothetical continent on his 1531 world map, as did Flemish cartographers Gerardus Mercator and Abraham Ortelius in 1541 and 1564 respectively. Mercator believed that some of Marco Polo's descriptions applied to the southern continent, and that such a large territory was necessary to balance the earth so that it would rotate properly.[22]

Magellan's 1522 passage through the strait near the southern end of South America demonstrated that a southern continent was not attached to America, and that a Southwest Passage to Asia existed. However, it was still conceivable that Tierra del Fuego (whose coast was seen to the south by Magellan) was connected to the southern continent. Mercator, in 1569, and Ortelius, in 1570, depicted this linkage, as it had not yet been ascertained that ships could sail around Tierra del Fuego on the way to Asia. A Spanish expedition headed by Garcia Jofre de Loaisa had gone south off the east coast of Tierra del Fuego in 1526. Notwithstanding, it was not until 1616 that a Dutch expedition headed by Willem Corneliszoon van Schouten and Jacob Le Maire rounded Tierra del Fuego and proved that it was not part of a southern continent. This information was kept secret because the Netherlands hoped to establish its Asia trade along this route. The separation between a southern continent and Tierra del Fuego therefore did not appear on European maps until 1630.[23]

The search for the southern continent led at first to what we know as Australia, and then to New Zealand. The historical record indicates the sighting of Australia by Dutch navigator Willem Janszoon in 1605 (although he assumed that it was part of New Guinea), and probable landfall in 1616 by Dirk Hartog. Nevertheless, there are tales of Chinese and Egyptian visits as far back as the sixth century B.C. and later Arab ones in the ninth century A.D. A map prepared by Mohammed ibn Musa al-Khwarizi of Baghdad in 820 reputedly portrays Australia, as may a 1542 map by Norman cartographer Jean Rotz, a 1611 map by the Dutchman Johannes Isacius Pontanus, and a 1602 map by Matteo Ricci.[24]

The Netherland played a major role in exploring Australia. In 1637, cartographer Jan (Joannes) Jansson relied on his country's data for his south polar projection depicting part of the continent, which he presented as distinct from *Terra Australis Incognita*. In 1642, Abel Tasman traveled to Australia and "discovered" New Zealand. His second voyage in 1644 led to the designation of "New Holland" for the larger area—later renamed "Australia" in 1817 by the British. Father Victorio Riccio, stationed in Manila, forwarded a map including New Holland to the Vatican in 1676.[25]

Europeans accumulated knowledge about New Holland, but clearer definition of the mysterious southern continent had to await the British expeditions of the late eighteenth century commanded by James Cook. These endeavors were stimulated by the Scottish geographer Alexander Dalrymple, who advocated British commercial control of the region. Dalrymple's 1767 book on a southern continent was surely off base in claiming that it had a population of fifty million, and that New Zealand was probably part of it, but it did encourage funding for Cook's 1768–71 voyage. Cook then proceeded to circumnavigate New Zealand, proving that it was not connected to Australia, and he named the southeastern portion of Australia "New South Wales." Both Australia and New Zealand were then settled by the British.[26]

Cook's second voyage in 1772–75 included extensive sailing off the coast of Antarctica. Although he never actually saw its mainland, he demonstrated that it was not attached to Australia. Visualization of the presumed "southern continent" was thus crystallized: Australia, New Zealand, and

Antarctica were separate entities. Yet Antarctica was still largely unknown. It was not until 1820 when a British expedition first established eye contact. The British, on a sealing venture commanded by William Smith and accompanied by navy surveyor Edward Bransfield, may possibly have landed there, but credit for this is generally given to an 1840 French group headed by Jules Sebastian Cesar Dumont d'Urville. Also crucial was the 1838–42 American scientific expedition led by Charles Wilkes. By following the Antarctic coastline for at least fifteen hundred miles, Wilkes proved that Antarctica was a huge territory—perhaps qualifying as a continent in its own right.[27]

Ironically, the "Age of Discovery" beginning in the fifteenth century featured European leadership in the exploration and mapping of the Pacific region. Inspired at first by commercial considerations, the Europeans then engaged in serious scientific inquiry that included advances in cartography. China and Japan may appear to have been likely candidates for such a role, but they both withdrew from probing their own part of the world. The Chinese had generally viewed geopolitics in terms of land rather than sea power, and drew maps depicting ocean waves as menacing and dangerous. The seven naval expeditions commanded by Zheng He during the years 1405–33 were an exciting departure in Chinese navigation, but the death of Emperor Yongle in 1424 soon led to restrictions on the construction of sea-going vessels and the destruction (about 1479) of Zheng He's records by the War Ministry. Security problems related to the Mongol and Manchu threats from the north assumed policy priority. The Japanese had a strong tradition of insularity, which became further accentuated in the seventeenth century when an imperial decree (approximately 1636) stipulated the death penalty for any Japanese attempting to return home from abroad. In 1689, another decree banned the building of ships capable of sailing the oceans and ordered the wrecking of existing vessels with that capability.[28] China and Japan had therefore narrowed their geographical horizons, abetting the extension of European empires and Continental dominance of mapmaking.

CHAPTER 8

The Geography of Empire

As exploration and colonialism accelerated, cartography came to be predominantly European as well. Maps from the fifteenth through nineteenth centuries emphasized territorial expansion, with science abetting power. Knowledge of latitude and longitude was frequently used to affix boundaries irrespective of existing political units or areas of common ethnicity, as the Ptolemaic grid was revived to buttress legal claims based on the rationalization of space. During the Middle Ages the emphasis had been on "things," such as land masses or islands, as abstract interpretation was not considered independently from the objects within it. Then, with the construction of globes and the perceived connection between Christianity and mathematics, the grid again became a vital component of cartography. Especially in the sixteenth century, Europeans looked upon the globe as a symbol of God's creation and upon mathematics as representative of the divine. God was attributed with organizing the world geometrically, as this field of mathematics returned to its original semantic roots of measuring the world.[1]

Societies lacking surveying and mapmaking skills were at a disadvantage as their lands were claimed by Europeans, and the foreign imprint was applied through the renaming of locations. At first, the European influence on cartography was in coastal regions as a consequence of the slave trade and commercial considerations. Later, when administration spread inland through the establishment of colonial governments and the development of resource extraction, the blank interior was filled in on maps.[2] In the case of America, there was a communications barrier between Europeans and the native Indians (in part because the Indian languages were not in written form), so maps were used as a common denominator for the purpose of conveying information. As part of this process, Indians provided maps for the Europeans that were then employed to the recipients' advantage in competition with other European rivals.[3]

The age of empire was based on "discovery" by the strong, whereas the weak were "discovered."[4] Oftentimes, territories deemed available for colonization ("virgin territory") were accompanied on maps by images of women—perhaps to indicate that those lands were suitable for seduction or rape.[5] Just what constituted "discovery" was ambiguous. Did it mean seeing a piece of territory, stepping on it, or inhabiting it? The outcome, however, was evident: European sovereignty, settlement, the advancement of trade, and the dissemination of European Christian values.[6]

FOUNDING FATHER

Gerardus Mercator (Gerhard Kremer) was the most outstanding figure in modern cartography, with his maps and method of projection dominating the field for over four hundred years. Born in 1512, Mercator worked in Flanders and Germany until his death in 1594. Although a religious believer, his approach to geography was mathematical and devoid of the influences of Christian cartography.[7] It also featured political units more than topography, and thus fit in well with the burgeoning of European empires. Mercator's projection was one of many developed in Europe during this "Age of Discovery," but its impact far exceeded that of other cartographers for several centuries thereafter.[8]

Mercator's maps maintained accurate territorial shape and were practical for navigators throughout the "Age of Discovery" due to their fidelity of direction and angles. They offered true compass readings along straight lines, especially for east-west voyages parallel to the equator.[9] The polar zones were more problematic, because Mercator drew meridians that did not narrow toward points at the poles, as they would on a globe where a degree of longitude at the equator is about 66 miles but at 60 degrees north or south latitude is approximately 32 miles. Mercator generally did not extend his maps to the poles, apparently as an outgrowth of this geometric difficulty, but additionally because of his lack of detailed knowledge of these regions. In any case, little polar navigation was possible in Mercator's time, so his polar map distortion was relegated to remote areas.[10]

Mercator presented precise scale along the equator, but distortion of size increased toward the poles. Everyone is familiar with his giant representation of Greenland (four times larger than China rather than less than a quarter its size, and similar to Africa instead of one-fourteenth its size!), a result of his maps incrementally exaggerating land size toward 600 percent when approaching 80 degrees of latitude. North America and Europe, at the

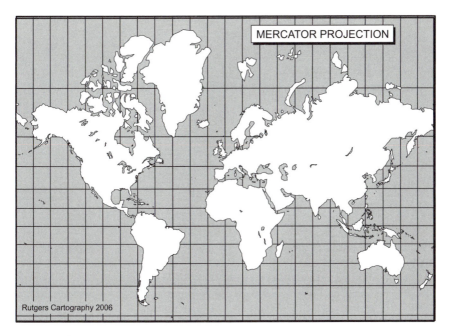

Mercator Projection

middle latitudes, appear too big and the Indian subcontinent too small. One would never imagine from an examination of a Mercator projection that North America is really less than two-thirds the size of Africa, or that Europe west of Russia is only roughly equal in area to the Indian subcontinent. If not cropped off the map, Mercator's Antarctica is larger than all other continents combined.[11]

Mercator had to support himself through the sale of maps, and his clients were European. He therefore produced more detailed maps of Europe than of other continents. Mercator, as had Ptolemy, drew the prime meridian through the Canaries—although he later moved it to Cape Verde to accord with his calculations on zero magnetic deviation.[12] In either location, it still passed through Europe. Some of Mercator's maps, including his famous world map of 1569, cut off at least one-third of the earth's surface at the largely unexplored southern end and thereby exhibited an east-west axis considerably north of the equator.[13] The Northern Hemisphere thus predominated over the Southern Hemisphere in terms of space allocation, and Europe moved into a more central location. Notwithstanding, Mercator also made many maps with the equator bisecting his frame. Yes, he was Eurocentric, but he was a European catering to European customers. His motivation was more commercial than an intentional attempt to marginalize equatorial and southern regions or promote colonial expansion.

The legacy of Mercator's projections is somewhat different. Students throughout the world learned their geography from his maps and emerged with a Eurocentric bias. This was demonstrated in a recent survey of 438 geography students at 22 sites, only 3 of which are in Europe. One of these was in Istanbul, which is mostly in Europe but part of a predominantly Asian state. Students were asked to draw from memory a map depicting the continents. Not surprisingly, the majority at 15 sites made their own continent larger that it was in reality. More revealing was that students at all 22 sites exaggerated the size of Europe, and those at 20 sites drew Africa as too small. This latter phenomenon was even evident at 4 of the 5 African sites used for the survey.[14]

Despite some distortions and European emphasis on his maps, Mercator contributed significantly to the mathematical development of cartography. He moved it in the direction of scientific inquiry for, as he wrote to his Flemish compatriot Abraham Ortelius, mapmakers had corrupted "geographical truth." Mercator was well trained in the sciences, having studied at Leuven University under noted mathematician and physician Gemma Frisius. One of his fellow students, also a pupil of Frisius, was the soon-to-be British royal cosmographer John Dee. Dee was a highly competent mathematician in his own right, and he and Mercator shared their knowledge with Ortelius, who was Mercator's friend and commercial rival at the same time. rtelius did not have a notable background in the scientific aspects of cartography but was still a mapmaker of high repute. Mercator and Ortelius had met in 1554, and they journeyed through France together in 1560.

Rounding out this prominent group of erudite scholars was Pedro Nunes (Petrus Nonius), a mathematician as well as Portugal's royal cosmographer. He shared his mathematical formulations with Dee and greatly influenced the geometry behind Mercator's famous projection via his publications of 1537 and 1566. Nunes discussed the relationship between rhumb lines and great circle arcs and was a major theorist of oblique courses that came to be known mathematically as "loxodromes." Insights gained from Nunes helped Mercator work out his system of parallel meridians accompanied by increasing distances between parallels approaching the poles. Although Mercator successfully applied mathematics to the mapping of the world, and produced the most well-known projection in the history of cartography, he never explained his calculations. This task of relating Mercator's geometry to his cartography was accomplished by British mathematician Edward Wright in 1599.[15]

FOR KING AND COUNTRY

Projection is not only a concept pertaining to cartography, cinematography, and psychology—but also to international politics. States engage in "power projection" overseas, seeking colonies, bases, and logistical rights. Mercator's geometric projections in mapmaking therefore had their counterpart in European expansionism, and maps were intrinsically tied to imperial designs. Blank space in an area implied that territorial claims could be made there, and information about travel routes served military and commercial enterprises. Representatives of vested interests frequently presented maps to British officials, since influence over state policy could enrich them. Maps of the British Empire, centered on a Greenwich prime meridian, often featured shipping and telegraphic links, since strategic power and entrepreneurship often went hand in hand. Components of the Empire were presented in striking red or pink, as coloring reinforced the concept of "Rule Britannia!"[16]

The "Kapp globe," made in Nuremberg about 1871–80, was produced for the British market, and it intentionally portrayed a British world image. The only country labeled in a Europe crowded with cities and rivers was "British Isles," and its size was enhanced. Africa had more space for labeling, but few locations were actually delineated. Tellingly, a great amount of detail was provided for Australia, the East Coast of the United States, and parts of North America. This was a reflection of British trade patterns.[17]

George Parkin's "British Empire Map of the World" was issued in 1893 by a Canadian secondary school teacher who was a self-proclaimed publicist for the Empire. The red and pink of Empire contrasted with grays for Russia and China, and British shipping routes in blue stood out from those used by other countries that appeared as faint dots. The emphasis was on logistics, control of the sea, and telegraph cables. British naval stations and bases were visually distinctive, and the only cities were those where Britain had an embassy, legation, consulate, or vice-consulate.

The Parkin map covered 420 degrees of longitude. This permitted Australia and New Zealand (components of the Empire) to be included twice, at eastern and western ends. Use of a Mercator projection also enabled Parkin to bloat the sizes of Canada, Australia, and South Africa so as to make the Empire seem huge. Parkin lobbied for the adoption of his map, and it was accepted by the 1894 Colonial Conference in Ottawa as the official cartographical representation of the Empire.[18]

France was a major competitor of Britain, and its mapmaking also reflected the expansion of empire. By the late seventeenth century, France had become the European leader in the field of cartography. Jesuit mapmakers and mathematicians were dispatched to survey Canada and the Great Lakes region, and they enjoyed the financial support of the French government due to their joint mission of mapmaking and converting native Americans. The Jesuits made a determined effort to learn "Indian" languages, which assisted them in charting the locations of these indigenous peoples. A royal cartographer of New France was appointed in

1686, and a law went into effect that all maps of the American interior had to be forwarded to the Ministry of the Marine in Paris. They were then published there. Later, in the nineteenth century, missionaries associated with the Religious Institute of the Oblatics of Mary Immaculate (such as Father Emile Petitot) played a major role in mapping the Canadian interior—especially in the northwest.[19]

Size mattered in the nineteenth century. James Wyld, royal geographer to Queen Victoria, exaggeratedly claimed in 1839 that Britain's Empire was 28 times larger than France's. Since Britain and France were small in comparison to their colonies, their territorial deficiencies could be overcome by boasting about their empires. In 1902, former royal geographer G. H. Johnston declared that the British Empire was 125 times the size of the homeland, and 55 times greater than France. At the time, France's empire had 18 times the land of the metropole, so Britain's empire was approximately only 3 times that of France's.[20]

Germany was not a participant in the colonial sweepstakes, but its ambitions changed after its 1871 victory in the Franco-Prussian War and the country's own unification. Since it was a latecomer, it sought to legitimize its acquisitions through agreements on maps, as did Belgium. Leopold II wanted to establish a Congo Independent State under royal control and convened an 1876 conference in Brussels toward that end. Germany's focus was also on Africa, since a great amount of land had yet to be claimed by European powers. This factor led Germany gradually to take over Kamerun, Togo, Tanganyika, and Ruanda-Urundi. At the Berlin Conference, held from November 1884 to February 1885, all major European countries plus the United States recognized these spheres of influence in Africa. This meant British and French acceptance of Belgian and German claims, including Leopold II's Congo Independent State. The Europeans divided Africa, in part based on the mathematical logic of the graticule, and formulated arbitrary spheres of influence that did not take traditional African political units into account. It is not true, however, that the actual boundaries within Africa were drawn at this conference.[21]

Also during the nineteenth century, the boundaries of Siam (Thailand) were delineated by the British, who wanted to establish a buffer between their sphere of influence in Burma and France's in Indo-China. Their concern was geostrategic, so the boundaries drawn did not reflect the local reality. Instead, Siam was restructured with European-prepared maps serving as a means of legitimizing what has been described as a "new discourse" based on "hegemony."[22] Siam was understandably unenthusiastic about this British endeavor, and its people living in border areas saw no reason why an invisible line should be drawn that would negatively affect their movement and trade. However, Siam was an independent country that felt threatened by the French, so King Mongkut (1851–68) quickly came to appreciate the power principles underlying European cartography. He therefore hired a Dutch surveyor and began to assert Siam's own influence over its country's maps. In 1882, Prince Damrong founded a school for cartography and, three years later, a Royal Survey Department.[23]

During the same period in India, the British created an "imperial space" by delineating their own conception devoid of reliance on a "natural" map. According to geographer and anthropologist Matthew Edney, the British imposed their power through surveying, as they defined territory mathematically. They didn't know much about the "real" India, leading many anti-British nationalists to challenge this supposed application of empiricism. Nevertheless, the British image of India geographically became institutionalized to such an extent that even the critics came to accept the validity of a geographically unified "British India"—and they started to maintain that it had pre-dated the British presence.[24]

The U.S. government had very little mapping capability and had to rely on publicly available maps and atlases. Among them were materials produced by the National Geographic Society, which had a major patriotic impact on American opinion in regard to the Spanish-American War. President Woodrow Wilson later recognized that maps served a useful political function, and he therefore wanted to be well prepared for the Versailles peace conference following World War I. Here was an opportunity to shape the world in terms of boundaries and sovereign control, so he secured the assistance of Isaiah Bowman to apply geography to the dictates of American public policy. Bowman, a distinguished geographer, had been director of the American Geographical Society since 1915, and Wilson appointed him to head the Inquiry Committee which prepared twelve hundred maps pertinent to the Versailles negotiations.

Bowman saw cartographical decisions as political, and he wanted the United States to gain leverage over the mapmaking at Versailles to compensate for its relative inexperience in diplomacy. He was personally active at Versailles in addition to his Inquiry Committee role, and he was the key figure in forging new states in Europe and the Middle East on the basis of the ethnic concept of national self-determination. Working in a parallel manner at Versailles on behalf of U.S. interests was the Intelligence Section, which was divided into 18 divisions, including one on "geography and cartography." The military conflict was over, but the peace was to be won with maps. They had an authenticity that commanded respect, and were often introduced when statistical data were not sufficiently impressive to win a negotiating point. So persuasive were maps that many countries resorted to the presentation of forgeries to make their case.[25]

FORGING A DISCIPLINE

The subject of geography was transformed during the nineteenth century in conjunction with the growth of European empires, a process generally known as "imperialism."[26] Of course the study of geography had existed for millennia, but it had been intertwined with theology, astronomy, navigation, and travelogues, so its practitioners were not working in a distinct field. The new approach to geography included biological theories of race and rather determinist concepts of racial behavior based on perceived climatic influences. The temperate zones supposedly produced energetic people who naturally spread out into the tropics inhabited by the indolent. Such an approach was used to explain exploration, justify empires, and buttress Eurocentrism.[27]

Geography also began to stress economics, with explorer and journalist Henry Morton Stanley describing it as "a science which may best be called the admonitor to commerce." The distribution and extraction of resources was studied, and areas were recommended for the export of surplus members of the lower class and criminals. The military, especially in Germany and Britain, pushed for geographical education so that officers could acquire information relevant to their foreign operations. Strategy grounded in map interpretation thus became an important discipline for planning wars, as militarism became fused with monarchism and Social Darwinism.[28]

Geographical societies that funded exploration and engaged in cartography were established in many European countries, with France's Geographical Society of Paris being founded in 1821, Germany's Berlin Geographical Society in 1828, and Britain's Royal Geographical Society in 1830. The RGS backed Stanley's expeditions in Africa, published advice on surveying, and sold surveying instruments. Its first two presidents had been ministers for the colonies, and several in later years were former diplomats. Twenty percent of the RGS's original members were military officers. As described by David N. Livingstone, an historian of geography and science, geography during the Victorian era was "the science of imperialism *par excellence*," and it did not just play a role in "*discovering* the world," but also in "*making* it." In the early twentieth century, the RGS contributed to British intelligence during World War I and organized polar and Himalayan expeditions that had implications for British strategic interests.[29] The Imperial Russian Geographical Society, constituted in 1845, included many military geographers and encouraged Russian expansion into Asia as part of the "Great Game" with the British.[30] In the United States, the American Geographical Society was formed in 1851 and the National Geographic Society in 1888.

It is no accident that "imperialism" in the late nineteenth century spawned in Europe the evolution of geography as an academic discipline.

German universities started to create geography departments in 1874. In Britain, the University of Oxford appointed its first geographer in 1887, and Cambridge in 1888. A chair in colonial geography was established in Paris in 1892.[31] At the same time, maps began to reflect imperial concerns about social and economic factors and to devote less attention to physical forces such as winds and currents.[32] Cartography became more didactic, an instrument linking geography and state power in a combination soon to be known as "geopolitics."

CHAPTER 9

Geopolitics

Geopolitics, which featured an analysis of geography from the standpoint of Social Darwinism, developed as a discipline toward the end of the nineteenth century. States were seen as in competition for space and survival, even during peacetime, and their power was determined by advantage in geographical positioning. Geography was destiny, and spatial dynamics was the key to geographical understanding.[1]

Geopolitics was firmly linked to foreign policy and served as a strong influence on strategic theory. It was a form of "applied political geography," or possibly "geographical politics," which recognized the need for states to master a constantly changing world environment.[2] Consequently, geopoliticians brought forth a new approach to maps emphasizing geographical struggle within an international arena. Cartography was no longer geared toward navigators, but rather military planners.

THEORETICAL FOUNDATIONS

Although the term "geopolitics" had not yet been formulated when most of his works were published, Alfred Thayer Mahan was the first major figure in this field. He was a captain in the U.S. Navy, president of the Naval War College, and a rear admiral after retirement. Mahan's voluminous writings on the strategic aspects pf sea power, especially his 1890 book *Influence of Sea Power upon History*, stressed geographical position as Mahan examined the linkages between colonies, commerce, and dominance of the oceans. From his perspective, the seas were critical, since they were contiguous and covered more than two-thirds of the earth. State power was therefore dependent on lines of communication, and the importation of resources, with control over narrow waterways was deemed particularly vital. Militarily, he believed that sea power protected the United States and minimized any need to send troops into overseas conflicts or to defend the United States at its shoreline. Mahan's views were immediately influential in regard to the colonial policies of Britain and Germany as well.[3]

Another important late nineteenth-century contributor to the foundation of geopolitics was German geographer Friedrich Ratzel. Originally trained as a biologist, and an advocate of political geography as a subdivision of natural science, he applied Darwinism to the functioning of states and concluded that there was an organic process of evolution that led them to compete for *lebensraum* (living space). For him, strong states were healthy organisms that were striving to acquire additional territory for their growing populations at the expense of weaker neighbors. Germany's own history impacted on Ratzel's outlook, as its borders were frequently changing due to persistent warfare. Ratzel therefore saw hope in the creation of a unified and powerful German state in 1871. Additionally influencing Ratzel's vision were his travels in the United States and Mexico in 1874–75, where he experienced the growing force of "Manifest Destiny." Ratzel's geopolitical perspective was later to be incorporated into Nazi ideology.[4]

Rudolph Kjellen, a Swedish professor of government, coined the word "geopolitik" in 1899. His approach paralleled that of Ratzel in accentuating organic states bent on expansion. Both men perceived limited human agency, as geography was seen as scientifically critical, and they shared a view that geography and eugenics worked symbiotically in a competitive evolutionary process. Furthermore, Kjellen was a Germanophile who advocated a Nordic-Germanic bloc against Russia, a country that he saw as a threat to his native Sweden. Kjellen's works were widely disseminated in Germany and became notably influential following Germany's defeat in World War I.[5]

STRATEGIZING

The grandmaster of geopolitics is Halford John Mackinder, who related the expansionist theories of Ratzel and Kjellen to critical geographical regions—yet recognized the policy choices available to policymakers by downgrading determinism. Mackinder studied natural science at Oxford, with a specialization in biology, but he was then attracted to geography and appointed at his alma mater in 1887 as the first full-time academic in that field in Britain. He later used his geographical knowledge to advise the British government on strategy. Although rooted in a country that controlled an empire firmly based on sea power, Mackinder eschewed Mahan's naval orientation and focused instead on land power. This interpretation derived from his observation that there had been a pre-Columbian dominance of land power, a Columbian period featuring sea power, and a post-Columbian era returning to land power. This latter era was to extend through the coming twentieth century.[6]

Mackinder lived at a time when the British suffered, in the words of geographer Robert Mayhew, a "crisis of confidence" in their future. Their days of discovery were waning, and British sea power was being challenged by the enhancement of land power based on railroad construction. Mackinder turned against the free-market policies of the Liberals and Conservatives, as his geographical grasp of international affairs led him to the conclusion that the free trade phase was over and was being replaced by a competitive system grounded upon national interest. As a British patriot, he was an advocate of continued Empire and therefore became a member in 1901 of the Victoria League, a pro-Empire organization.[7] He saw his country's privileged world status as under siege, and the threat as emanating from central Eurasia. Russia and Britain had been playing their "Great Game" throughout the late nineteenth century and, as described by geopolitical analyst Milan Hauner, "Mackinder's view of Russia was originally founded on the typical perception of an Edwardian imperialist who contemplated Tsarist Russia as the perennial aggressor ready to seize the Dardanelles and descend on India."[8]

A new dimension was then added by the construction of the Trans-Siberian Railroad from 1892 to 1902, with Mackinder maintaining that railroads enabled landlocked peoples to become more mobile.[9] Russian power was therefore on the upsurge, and the British geographer was alarmed by an impeding Russian war with Japan. It was necessary for an insular Britain to act in order to sustain its position, and this meant focusing on the land threat evolving on the "Continent." Russia had previously been viewed as peripheral by most Europeans, but Mackinder had promoted it to a central role. Germany represented, in his opinion, less of a danger to Britain—but a Germany allied with Russia was the worst doomsday scenario. Japan, even though it was soon to defeat Russia in 1905, did not figure prominently in Mackinder's thinking. He was therefore somewhat off the mark (or premature) on Russia's power and on Germany's growing military might, which was evident during World War I.[10]

In 1904, Mackinder presented a paper to the Royal Geographical Society on "The Geographical Pivot of History." It was predicated on his evaluation that British strength could no longer be maintained through sea power, and that protection from any dominating force in Eurasia required an alliance system grounded on the British Empire.

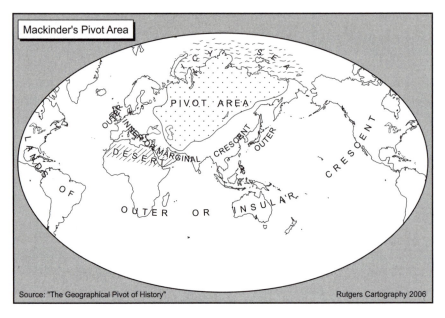

Mackinder's Pivot Area

The challenge came from the "pivot area" in central Russia, which was protected from the sea by impassable Arctic ice. Russia was therefore employing the new railroad to develop a military juggernaut menacing European civilization.[11]

Mackinder's global image was of a powerful "pivot area," then an "inner crescent" of lands in Eurasia and North Africa, and, lastly, an "outer crescent" of additional continents and islands—including Britain. The "pivot area" was visually accentuated cartographically in several ways. One was the use of a Mercator projection, which exaggerated territorial size at northern latitudes. Then there was the centering longitudinally on the "pivot area" rather than on the Greenwich meridian. Also contributing to this effect was the placement of the "pivot area" at a more prominent location latitudinally, achieved by eliminating southern latitudes beyond Cape Horn at the tip of South America. Mackinder did not believe that the United States would be crucial to the defense of Britain. As a result, his world map marginalized the United States in an unusual manner—having it appear at both eastern and western extremities. American vigor within the Western Hemisphere and a growing naval role were not sufficiently recognized, perhaps because Mackinder's concentration theoretically was on the importance of land power in the "pivot area."

After World War I, Mackinder renamed the "pivot area" the "Heartland" and declared that whoever controlled it would control the world. He also redefined the boundaries of the "Heartland," extending it further westward toward Germany. This incorporation of what he called "East Europe" into the "Heartland" made this region a buffer against potential German expansionism and reduced the importance of Central Asia.[12] Mackinder was not a participant at Versailles, but he attempted to influence the terms of a peace treaty through his 1919 book *Democratic Ideals and Reality.* Although Germany had been defeated, the British geographer came to acknowledge its strategic importance and he made the Russo-German relationship the key to his analysis of the post-war settlement. Mackinder wanted to prevent the formation of a Russo-German alliance, or a bloc in which one imposed its power over the other (as had happened in the 1918 Treaty of Brest-Litovsk). Furthermore, Mackinder was anti-Bolshevik, and he feared communist control over the "Heartland." His proposal to the British Cabinet to overthrow the Bolsheviks was rejected, but he was appointed British High Commissioner to Southern Russia in 1919 and worked closely with a "White" leader Anton Denikin.[13] His efforts, however, did not bear fruit as the Bolsheviks triumphed in Russia's Civil War and, in 1922, signed the Treaty of Rapallo with Germany.

Beginning in 1925, the newly constituted Soviet Union and Germany engaged in secret military collaboration, which led eventually to the 1939 Nazi-Soviet Pact. During this pre-World War II period, Mackinder's geopolitical concepts were studied widely in Germany, but not in the Soviet Union. The communist government decried geopolitics as an "anti-Soviet pseudoscience" since the economic "base" and "means of production" were considered more critical to behavior than geographical attributes.[14] This outlook was ironic since Mackinder considered the Soviet Union to be the country most amply endowed by its geographical location.

World War II brought about another change in Mackinder's perception. Whereas the war had constituted the expected battle for the "Heartland" between the Soviet Union and Germany, Mackinder's fear turned toward Germany. He therefore acknowledged the importance of American and British sea power in alignment with Soviet land power, and anticipated continued Soviet-American cooperation after the end of hostilities. He thus revised his estimation of America's strategic might, and came to view the United States as a key player in the "Midland Ocean" (North Atlantic) that could contribute to the restraint of Germany. Mackinder claimed that the defeat of Germany would make the Soviet Union the greatest land power, but he also removed much of eastern Siberia from his "Heartland." This gave it a more westward orientation, relating it more directly to Germany.[15]

Mackinder had underestimated the strategic roles of the United States, the Arctic, and air power. Also undercutting his theory was the strategic analysis of Nicholas Spykman, a Dutch–born American professor of international relations. Spykman was concerned about U.S. geopolitical interests, and he developed the concept of a "Rimland," which was to prove prescient in the postwar era. It was the reverse of the "Heartland" approach in that the dominant area was similar to Mackinder's "inner crescent," and whoever controlled the "Rimland" was to control Eurasia. The "Rimland" was basically Eurasia minus the "Heartland," with Britain and Japan labeled "off-shore islands." Also significant was that Spykman rejected the prime role of land power and presented a more balanced analysis of geopolitics. The "Rimland," located between the "Heartland" and the sea, was considered strategic in terms of both land and sea power and would serve to protect the United States from the "Heartland."[16]

By the time of his death in 1947, Mackinder had revolutionized geostrategic analysis through his fluid image of the world that rejected static compartmentalization. For him, all of the oceans were interactive as one sea—and continents gave way to a "World Island" plus "inner" and "outer" crescents. Mackinder's "pivot area" map, and his two subsequent cartographical adjustments, reflected an ongoing historical process that made geography both critical and palpable—and would continue to do so into the period of the Cold War.

THE FASCIST IMPULSE

Geopolitics, and a chauvinistic mapmaking tradition, combined in Germany even prior to the advent of Nazism. Ratzel was a German, Kjellen was pro-German, and Major-General Karl Haushofer advanced geopolitical concepts from his academic post at the University of Munich throughout the Weimar Republic. Atlases used in the German school system before World War I had used differing scales so that Germany appeared to be as large as the United States. After the war, territorial losses under the Treaty of Versailles were accentuated through the distorted use of scale and alarmist inclusion of arrows directed at Germany. By the late twenties, former colonies that had been taken away and made League of Nations mandates were presented on maps with their previous names. Their mandate status was sometimes delineated, but in small type. Nazi maps later pointed out the Versailles-imposed demilitarized zone in the Rhineland, expatriate German minorities in neighboring countries, and substantial armaments possessed by Germany's neighbors.[17] Haushofer contributed to Germany's propagandistic cartography through what he called "suggestive maps" that stressed the points that he wanted to highlight and eliminated, or toned down, others.[18]

Karl Haushofer, with his doctorate in geography and expertise on military history, was the doyen of German geopolitics. He was indebted to Mahan for the latter's linkage of geography to power, but he became a disciple of Mackinder's land-based approach and a supporter of the "Heartland" concept.[19] Like Mackinder, Haushofer somewhat marginalized the Western Hemisphere by placing it at both ends of his world maps. His heavy reliance on Mackinder even enhanced the importance of the British geographer, who was not well known outside his academic field. In particular, great attention was drawn to Mackinder when the British periodical *New Statesman* on August 26, 1939, cited Haushofer's attraction to his ideas and maintained that the German geopolitical strategist exerted extensive influence over Hitler. Haushofer had originally been introduced to Hitler by Rudolf Hess, who was his aide-de-camp during World War I and subsequently his pupil in geopolitics at the University of Munich. Hess was Hitler's personal secretary, and eventually a deputy leader of the Nazi Party.

Haushofer was the driving force behind the theory of *lebensraum,* which was a persistent theme of Hitler's. He borrowed the concept from Ratzel, who was a close friend of his father—himself a geography teacher. Little Karl often joined Ratzel and his dad in conversation, and was influenced by the idea that boundaries between states were changeable because some countries expanded. Haushofer later observed: "Survival of small states is a clear sign of world-political-stagnation. Absorption, on the other hand, indicates life and development." Echoing Ratzel, he described borders as "state-biological organisms" that envigorated "lifeless lines" and pulsated "like the skin and other protective organs of the human body."[20] Haushofer also distinguished between political and military boundaries, averring that the former applied to territory of a cohesive cultural group and the latter to defensive depth needed to protect the homeland from enemy shelling. Military boundaries therefore extended further than political boundaries.[21]

Haushofer related *lebensraum* to Germany's historical circumstances after World War I. Germany's defeat rankled, and the antidote, he believed, was to turn to geopolitics to redress the perceived inequities of Versailles. He therefore arranged for his academic position in 1919, and developed a program of research and publications that substituted for the general staff that had been decimated by the Versailles provisions.[22] Haushofer, in part, blamed American mapmakers for the terms of a treaty that had truncated his country, and he advocated a greater Germany. The German geographer maintained, apparently as an attempted justification, that *lebensraum* had to be acquired to protect Germany within a hostile environment and that geopolitics should be the means to assert "the geographical conscience of the state." Haushofer recommended that Germany publicize *lebensraum* as "an inevitable natural necessity" due to the population's outstripping of the food production. He pointed to Japan's annexation of Korea as an appropriate model for Germany.[23]

Haushofer advocated a coalition of the Soviet Union, Japan, and Germany, and praised the 1939 Nazi-Soviet Pact. From his "Heartland" perspective, offensive action proceeded outward from the center, so Germany had to align with the Soviet Union. This meant by treaty or, as in 1941, by means of conquest that noted American mapmaker Richard Edes Harrison described as a "Genghiz Khan invasion in reverse."[24] Underlying much of Haushofer's thinking was his belief that Germany had to avoid a two-front war, the main cause in his eyes of Germany's defeat in World War I.

Japan was always critical to Haushofer's geopolitical analysis. In 1908, as a young officer, Haushofer was dispatched to Tokyo to study the training and organization of the Japanese army. En route by sea, he was impressed with the logistics enjoyed by Britain and came to understand that the naval power of Britain and Japan could be balanced militarily by Germany if it were aligned with Russia. Interestingly, from a different angle, Mackinder had looked at potential Russo-German collaboration as a threat to Britain. Haushofer arrived in Japan in 1909 and remained for over a year. He was there when the Japanese were in the process of engulfing Korea, and this action helped crystallize his thinking about the relationship between geopolitics and *lebensraum*. The German officer also came to recognize Japan's regional dominance and the importance of Russia as a land link connecting an envisioned German-Japanese entente. Haushofer wrote his doctoral dissertation on the development of a Japanese empire in Asia, and he afterwards pressed his country to join with Japan in the Anti-Comintern Pact of 1936.[25]

Haushofer favored German expansion but, unlike Hitler, he did not look to Britain as a potential ally. In addition, his main concern was territory. Race or anti-Semitism did not play a role. Of course, Hitler approached international politics from an ethnic perspective and did not endorse geopolitics based solely on geography.[26] As the war progressed, Haushofer realized that the horizontal emphasis of maps fostered by Mercator's projections was no longer relevant. The Soviet Union was seeking access to the Indian Ocean, and the United States was including South America within its sphere. The age of verticality had arrived.[27] Such a perspective was attuned to Haushofer's vision of a world composed of pan-regions rather than continents. He had maintained throughout the nineteen twenties and thirties that there were three basic longitudinally configured zones—with each dominated by one power: Germany in the Eurafrican pan-region, Japan in the pan-Asian, and the United States in the pan-American. He had pointed out that the Soviet Union could emerge as the hegemonic power of a fourth pan-region.[28]

Due to Haushofer, geopolitics came to be considered a German discipline linked to Nazism. Its focus on geographical location had shifted to one of state enlargement, and its metaphysical notions had moved it away from the mainstream of social science.[29] Geopolitics and totalitarianism had formed an unholy partnership, but Haushofer was decidedly less deterministic than Hitler in regard to geopolitics as he argued that 75 percent of history may be explained by human initiative rather than geography. In his last testament, written after World War II, Haushofer claimed that the Nazis had not understood geopolitics but had only developed slogans ostensibly based upon it.[30]

Actually, it was not only the Nazis. Germany's ally Italy had also jumped on the geopolitical bandwagon. In 1939, the journal *Geopolitica* was launched in Italy. There had been numerous contacts between German and Italian advocates of geopolitics, and it was not surprising that the first issue sported a greeting from Karl Haushofer, who called for "living space," and proclaimed that the powerful have the right to expand. Haushofer was also a member of *Geopolitica's* editorial board.

Premier Benito Mussolini portrayed Italy as the heir to the Roman Empire, and he had marble maps of both the Roman Empire and contemporary Italy placed beside major roads. The primary geopolitical context for Italian expansionism was in reference to Africa, with *Geopolitica* frequently referring to "Eurafrica." Africa was seen as an area rich in resources, and Italian maps depicted this continent as strategically oriented along a north-south axis connecting it to Europe. Arrows and black lines were used to emphasize this perspective, and to demonstrate Africa's isolation along an east-west axis. The key to Africa's linkage to Europe was deemed to be Libya, which was already under Italian control by World War II. Mussolini's mapmakers thus displayed hypothetical rail lines and hydroelectric grids extending from Africa to Italy, via Libya. Such a strong geopolitical bond between Africa and Europe, built upon the Italian-Libyan relationship, was presented in conjunction with the claim that the Mediterranean was an Italian sea serving as a *spazio-vitale*, or "living space."[31]

Geopolitics also developed in Japan during the twenties, and its theories were used to justify the 1932 invasion of Manchukuo (Manchuria) and the establishment of a greater East Asia Co-Prosperity Sphere. Kjellen was an important influence on the Japanese, as was Haushofer, whose expertise on Japan was greatly appreciated there. Many of his works were translated into Japanese. Haushofer's pan-regional approach struck a vital chord as Japan was recognized as the dominant power in the Far East. The Japanese called for a "right to live," which was related to expansionism in the quest for raw materials and applied especially to Manchukuo. After World War II, the Allies purged Japanese administrative personnel and academics, including advocates of geopolitics.[32]

Geopolitical analysis was prevalent during World War II, with American theorists adopting an approach based less on land power than that of the Europeans. U.S. geographical separation from the major war fronts critically affected cartographical perceptions, as did recognition that the air age had started to supplant Mercator's emphasis on navigation.

CHAPTER 10

Defending the Western Hemisphere

The advent of World War II challenged American geographical and cartographical assumptions as the United States pondered its possible involvement in a European conflict. Isolationists emphasized the security afforded by the Atlantic Ocean and concluded that deployment in Europe would not be essential to American defense. For them, a Pan-American security zone buttressed by the 1823 Monroe Doctrine was sufficient. Interventionists countered by describing the seas as highways rather than barriers, and by maintaining that a Western Hemispheric defense line could only be secondary. American security had to be preserved by extending this line and participating in the European balance of power framework. Geography alone could no longer protect the United States, so alliances with European states were required. The Monroe Doctrine concept of two distinct hemispheres, which would not interfere in each other's affairs, was outmoded as geopolitical self-interest dictated against isolationism.[1] Based upon this outlook, polar projections not incorporating any east-west divide were widely disseminated by the interventionists.

The Monroe Doctrine was not based on historical claims or international law, but was grounded instead on the application of a geographical vision to U.S. security needs. Isolationists endorsed it, whereas interventionists chafed at its provision pertaining to non-intervention on the European continent.[2] However, those favoring engagement in World War II cleverly undercut the isolationists by linking the Monroe Doctrine to a widened hemisphere that stretched out the security zone even further. Henry Stimson, at his July 1940 Senate confirmation hearing for appointment as secretary of war, consequently called for American aid to Britain on the basis of the Monroe Doctrine, arguing that the U.S. defensive perimeter could be maintained with British support. Protecting the sea route to Britain was also essential to his interpretation of the Doctrine. Therefore, as the United States moved toward war, hemispheric defense became the keynote of the interventionists and was emphasized by President Roosevelt much more than any moral obligation to preserve the freedom from Nazism of European states.[3] The United States was prepared to back the Monroe Doctrine up to the shores of Europe, but the World War I disregard for the nonintervention in Europe clause was repeated. Not only that, but this provision of the Monroe Doctrine was even considered inconsistent with Western Hemispheric defense.

GEOGRAPHY AND AMERICAN POLICY

If hemispheric defense is the basis of foreign policy, then defining the boundaries of the hemisphere is crucial.[4] The Monroe Doctrine referred to "this hemisphere," but made no attempt to formulate its extent. At that time, there was no common agreement on a prime meridian but, once Greenwich became standardized, we may possibly assume that the two hemispheres became separated there. Yet this would not make sense, as Spain, Portugal, and parts of both West Africa and Britain would then be assigned to the Western Hemisphere. A dividing meridian therefore had to lie someplace to the west of Greenwich, but where? During World War II, the U.S. government grappled with this issue, since its implications were not just cartographical—they were critical to American war strategy as it related to Greenland and Iceland. If these islands were deemed to be in the Western Hemisphere, then they would be covered by the principles set forth in the Monroe Doctrine.

Basically, cartographers working for the Roosevelt administration backed the concept that the Western Hemisphere began at 20 degrees west longitude.[5] This formulation presented an ambiguous interpretation of whether Iceland was subject to the Monroe Doctrine, since this meridian cut through its territory. Greenland clearly lay to its west. Also problematic was where the Western Hemisphere ended. If it was at the international dateline, then it would be 20 degrees short of a complete 180 hemisphere. Therefore, Washington postulated that the Western Hemisphere went beyond the international dateline to a longitude of 160 degrees east. This meant that the Monroe Doctrine was applicable in much of the Pacific. In June 1940, Joint Army-Navy Plan 4 was approved by the secretaries of war and the navy and endorsed by President Roosevelt. This document described the Western Hemisphere as including Greenland, but not

Iceland, and it additionally listed places distant from American shores such as Western Samoa, Pitcairn Island, and the Tuamotu Islands. These territories were east of the international dateline. On the other hand, the Gilbert and Ellice Islands were also noted. They lay west of the dateline, but within a hemisphere terminating at 160 degrees east.[6]

Cartography and the Monroe Doctrine had a direct bearing on activation of the no-transfer principle. At the turn of the nineteenth century, the United States feared that Britain would acquire Florida or Cuba from a weakened Spain. Consequently, Congress in January 1811 passed a no-transfer resolution pertaining to Spanish territories adjacent to the United States and authorized the president to carry out the occupation of such lands to prevent them from passing from one colonial power to another. This principle was thus critical to American policy prior to the Monroe Doctrine, and there was no need to mention it explicitly in that document. Then, in 1870, President Ulysses Grant permanently linked the principle to the Doctrine with his statement that "the doctrine promulgated by President Monroe has been adhered to by all political parties, and I now deem it proper to assert the equally important principle that hereafter no territory on this continent shall be regarded as subject to transfer to a European power."[7]

In June 1940, in conjunction with Joint Army-Navy War Plan 4, the State Department reiterated the no-transfer principle.[8] This statement was made to establish a framework for July's Havana Conference of American states, since France, Denmark, and the Netherlands had already been occupied, leaving their possessions in the Western Hemisphere vulnerable to transfer to Germany. The Act of Havana, as an aspect of Western Hemispheric defense, then endorsed the no-transfer principle and authorized any country in the Americas to engage in "preemptive occupation" as a means of self defense—subject to prior consultation with other American states. The Act made clear that occupation would only be temporary, and that territorial acquisition would not be allowed. Sovereignty was to be restored to the original European administrators once this became possible.

The Act of Havana did not consider whether Greenland and Iceland, the former a Danish colony and the latter a self-governing Danish territory, were part of the Western Hemisphere. The main concern was the fate of European possessions that were undoubtedly in the Americas such as the Guianas, Martinique, and the Netherlands Antilles. One interesting byproduct of this endeavor is that British and French troops joined the United States in countering German designs on Curacao in the Netherlands Antilles. Such action was aimed at securing that island's oil refineries and protecting tankers from frequent German submarine attacks, since the Venezuelan crude oil processed in Curacao was vital to the Allied war effort. As part of this operation, control over all shipping in Curacao was placed in the hands of U.S. naval headquarters in Washington.[9] Thus, while invoking the Monroe Doctrine and the no-transfer principle, potential foxes (albeit anti-German ones) from Europe were brought in to help guard the American chicken coop.

THE GREENING OF AMERICA

Greenland proved to be a test case for both the Monroe Doctrine and the no-transfer principle. Its location at the fringe of North America, and its lengthy status as a Danish colony, had traditionally separated it from Western Hemispheric affairs, and few in the United States really thought about Greenland when contemplating Washington's policies toward the Americas. Similarly, who would ever think of the "discovery" of Greenland by Icelanders as the "discovery" of America?[10] However, as World War II increasingly threatened U.S. security, Greenland's significance was enhanced and this territory came to be considered by the U.S. government as an integral component of the Western Hemisphere.

Where Greenland belonged geographically had always been controversial as it may have been connected to North America. Greenland wasn't actually proven to be an island until Admiral Robert Peary's 1909 circumnavigation. In 1868, a report commissioned by Secretary of State William Seward had recommended that the United States purchase Greenland as well as Iceland, but no action was taken. Then, in 1916, the United States agreed to relinquish rights there as part of an agreement to buy the Danish West Indies (Virgin Islands) the following year. Peary objected, claiming that Greenland was within North America and should be covered by the Monroe Doctrine. He also recognized Greenland's importance due to the advent of air power.[11] Ironically, Secretary of War Harry Woodring later concluded in May 1939 that the United States should not attempt to purchase Greenland because it lacked strategic value in terms of either air or sea defense.[12]

On April 9, 1940, Denmark was occupied by Germany. That same day, a report prepared for Undersecretary of State Sumner Welles maintained that Greenland was in the Western Hemisphere and should be covered by the no-transfer principle. Security concerns surely precipitated this judgment, but Greenland did indeed lie to the west of the 20-degree west hemispheric line used by the U.S. government. Roosevelt adopted the report's position three days later, and it was presented to British Ambassador Lord Lothian by Secretary of State Cordell Hull, who warned that British intervention there would violate the Monroe Doctrine.[13]

The United States planned a preemptive occupation of Greenland to forestall the Nazis, but delayed because it could conceivably establish a precedent convenient for Japan in the Netherlands East Indies should the Netherlands come under German control. Japan had in April 1934 issued the Amau Doctrine, which was modeled on the Monroe Doctrine. It proclaimed "special responsibilities" to act unilaterally in East Asia "to preserve peace and order." Once Denmark had fallen to the Germans, Hull placed the Japanese ambassador on notice by telling him: "There is no more resemblance between our Monroe Doctrine and the so-called Monroe Doctrine of Japan than there is between black and white."[14] Germany conquered the Netherlands in May 1940, but Japan did not seize the Netherlands East Indies until March 1942.

Actually, a "Japanese Monroe Doctrine" had been developing since 1905. Theodore Roosevelt had recommended its adoption by Tokyo as part of a defensive maneuver against the Europeans after the Russo-Japanese War, and he had discussed the matter with former Harvard classmate Viscount Kentaro Kaneko. Japanese authorities used this term frequently and believed that Japan was entitled to a special role in Asia similar to that of the United States in the Americas. Japan was to be responsible for security in the Far East, especially in regard to China and Manchukuo (Manchuria). Thus the Amau Doctrine represented continuity in Tokyo's policies. It was announced by Foreign Office spokesperson Eiji Amau in the context of Sino-Japanese relations, and was directed against any "Open Door Policy" in East Asia or non-hemispheric assistance to China.[15]

As soon as the Nazis had occupied Denmark, envoy extraordinaire to the United States Henrik de Kauffmann had pressed Roosevelt to set up a protectorate in Greenland because it was in the Western Hemisphere. Kauffmann's loyalty was to the previous independent Danish government, and he was the key figure in negotiating a deal with Washington on the Greenland issue. There was a coincidence of interest since, from its perspective, the United States recognized Greenland's importance to Western Hemispheric security. It was on the great circle air route to Europe, it could prove vital logistically if the United States entered the war in Europe, and potential German control of Greenland would militarily threaten North America. Already, German aircraft were flying reconnaissance missions there. Furthermore, Germany's weather could be predicted on the basis of Greenland's weather, as the atmospheric conditions shifted eastward. A U.S. presence in Greenland would therefore provide critical meteorological information that could be used to select bombing targets in Germany.[16]

On April 9, 1941, the anniversary of Denmark's fall to the Nazis, Hull and Kauffmann penned an agreement on the American occupation of Greenland that cited the Act of Havana and defense of the Western Hemisphere. An accompanying letter signed by Hull asserted that Greenland was within the area covered by the Monroe Doctrine. On this matter, Washington was proceeding unilaterally without consultation with other American states. However, in accordance with the Act of Havana, the agreement acknowledged that the U.S. occupation was temporary, that Denmark retained sovereignty, and that Danish administration would be restored when conditions allowed. Basically, the U.S. government was invoking both the Monroe Doctrine and the no-transfer principle on the ground that there was a German threat to the hemisphere. White House spokesperson Stephen Early conceded that a small part of Greenland east of the 20-degree west meridian may have been outside of the Western Hemisphere, but that, in practice, the United States would consider all of Greenland within the hemisphere. Germany, and collaborationist authorities in Copenhagen, proclaimed that the agreement was invalid because Kauffmann had acted without the approval of his government or King Christiaan. He was summarily dismissed.[17]

The United States occupied Greenland immediately, justifying its action on the combined factors of cartography and security. Once Danish control was reasserted after the war, Greenland's hemispheric location soon became moot, since its protection by the United States was assured by Denmark's 1949 entrance into NATO. Under a 1951 agreement, American troops remained in Greenland but the United States no longer continued to describe that island as part of the Western Hemisphere.

ON THE EDGE

The fate of the self-governing Danish territory of Iceland also became an important concern pertaining to Western Hemispheric defense. In a book published in 1939, Vilhjalmur Stefansson had averred that Iceland was in the Western Hemisphere, and he quickly became the main protagonist in an effort to include it under the American umbrella. Especially influential was his January 1941 article in *Foreign Affairs* proposing that a security line should be established east of Iceland.[18] Stefansson's parents were Icelandic, but he was born in Canada and moved to the United States when he was one year old. He was an Arctic explorer and writer who later worked with the U.S. military in Alaska. Stefansson's ethnic heritage attracted him to Icelandic affairs, and it should be noted that he had been a consultant to Transamerican Air Lines, which wanted to develop a route from the United States to Denmark via Greenland and Iceland. In 1931, Pan American Airways purchased Transamerican and he then served it as a consultant during the period 1932–45.[19]

In May 1940, a month after Germany's takeover of Denmark, British (and some Canadian) troops moved into Iceland. London was reacting in part to the Nazi assault on the Netherlands and Belgium, and the United States did not invoke the Monroe Doctrine to challenge Britain's military deployment because it wanted protection for Greenland's eastern flank. At this time, Iceland was still under the Danish crown (it became a republic in May 1941) and was pledged to neutrality under its self-governing agreement with Denmark. Copenhagen handled Icelandic foreign policy but, as a response to the German occupation of Denmark, Iceland began conducting its own foreign affairs in April 1940 and set up a foreign ministry the following year.[20]

By December 1940, Iceland feared that Germany would occupy Britain and that its troops would be withdrawn from Iceland's defense. Iceland therefore sought U.S. intervention under the Monroe Doctrine, an idea backed by the American consul Berbel Kuniholm. Secretary of State Cordell Hull objected to extending the hemisphere, but the United States did proceed with plans for military intervention. In February 1941, German planes attacked the Reykjavik airport. Then, in June, Britain informed Iceland that its troops were to be transferred to North Africa. In sum, Washington intended to protect Iceland militarily, but wanted advance official approval from the government in Reykjavik. Roosevelt and Prime Minister Hermann Jonasson then exchanged letters, and an agreement on intervention was formulated on July 1. Jonasson justified it with the argument that Iceland's neutrality would not be violated since the United States was not at war.[21]

Roosevelt informed Congress on July 7 that American soldiers had landed that day in Iceland at the invitation of its government. The president pointed out that Iceland's sovereignty would not be affected, and that the country was a "strategic outpost" in the Atlantic crucial for establishing "our defense frontier" for the New World. He therefore endorsed Western Hemispheric defense, yet did not claim that Iceland was itself within the hemisphere nor that it was covered by the Monroe Doctrine or by the Act of Havana. Roosevelt surely believed that German occupation of Iceland would jeopardize the Western Hemisphere. Nevertheless, he didn't want to get embroiled in a confrontation with American isolationists who were wary of stretching out the hemisphere toward Europe. Placing Greenland in North America had gone far enough. As a concomitant of this decision, Roosevelt made certain that no conscripts were assigned to the Icelandic intervention, as there was then a restriction on their deployment outside the hemisphere.[22]

Cartographically, Roosevelt interpreted maps in a manner supportive of his military and political interests. Thus Greenland was in the hemisphere and Iceland was not, despite the fact that part of it lay to the west of the twentieth meridian. On the other hand, the American security line was to be delineated apart from hemispheric considerations. In April 1941, a week before the Greenland intervention, Roosevelt had imposed a defense line at 25 degrees west longitude—based on the midpoint line between Africa and South America. It included almost all of Greenland, but not Iceland, and he additionally had established a neutral zone closed to the ships of combatants. Of course, Germany was the target. Then, a few days after U.S. troops entered Iceland, the president bent the line eastward around Iceland so that it fell within the zone. Clearly, if American military personnel were stationed there, the United States was intent on providing naval security. Iceland therefore found itself enclosed by the U.S. defense perimeter even though Washington did not recognize it as a Western Hemisphere state.[23]

Iceland declared its independence in June 1944 and joined NATO in 1949. Like Greenland, it therefore came under U.S. protection irrespective of the Monroe Doctrine. American troops are still deployed there as part of NATO as, quite unusually, Iceland is a member of a military alliance even though it has no army of its own.[24]

WAR OF THE MAPS

In July 1941, President Roosevelt appointed William Donovan as Coordinator of Information. Donovan therefore played a major role in the area of national security and intelligence, and he advised FDR that "Geography has been neglected in this country's policy planning. Close study of geography is invaluable in outguessing the enemy. The Nazis make what they call 'Geopolitics' a vital arm of military policy. Their Geopolitical Institute is an integral factor in the development of that policy." That October, Donovan encouraged Vilhjamur Stefansson to set up a research center to focus on the Arctic. Donovan recognized the growing importance of the far northern latitudes as, potentially, the United States could deliver supplies to Murmansk by sea to assist the Soviet Union in its war with Germany. In the Far East, Donovan expected increased Japanese aggressiveness now that the Soviet Union was bogged down in a conflict on the Western front. The security of Alaska and the Aleutians was therefore in jeopardy. In mid-November, Donovan notified FDR that Stefansson had agreed to found a Center of Arctic Studies, and it was in operation by the end of the month.[25]

Following the December attack on Pearl Harbor, the United States entered the war against Germany and Japan. On February 23, 1942, President Roosevelt made a national radio address (a "fireside chat") to explain why involvement was necessary. He asked his listeners to follow along at home on their world maps (which, in a radio broadcast two days earlier, he had urged Americans to buy), and he encouraged them to study geography. Roosevelt clearly understood that maps could be used to influence public opinion, and attitudes toward postwar arrangements. Furthermore, Roosevelt had a great personal interest in maps. Eleven days after Pearl Harbor, he had requested a map of Sinatang Island off the northwest coast of Sulawesi in the Netherlands East Indies. None was available within the government, so he secured the needed map from the National Geographic Society. Six days later, the N.G.S. provided the president with a cabinet filled with maps on rollers, and it was placed in his White House study. The inspiration for this portable collection had been Winston Churchill, who had brought such a map collection with him on his visit that month to Washington. In January 1942, Roosevelt's "Map Room" was established, again modeled after Churchill's "Map Room" within his underground Cabinet War Rooms in London.[26]

Maps also played an integral role in the internal debate over war policy. Mercator projections had for long dominated American perceptions of the world, and they buttressed isolationist contentions that the United States was geographically removed from the regions of conflict. Many American Mercator projections put the United States at their longitudinal center, thus accentuating separation from Europe and Asia by oceans. Maps centered on the Greenwich meridian portrayed the same separation from Europe and cut off America from Asia entirely. These continents were at opposite ends of the map, and the Pacific Ocean was bifurcated.[27]

Based on Mercator projections, the United States had considered Hawaii to be the geostrategic key to the Pacific. It served as a bridge to the Philippines, which had become an American colony in 1898 and was considered to be a bastion for defending the West Coast from attack. The Pacific fleet was thus headquartered there, and the Japanese targeted Pearl Harbor when they initiated hostilities against the United States. Nevertheless, both the United States and Japan had failed to recognize the fallacy of their Mercator oriented outlooks. The most direct route between the Philippines and the United States actually ran two thousand miles north of Hawaii, and the most geographically crucial link in the air conflict between the United States and Japan was the Aleutian Islands. Verticality had superseded Mercator's horizontal naval-based image, so Japan was remiss in not concentrating on seizure of the Aleutians. Had it carried out a successful military action there, Japan would have threatened the U.S. mainland and would have been able to stop the Americans from bombing the Japanese northern Kuriles from only 750 miles away. Japan did belatedly capture the U.S. western Aleutian island of Attu in 1943, but American forces reasserted control that same year.[28] As previously noted, Haushofer and the Germans also had a Mercator mentality that underestimated the criticality of potential U.S. intervention in the war. A study of the 20 world maps appearing in *Zeitschrift fur Geopolitik* during the period 1934–40 found that 17 were Mercator projections, and none were polar projections.[29]

Interventionists wanted to emphasize American proximity to Europe, so they favored polar projections, which depicted the closeness of the continents via the Arctic. These projections were much more accurate than Mercator's in representing the size of northern territories such as Greenland and Iceland, and their round features were more suitable to an air age featuring great circle routes. Such azimuthal projections displayed a constant scale for lines drawn outward in any direction

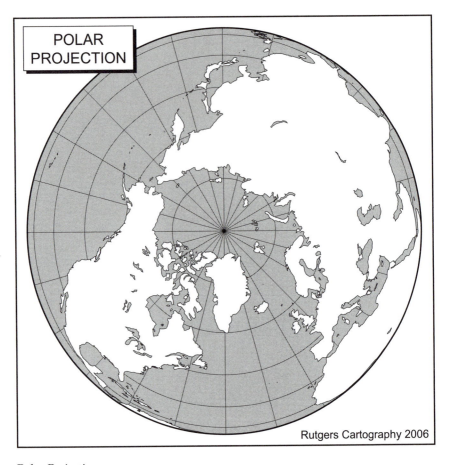

POLAR
PROJECTION

Rutgers Cartography 2006

Polar Projection

from the North Pole, and indicated the shortest distance. Clearly, these characteristics were highly functional to bombing and missile targeting. The deficiency of polar projections was their shape distortion as one progressed away from the center. This was not decisive in regard to the European war, fought mainly at northern latitudes, but it did render them less useful for the Pacific war, which to a great extent took place in equatorial and southern regions.[30]

Polar projections were not new, having been invented by the Swiss cartographer Heinrich Loriti (Glareanus) about 1510.[31] However, they had not been used extensively—in part because much of the Arctic had yet to be surveyed until the twentieth century. Interventionists started to advocate this type of projection early in World War II, and maps employing it became even more common after 1941 since they enabled one to follow the war more easily, especially in the Arctic. Rand McNally, a leading publisher of maps in the United States, released its first polar projection of the world in 1942.

Reflecting the shrinking of the world, polar projections presented great circle routes that came to be recognized as more concise than parallel-hugging sea routes. Although somewhat difficult to comprehend at first, the shortest distance between two points on a flat map is not a straight line, and great circles through northern latitudes are more direct than the traditional east-west sea lanes. The Arctic had become a transit hub, and polar projections made the Arctic Ocean look like an inland sea crossroads resembling the Mediterranean.[32] An editorial in the pro-interventionist *New York Times,* unusually broaching a cartographical controversy, proclaimed that air power had made Mercator projections obsolete, as they were geared toward the shipping trade. The old east-west emphasis should therefore be redirected to a north-south perspective.[33] Actually, air power and the shipping trade were in tandem as far as Allied trans-Atlantic convoys were concerned. Air cover was required to protect the northern sea-lanes, and it was projected out of bases in Canada, Iceland, and Britain.[34]

Advocates of polar projections helped transform the global geographical image of the United States, and they often appealed to American opinion by placing the United States along a map's central vertical axis. Nevertheless, interventionist Nicholas Spykman rejected these projections and contended that east-west connections across the Atlantic and Pacific at middle latitudes would remain more important than the Arctic. For him, the Arctic region was a relatively unpopulated barrier to contact that had temporarily assumed a major role because enemies of the United States had cut transoceanic routes. He labeled this development a "detour" and iterated his support for Mercator projections.[35] Another valid concern was raised by Columbia University geographer George Renner, who postulated that the Western Hemispheric defense concept was based on "ship geography," whereas the air age had already begun. Consequently, polar projections were strategically relevant, but their visual elimination of distinct Eastern and Western Hemispheres was not in synch with U.S. foreign policy formulations.[36]

Richard Edes Harrison, a mapmaker for *Fortune* and other American publications, was the person who most profoundly recognized the cartographical implications of air power and strategy during World War II. Majoring in zoology, and then earning a master's degree in architecture, Harrison was not a professionally trained cartographer. However, as a journalistic cartographer, he influenced a public that had previously been exposed mainly to photographs as accompaniments to articles in the written media. Harrison exhibited what he described as a "freedom from cartographic traditions," and drew upon his architectural background to make maps that appeared to be three dimensional. They also featured bird's-eye views, which stressed the sphericity of the earth and gave the impression that the observer was hovering above it like a bird or pilot. This approach led to unusual angles, elevations, and orientations and may have derived from Harrison's extensive devotion to ornithology.[37]

Harrison believed that mapmaking was part of the American war effort, and that knowledge of geography was essential to understanding political, military, and economic relationships. His maps were therefore drawn to accentuate strategic aspects of World War II, and Harrison was selected to prepare the maps for Chief of Staff George Marshall's biennial report for 1943–45.[38] Harrison's maps were provocative and emotive, surely not promoting dispassionate geometry. He was pro-interventionist and tried to portray the United States as geographically part of an interconnected world. His August 1941 comprehensive world map "One World, One War" (first published in *Fortune*, and then reprinted in his 1944 atlas *Look at the World*), and his polar-centered azimuthal equidistant projections, stressed U.S. proximity to both Europe and Japan. The U.S. Army was so impressed with "One World, One War" that it ordered 18,000 copies.[39]

Harrison saw the United States threatened by "external dangers" that belied any proclivity toward isolationism. Germany loomed in the North Atlantic, and Japan in the North Pacific near Alaska and the Aleutians. He asserted that whoever controlled Iceland would dominate the North Atlantic, and that this island nation was critical in blocking any German designs on the St. Lawrence River which led toward American defense industries in Chicago, Detroit, and Pittsburgh. One map in his atlas, a globe-like orthographic projection with Iceland at its visual center, was therefore labeled "Iceland: Kingpin of the North Atlantic." Alaska, referred to as the "causeway to the World Island," was deemed to be the strategic heart of the North Pacific, and the proximity of the Aleutians to Japan was accentuated.[40]

In essence, Harrison was an advocacy journalistic cartographer who had brilliant insight into both strategy and geography. His unorthodox perspectives were not only fresh in terms of ideas and presentation, but they concomitantly encapsulated the air age, the growing importance of the Arctic, and a post-Mercator vision highlighting the earth's sphericity.

CHAPTER 11

Cold War

As the Cold War unfolded after World War II, a bipolar ideological image oriented east-west developed alongside a strategic vision aligned north-south. The Soviet Union and the United States emerged as the dominant superpowers, and the blocs they established became known as the "East" and "West" due to doctrinal differences and the geographical division of Europe. Simultaneously, the military prominence of air power and the advent of intercontinental ballistic missiles contributed to a "north-south" polar view of warfare based upon great circle arcs.

Although the terms "East" and "West" persisted, they gradually lost any geographical meaning as communist rule eventually spread to Cuba, and Japan became part of the "West." In Africa, Angola and Ethiopia came to adhere to the "East," and Zaire and Ivory Coast to the "West." Furthermore, the old Eastern and Western Hemispheres lost much of their significance once there was a political fixation on Soviet-American rivalry. This was recognized quite early by U.S. Secretary of State Dean Acheson, whose December 30, 1951, speech on world affairs concentrated on the Northern Hemisphere even though he pointed out that the United States was in the Western Hemisphere as well.[1]

The Atlantic Alliance survived World War II, and the creation of NATO linked the United States and Western Europe in a "Western" coalition. For Washington, hemispheric defense of the Americas became secondary to the trans-Atlantic arrangement. Since the Soviet Union was seen as the main threat, the defensive perimeter was extended to Europe. Note also the vital location of Europe in the air age. If one relates access to the world's land masses to flight, then Europe has the greatest centrality. It is the geographical hub of aviation and, in particular, France has the prime placement.[2]

Therefore, "East-West" competition was focused on Europe, but strategic defense was directed toward the Arctic, since it served as the connection between the two superpowers. Polar projections, just as they had during World War II, portrayed the proximity of the United States to Europe—and it is no accident that the U.N. flag adopted in 1947 displays a map with a polar projection.

AMERICAN EUROCENTRISM

Noted journalist James Burnham observed at the end of World War II that, both geographically and strategically, "Eurasia encircles America, overwhelms it." The Soviet Union had gained control over the "Heartland" and was in a position to dominate Eurasia and Africa. It possessed the most favorable location in the world due to its invulnerability to sea power, and additionally had a large population and effective political organization. It also occupied the eastern sector of Germany, a key to hegemony over Eurasia. Nonetheless, Burnham saw hope in an American-British-Commonwealth alliance, and cited U.S. air power and possession of atomic weapons as means of challenging continued domination of the "Heartland" by the Soviet Union.[3]

George Kennan, the originator of the "containment doctrine," depicted Soviet control of the "Heartland" as menacing to the "Rimland," so American power had to be directed at blocking any such territorial advances.[4] In April 1947, the Joint Chiefs of Staff concluded that Europe had to be the focus of such a strategy and that the United States should firmly align with Britain and France. Containing the Soviet Union was the motivation, but establishing a trans-Atlantic defense for the United States in collaboration with European states was also a vital aspect of this endeavor. In ranking the importance of specific countries to U.S. security, those in Europe were clearly deemed the most critical, as the list was headed by Britain, France, Germany, Belgium, the Netherlands, Austria, and Italy.[5]

In May 1947, Kennan was appointed as the first director of the Policy Planning Staff of the Department of State. Preventing Soviet expansion in Europe was the main concern, with the United States and its European partners asserting that the Soviet Union had extended its might westward since the end of the war and was "strategically capable at the present time of dominating the continent of Europe by force."[6] Accordingly, the first of Washington's anti-Soviet alliances to be formed was NATO in April 1949. Paul Nitze replaced Kennan in January 1950, but the study group Nitze headed continued to apply the principles of "containment" and concluded in April that "Soviet efforts are now directed toward the domination of the Eurasian land mass."[7] This report averred that the United

States was the crucial power capable of countering Soviet expansion in this region.

Europe was primary. East Asia was considered secondary strategically, with China, Japan, Korea, and the Philippines far down the April 1947 list of rankings. In 1946, General Douglas MacArthur had maintained that the U.S. Pacific Fleet's chief role should be support for the American occupation of Japan and South Korea. Not surprisingly, MacArthur wanted to control these naval forces through a unified command headquartered in Tokyo—but General Dwight Eisenhower had a different perspective regarding American deployment and military "turf." He argued that the Navy's basic concern should be the defense of Alaska and the West Coast, with the Western Pacific relegated to a lesser status pertaining to American security. Eisenhower had won.[8]

Eisenhower's low regard for Asia may possibly be related to his background as Allied commander in Europe and to his rivalry with MacArthur, who headed the post-war occupation of Japan. However, his outlook was consistent with that of Kennan, who had written in November 1947 that South Korean forces could not hold back communist expansion by themselves, that Korea "is not of decisive strategic importance to us," and that Americans should "extricate ourselves without too great a loss of prestige."[9]

A similar situation was soon evident in China, where the communists had come to power in October 1949. The new government was threatening to seize the offshore Nationalist stronghold of Formosa (Taiwan), yet the American stance was to avoid conflict there. In a December 1949 report, the National Security Council maintained that only American occupation could forestall a communist takeover—but that such an effort should not be attempted due to Formosa's limited strategic importance. The recommendation was to stand aside since administering Formosa "would not be in the U.S. national interest."[10]

As Europe, NATO, and the Western Alliance took precedence, Latin America and the Monroe Doctrine were placed on the back burner. The April 1947 rankings had placed Latin America far down the list, and the region as a whole had been cited rather than any particular countries that could possibly be vital to U.S. security. Certainly, alignment with European states superseded the concept of Pan-American defense, because Latin America was only an "aerial backyard" (surely as presented on a polar projection) removed from the Soviet line of fire.[11] Concomitantly, the Monroe Doctrine had been undermined by NATO's existence. Britain, France, and the Netherlands still had colonies in the New World, but the United States was no longer concerned, as these European states were now military partners rather than continental interlopers. Parallel to this development was that U.S. troops were stationed in Western Europe as part of NATO, yet their hosts generally appreciated their commitment to Europe's defense and did not raise the issue of Monroe Doctrine violations.[12]

In September 1947, the United States tried to eliminate the World War II confusion over the extent of the Western Hemisphere and yet maintain the commitment to its defense. The Rio Pact (Inter-American Treaty of Reciprocal Assistance) therefore referred to "American States," "the Continent," and "the region covered by the treaty"—but not to "the hemisphere." Greenland and part of Antarctica were included within the framework, as lines defining the treaty area extended to the poles. In essence, the Rio Pact was the application of the principle of "collective self-defense" to the Western Hemisphere in accordance with the new charter of the United Nations. As drawn, the zone stretched across 180 degrees of longitude but this expanse was basically from 170 degrees east to 10 degrees west so as to provide coverage for the Aleutians. In some places, the longitudinal range narrowed to only 90 degrees west and 60 degrees west.[13]

STRATEGIC CONSIDERATIONS

Mackinder had used a Mercator projection to demonstrate his "Heartland" theory. This method emphasized the great expanse of Eurasian land at northern latitudes, as well as the "Heartland's" lack of vulnerability to sea power. Air assault on the "Heartland" was not possible at the turn of the twentieth century, but this consideration moved to the forefront after World War II as polar projections accompanied the new age of air power. Also, with the defeat of Germany, Soviet control of the "Heartland" had become the major preoccupation of American strategists. Such a geopolitical conception was attuned to an historic American fear that dominance of Eurasia by one power would pose a threat to the United States. Jefferson had been wary of Napoleon's advance into Russia, and alarm about German dominance in the region had prompted American intervention in Europe during both twentieth century world wars. Kennan's "containment doctrine" was based on similar considerations.[14]

Air Force General James Doolittle had argued in a fall 1945 presentation to the Senate Committee on Military Affairs that the Mercator projection had been responsible for "fallacious theories." He then proceeded to use a polar projection to stress the importance of air power, and his references to enemies of the United States had left little doubt that Soviet proximity via the Arctic constituted a military challenge to the United States.[15] A polar image of the world enhanced the view that mutual targeting across the Arctic would be fundamental to the Cold War. American aircraft designer and pilot Alexander De Seversky referred to the polar region as the "area of decisions," and maintained that air power could be used in "interhemispheric warfare" to undercut the outmoded protective shield of the "Heartland." Whereas the United States had applied a "stepping-stone" approach to air power in the course of World War II, De Seversky proclaimed that planes could now strike the Soviet Union directly from American territory. He argued that Mercator projections had to give way to polar projections, as Europe and Asia had to be viewed as north of the United States, not east or west of it.[16]

The Strategic Air Command clearly operated on this basis throughout the Cold War. However, air power could not be isolated from land power. Their relationship had to remain symbiotic, since land bases were required for the aircraft, and aircraft were needed to protect land bases.[17] Also pertinent was that the Arctic had become a crossroads for military aircraft, but not commercial flights. The latter were following great circle routes, but not over the North Pole. Consequently, most commercial airlines illustrated their routes on Mercator projections, while strategic planners in the military preferred polar projections.[18]

Mercator or polar? Each was a double-edged sword, depending on offensive or defensive mentalities. Mercator projections presented a huge Soviet Union. As perceived from the United States, the map image accentuated a Soviet threat—and it was often enhanced by the use of red for Soviet territory. Such an imminent menace could also be exaggerated through framing, as areas at sea could be cut off. This technique would thus emphasize Soviet land superiority.[19] Since the United States was distant from the Soviet Union on a Mercator projection, the threat was more toward Western Europe than toward the United States itself, so Europeans had to be concerned about whether they could count on American commitments to their defense within the structure of NATO. Establishing U.S. military bases in Europe thus compensated for American geographical isolation. At the same time, the Kremlin saw these bases as a form of intimidation directed at its East European sphere of influence and at the Soviet Union proper. There were also no Soviet bases near the United States (until Cuba), so Moscow held an inferior geostrategic position. Even though the Soviet Union appeared to be dominant on a Mercator projection, its apparent advantage was lost once American military power was more capable of striking Soviet targets than vice versa.

From Moscow's perspective, encirclement of the Soviet Union was the flip side of the "containment doctrine."[20] This could best be portrayed on a polar projection, which visually reinforced circular images. Of course, Washington looked at NATO, SEATO, ANZUS, and the Baghdad Pact (later, CENTO) as defensive measures consonant with containment. For both superpowers, polar projections brought Europe and America closer together geographically—and this meant U.S. involvement in any major European war. Focusing on the Arctic also demonstrated that the superpowers were able to target each other in accordance with a North-South alignment—an interpretation with offensive as well as defensive connotations. In effect, the United States was carrying out a dual policy based on both geopolitics and nuclear deterrence. The "containment doctrine" and anti-Soviet pacts represented the geopolitical dimension, whereas the growth of atomic weapons and airborne delivery systems negated the salience of territorial space. In the nuclear age, the time factor had become paramount, as technology to a great extent had superseded geography, but the polar image had retained its pertinence and resilience.[21]

FAULT LINES

The bipolar image of the world, prevalent during the early stages of the Cold War, was soon replaced by a more nuanced recognition of greater global diversity. The United States and the Soviet Union retained their alliance structures and spheres of influence, but the impact of decolonization in the 1950s engendered a new grouping of states proclaiming their neutralism and nonalignment. This "Third World" concept, forged most strongly at the April 1955 Bandung Conference, was originally an affirmation of the independence gained by former colonies in Asia and Africa, but it gradually came to include Latin America. At the same time, economics became linked to the political doctrine of nonalignment as development assumed importance as a delineator of identity alongside membership in Cold War ideological military blocs.[22]

This tripartite schema was based on a "First World," also known as the "West," which was mostly democratic, capitalist, and pro-American; a "Second World," called the "East," which was composed of countries under communist rule; and a "Third World" of generally poor authoritarian states seeking their economic path to development. Geographically, the meaning of "East" had shifted away from Asia to the Soviet Union and Central Europe and, further complicating the situation, China (and later Cuba) was identified with both the "Second" and "Third" worlds. Australia, New Zealand, and Israel were deemed "First World," with Japan entering that category as its economy boomed. South Korea, Taiwan, and Singapore were pro-Western and increasingly prosperous, so they too became detached from the "Third World" and entered the "First World."[23]

Historian Carl Pletsch explains the "three worlds" image in a Cold War context, maintaining that the spread of communist-ruled systems ("Second World") necessitated a "Third World" that was less developed economically and nonaligned. In turn, the "First World" could not be in the same category as the "Second" despite their shared modernity, because the former was "guided by invisible hands" while the latter was highly centralized and ideological. Analyzing in terms of "three worlds" was therefore a convenient way to avoid derogatory labels, yet accentuate systemic differences. Modernization theory was applied to all "three worlds," but there were no characterizations pertaining to being "primitive" or "non-civilized." Pletsch additionally relates the "three worlds" framework to academic and governmental programs in the United States such as communist studies, area studies, and federal contracts in the social sciences and then expounds upon the shift toward "disciplinary generalists" that was triggered by the movement toward détente.[24]

After World War II, the Stalinist global framework was that of two ideological camps as political economy took its place alongside geopolitics. Neutralism was not recognized, and the countries of Asia and Africa (apart from communist-ruled China, Mongolia, and the northern part of Vietnam) were viewed as "reserves of imperialism." Stalin's death in 1953, and the Bandung Conference, then led to a new Soviet interpretation in which Asian and African states were labeled "anti-colonial" and "anti-imperialist," and their leaders were classified as "progressive" and capable of enacting socialist reforms. First Secretary Nikita Khrushchev hosted Indian Prime Minister Jawaharlal Nehru in June 1955, and then traveled to India, Burma, and Afghanistan in November. In February 1956, Khrushchev introduced the "peace zone" concept, according to which the "socialist community" of communist-ruled states was considered to be aligned with former Western colonies in Asia and Africa on the basis of an "anti-imperialist" platform. The two-camp, "East-West" dichotomy was greatly altered as the "Third World" in Western parlance came to be linked to the "East" within a common "peace zone." Acting upon this perspective of realignment, the ruling parties of Ghana, Guinea, and Mali were represented at the Twenty-Second Congress of the Communist Party of the Soviet Union in 1961, and the leaders of these newly independent states were the recipients of Lenin Peace Prizes in 1961, 1962, and 1963 respectively. Also keep in mind that Soviet connections to the "Third World" were strengthened by the 1959 Cuban revolution, Castro's 1962 adherence to the Soviet bloc, and the conclusion of "friendship treaties" with countries such as Egypt, India, Iraq, Angola, and Somalia.[25]

The split between the Soviet Union and China, which became especially virulent during the years 1960–63, created a rift in the "Second World" and precipitated Beijing's close identification with the "Third World." Trying to undercut Moscow's relationship in that area, the Chinese stressed their Asianness both geographically and racially (they had indeed participated in the Bandung Conference) and portrayed the Russians as white, status quo Europeans who had forsaken revolution and entered into "peaceful coexistence" with the capitalists. China also presented itself as a model for "Third World" development as the strategic and ideological division between "East" and "West" started to be replaced by a more economically focused configuration of "North" vs. "South."

World Bank President Robert McNamara suggested that a commission should be established to deal with the division of the world into economic haves and have nots, and proposed that it be headed by former West German Chancellor Willy Brandt. In 1977, an Independent Commission on International Development Issues was announced—and it had the endorsement of U.N. Secretary-General Kurt Waldheim. Its report, completed in 1979, was entitled *North-South: A Programme for Survival.* Reinforcing this "North-South" perspective was another independent commission recommended by Malaysian Prime Minister Mahathir Mohamad and formed in 1987 under the chairmanship of Tanzanian President Julius Nyerere. It was known as the South Commission, and its 1990 report was called *The Challenge to the South.* The South Commission advocated a restructuring of the international economic system so there would eventually be no "North" or "South."[26]

Soviet-American "peaceful coexistence" (later "détente"), and the collapse of communist rule in the Soviet Union and Eastern Europe, brought about the death knell of the "East-West" dichotomy.[27] Post-communism soon came to feature extensive capitalism, and several former communist-ruled states have been accepted for membership in NATO and the European Union. Furthermore, Russia has joined the leading capitalist G-7 powers in an enlarged G-8. A "North-South" division of the world thus predominates, and it is not surprising that all G-8 members are in the "North" both economically and geographically.

The Cartographical Revolution

CHAPTER 12

Social Protest and Deconstruction

Fireworks erupted on the mapmaking scene due to the changing nature of the political left in the West. For long it had focused on events such as the Russian Revolution and the Spanish Civil War. Such a European orientation was then upset intellectually by the impact of decolonization and the linkage developed between communism and the "Third World." Fidel Castro, Mao Zedong, Ho Chi Minh, and Che Guevara became icons of the radical left, which had largely abandoned the Soviet cause in favor of "Third World" liberation struggles. Moscow's so-called "revisionism" was eyed suspiciously as being status quo and statist, while "Third World" movements were deemed "progressive" and "participatory."

These interpretations influenced many geographers, particularly those identifying with the New Left, as they challenged basic cartographical assumptions considered to be Eurocentric. For leftist geographers, maps were part of the ideological battle and should therefore reflect social concerns and justice. Among the leading figures in this reevaluation of cartography was J. B. (John Brian) Harley, the noted British historical geographer, who described the designation of place names by colonialists as "cultural genocide" and rued the "silences" in maps produced by the exclusion or concealment of information about minorities or subject populations. Harley viewed cartography as subjective and culturally biased, and he referred to maps as rhetorical texts that had to be deconstructed to conform to values he believed to be ethical.[1] Thus the leftist dissection of perceived capitalist and European hegemony came to be applied to cartography, and an assault was launched on traditional geographical and cartographical postulates. Maps, however, as a form of "graphic language and visual representation" continue to be used extensively.[2]

THE RADICAL CRITIQUE

The late twentieth-century leftist approach to geography was conditioned by intellectual movements as diverse as Marxism, structuralism, poststructuralism, deconstructionism, postmodernism, postcolonialism, critical theory, feminism, and environmentalism. The "new geography" of the fifties led to the "radical geography" of the seventies, with each focused on societal relevance and change as well as political activism on behalf of the powerless.[3] As explained by Richard Peet, "radical geography" started to change in 1972 from "an attempt to engage the discipline in socially significant research to an attempt to construct a radical philosophical and theoretical base for a socially and politically engaged discipline."[4] Concepts such as "hegemony," "marginalization," and control of "space" came to be emphasized and, in one rather hyperbolic expression of anger at traditional mapmaking, a scholar in postcolonial studies wrote that "the construction of Australia as tabula rasa joins with its production as antipode to produce the continent as an empty, inverted space desperately requiring rectification and occupation."[5] For the radicals, cartography was a form of "discourse" in which the existing values had to be confronted by dynamic social forces seeking redress, and definitions became the means to cultural power.[6]

Maps were attacked on the ground of state-centrism. Their division of the world into political units with distinct boundaries was seen as unnatural, since dominance over territory led to alteration of the human environment.[7] War, "geographical violence," and the power of "discovery" were de-legitimized as terms such as "exchange" and "encounter" entered the historical and social science lexicons. Thus cartographers were implored to take into account the processes underlying mapmaking rather than concentrate primarily on the finished product.[8]

As colonialism declined, the radicals maintained that Eurocentrism had to be eliminated from cartography to make way for the new order. Disparate cultures should no longer remain reliant on Western values, as "objectivity alone" ought to prevail.[9] Consequently, a word such as "Oriental" should not be applied to East Asia, as it is reflective of a European perspective in which the East really means east of Europe. So too should "Oriental" not be used to describe people, as they should be identified by their culture, not their direction.

Sexism was decried along with Eurocentrism because maps were considered the creations of male chauvinists. Gillian Rose, a feminist geographer, lambasted the "white bourgeois heterosexual masculinities which are attracted to geography, shape it and are in turn constituted through it, imagine their Other in part as feminine." Simon Ryan, a postcolonial scholar, had similar observations as he recognized themes of penetration and unveiling pertaining to land described as representative of the female body. Too often, according to Ryan, exploration was presented as a male forcing himself upon "the inert yet resistant female land."[10] There was also an ecological dimension. Radical geography was based on an "organic relationship" between humans and the earth, and social processes were viewed as interconnected with the natural environment. Maps started to impute this interpretation, with great attention during the "cartographical devolution" being paid to ecosystems.[11]

Geographers Mona Domosh and Joni Seager argue that nature, generally viewed as female, was intellectually put under the control of males during the sixteenth and seventeenth centuries through the development of mechanistic laws of nature. This led to exploitation in the name of science and culture, and the emergence of a gender issue. What these feminist geographers see as the "nurturing" aspects of nature were then overwhelmed by images of rational control by men, and new metaphors such as "raping the wilderness, penetrating virgin lands, conquering a capricious nature, mastering the wild, and subduing untamed lands" were popularized.[12]

Australian geographer Louise Johnson cogently summarizes several feminist approaches within her discipline, which have in common the belief that women are subordinated to men. She distinguishes between "liberal," "socialist," "radical," "postmodern," and "postcolonial" types of "feminist geography" and expresses her preference for a strong feminist agenda that does not get sidetracked by matters of class and race. Her own perspective is that sexual differences related to power negate any notion that geographical space is neutral, as there are "gendered spaces" in which women are relegated to an inferior status.[13]

Contributing to the changing cartographical image was Emmanuel Wallerstein's "world systems analysis." Grounded on political economy and ideology, rather than geography and geometry, it nevertheless had an impact on map interpretation through its delineation of core, peripheral, and semi-peripheral areas. Wallerstein presented a "capitalist world-economy" dominated by core states producing manufactured goods, and a dependent grouping of peripheral states providing agricultural commodities.[14] In some respects, his vision conceptually paralleled the "Heartland" theory even though it was based on economics rather than geopolitics.

In the United States, university departments of geography came under assault by the radicals—and many were closed down. They were accused of "Eurocentrism," "imperialism," and "racism." Behavioral geography was hit hard for propounding biological and climatic linkages to race, as well as notions of competitiveness and territoriality that made humans appear animalistic.[15] Such Social Darwinism was alleged to be "fascistic." Geopolitics was denounced for being state-centric, determinist, and expressive of a Cold War mentality based on the perception of the "other" (namely the Soviet Union) as an "unchanging," "perpetual adversary" representing an "expansionist threat" to the United States. In a similar vein, area studies programs focused on geographical regions came to be challenged by "world systems analysis," "rational choice theory," and research on diasporas.[16]

David Landes, a Harvard historian and economist, recognized that geography had been discredited by "relativistic values and moral equality," but that this was rather inevitable since "nature like life is unfair." He agreed that there was Eurocentrism, but postulated that this was due to Europe's dynamism and sense of discovery. Landes perceived a great strength in European culture, yet admitted that culture "frightens" scholars with its "sulfuric odor of race and inheritance, an air of immutability."[17] Development expert Ricardo Hausmann has described the recent comeback of economic geography after its subjection to charges of racism. In his sobering analysis, geography implies an "immutable destiny" of riches or poverty. Hausmann maintains that, as of 1995, tropical countries had incomes only one-third of those in temperate-zone countries and that none of the leading 24 industrial countries were located between the Tropics of Cancer and Capricorn except for parts of Australia and the U.S. state of Hawaii.[18]

Overall, radical geographers contributed some keen observations—but did so in an overly shrill and exaggerated manner. Yes, cartography was Eurocentric—but the most critical strides in mapmaking did in fact take place in Europe. Yes, maps project state power—but they may "liberate" as well.[19] Just look at contemporary Kurdish cartography, which includes a greater Kurdistan stretching across Iraq, Iran, and Turkey. Yes, environmental concerns are important—but disparaged concepts arising out of nineteenth-century human geography were also environmental. And, yes, geopolitics contains an element of spatial determinism—but Marxist radical geographers are themselves quite deterministic in assessing economic factors.

PETERS' PRINCIPLES

The best publicized and most controversial advocate of radical geography was Arno Peters, a West German whose father had been imprisoned by the Nazis for his leftist activities. The younger Peters earned a doctorate in history in 1945 with a dissertation on film as a medium for propaganda and, in 1952, he published a Marxist-oriented world history that gave equal coverage to all regions. Peters then became interested in the use of cartography as a political instrument, emphasizing the importance of maps in the struggle for social justice. In 1967, he addressed the Hungarian Academy of Sciences on this subject and revealed the first version of his world map. Peters then issued it in 1972 and followed with a 1973 press conference in Bonn and a 1974 lecture to the German Cartographical

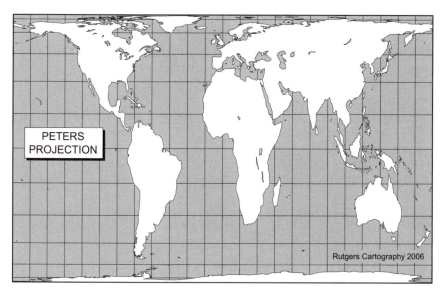

PETERS
PROJECTION

Rutgers Cartography 2006

Peters Projection

Society. Peters' atlas was published in 1980. Peters shook up the map establishment to such an extent that terms such as "pre-Peters" and "post-Peters" entered the cartographical lexicon.[20]

Peters' equal-area projection was a response to Mercator's exaggeration of northern land masses, which had for long provided a Eurocentric image. Peters did not charge Mercator with intentional distortion for ideological reasons, but he was perturbed by the consequences of his projection and sought to develop a counter-cartography based on egalitarian principles.[21]

Peters argued that "new maps" should help us understand "the deep gulf between the poor and rich people and nations," as contrasted with "the old world map with its bases of white superiority and xenophobia." He described any effort to retain traditional geographical concepts as "an attempt by the European colonial powers to maintain the old exploitation under a new disguise," and he proffered his own approach as "the expression of the worldwide consciousness of solidarity" that he saw growing in opposition to Eurocentrism.[22]

To replace Mercator's size distortions, Peters substituted accurate representations of area; to overcome bias in atlases, he used the same scale for all maps. At the same time, he was rather conventional in making rectangular maps oriented to the north that had straight lines for both parallels and meridians. Peters, like Mercator, couldn't display polar regions very precisely because the meridians did not narrow to a point at each pole. He also longitudinally centered his maps on the Greenwich meridian, a procedure that when combined with true size representation produced a large continent of Africa at the most prominent visual location.[23] Peters additionally adopted the international dateline, but suggested that it be moved slightly so as not to bisect so much inhabited land. He further recommended that the 360 degrees of latitude should be decimalized to 100 degrees.

Map coloring also concerned Peters. He rejected green for lowlands and brown for highlands, because this implied that lowlands were more fertile. In North Africa, lowlands are often deserts and the most fertile areas are the highlands. Green and brown should therefore signify vegetation, not altitude, and mountainous regions may thus appear as either green or brown.[24]

Peters' leftist sympathies affected his cartographical choices. In the 1990 U.S. edition of his atlas, maps of the Americas are placed first—but Canada is depicted before the United States. North and South America are illustrated in tandem rather than as separate continental sections, while "Australasia" and Antarctica each has a section of its own. "Thematic world maps" follow those of regions, and Peters' ideology is made abundantly clear when his presentation on women's rights refers to abortion as "rights over their own bodies." Peters' usage of "Arabian Gulf" rather than "Persian Gulf" is interesting, but not problematic. However, the area known as the "West Bank" ("Judea and Samaria") is not labeled and is portrayed as part of Jordan. In fact, this land had been under Israeli administration since 1967, and Jordan had renounced its territorial claim in 1988 to clear the way for its inclusion in an eventual Palestinian state. Even more curious is Peters' decision to portray Gaza as part of Israel. Gaza was surely administered at the time by Israel, but had never been incorporated into the Jewish state.[25]

CROSSFIRE

Peters created a furor, in part because he was not a cartographer by training. British cartographer D. H. Maling wrote that the Peters projection had the likelihood of being the "biggest cartographic non-event of the 1970s," and that it was impossible to apply a scale that is "constant at all points and in all directions."[26] Professionals viewed Peters as an academic interloper who appealed to public opinion on the basis of "political correctness" and a fashionable pro-"Third World" attitude that impressed educators, churches, and U.N. agencies. His projection was adopted by many textbook publishers, the World Council of Churches, UNESCO, and UNICEF. It was also featured on the cover of the commission report on "North-South" relations prepared by Willy Brandt's study group.[27]

Peters' contention that his equal-area projection represented a cartographical advance was ridiculed by the experts, who pointed out that size-accurate projections were even used by Mercator (although not on his 1569 world map)—and were applied by German cartographer Johann Lambert in the late eighteenth century. Furthermore, the Peters projection was almost identical to one published in 1885 by James Gall, a Scottish minister. Peters denied knowledge of Gall's work, but many cartographers began to use the term "Gall-Peters projection."[28]

Mercator's projection had undoubtedly exhibited Eurocentrism, but map scholars did not readily accept the Peters projection as an objective alternative due to his own ideological agenda. American geographer Mark Monmonier maintained that Peters was using Mercator as a "straw man," and church activist and educator Ward Kaiser pointed out that Mercator had indeed produced maps with other projections that did not have size distortion of the Northern Hemisphere land masses.[29] Basically, Peters was replacing a projection exaggerating the size of Europe with one accentuating the "Third World" via shape distortion in the equatorial zone. Peters was shape accurate in temperate zones, with no distortion at 45 degrees latitude either north or south, but he offered extensive north-south shape elongation near the equator. Furthermore, his projection offered no improvement over Mercator's in regard to polar regions as both relied on parallel meridians. This resulted in east-west shape distortion.[30]

The Peters projection, unlike Mercator's, is impractical for navigation due to its equatorial elongation and the shape distortion of coastal areas. Notwithstanding, Peters made no pretense that his maps could be beneficial to navigators. Intended usage must be considered. Peters was trying to challenge basic assumptions inherent in the Mercator projection with the aim of influencing social and political attitudes. His elongated images were shocking, and made people examine their cartographical frame of reference. On the other hand, Mercator had loudly declared that his projection was prepared as a guide to navigators. It was not meant to be a political representation of the world, nor was it absolutely conformal regarding true shape. Size distortions in the Arctic affected the accuracy of shape, but were a necessary consequence of the desire to present straight rhumb lines for navigators. Mercator was not inherently racist or Eurocentric, yet his famous projection could be misapplied toward such an interpretation. Peters effectively counterpoised Mercator, but the projections of these men should be viewed as complementary rather than antithetical, as they serve different purposes.[31]

CHAPTER 13

Rearranging the Pieces

Despite technological advances, the forefront in cartography is not the devising of new geometric projections but, more properly, new creative renderings reflective of the rapidly evolving world scene. There are few empty spaces left to fill, yet maps are being transformed perceptually by the impact of dynamic transnational globalism as a replacement for quiescent state-centrism. The "East-West" and "Three Worlds" images, based on territorial zones of influence, have broken down along with the collapse of the Soviet bloc. Cultural factors have now become the driving forces of international relations, transcending mapmaking's previous emphasis on sovereign political units. Consequently, fluid innovative ways of viewing the planet are burgeoning. Ethnicity lies at the heart of this trend, as there is a growing recognition of pan-regions, diasporas, irredentism, non-jurisdictional religious law, and both the fragmentation and re-amalgamation of existing state entities. The familiar continents, countries, and borders must therefore be reconsidered as essential building blocks pertinent to the emerging world order of the twentieth-first century.

RECONFIGURATION

The crumbling of the Habsburg and Ottoman empires in World War I ushered in a period showcasing ethnic claims on territory in accordance with the concept of national self-determination. Such a development reached its most pernicious and violent zenith in the form of Nazism, which then led to a post-World War II ideological backlash against rampant racialism and xenophobia. The Cold War, especially in Europe, served as a brake on ethnic passions but its demise engendered a revival of separatist chauvinism and the breakup of multinational states such as the Soviet Union, Yugoslavia, and Czechoslovakia. In other parts of the world, where the communist-capitalist superpower struggle was less pervasive, nationality differences had already been accentuated: In Pakistan, the Bengalis had seceded to set up their own country of Bangladesh; in Sri Lanka, the Tamils were attempting to do likewise.

Now, secondary ethnic fragmentation is evident as Chechens fight to withdraw from Russia, Abkhazians from Georgia, and Kosovar Albanians from Serbia. This process is reminiscent of the turn of the twentieth century, when the views of Ratzel and Kjellen were influential, and space started to be identified in ethnic terms. In gist, blood and culture help forge our image of cartographical units as new states defined by ethnicity are proliferating. In many cases, existing borders are being challenged from within, rather than from outside.[1] Ingrained is the issue of fairness. After all, why should there be independent countries like Tuvalu and Nauru, with populations of 10,000 and 12,000 respectively and seats at the United Nations, when the roughly twenty-five million Kurds have no state of their own? Thus our mental picture of the world has come to include "Kurdistan," an ethnic construct not consistent with current administrative realities, and magnifies sub-sovereign territories such as "Tibet" and "Kashmir."

There is, however, a seeming conundrum. Centrifugal forces are partitioning the globe on the basis of diversity, yet some centralization is also evident through the European Union—and, potentially, through the African Union. Actually, analytic compatibility may be discerned if we consider that both actions entail the definition of space culturally. Ethnic minorities seek independence in order to assert their identities but, in fact, are strong supporters of broader federalist mechanisms to assist in the maintenance of their rights. Distrustful of Russia, former Soviet satellites in Eastern Europe are eager to belong to the European Union and NATO. The Scots and Welsh, who have generally accepted devolution rather than press for sovereignty, also tend to look favorably upon the European Union because it provides legal remedies outside of London's control. Interestingly, the establishment of new states and additional borders helps drive the movement toward federal amalgamation. So too does integrative globalization evolve simultaneously with an increase in ethnic assertion.[2] Three Swedish scholars have asserted, "As the bonds with the national center are weakened, regional and local self-identities tend to be strengthened. This trajectory does not contradict the globalization trend. On the contrary, when mobility across national boundaries increases, the significance of local identities seems to grow as well." They point out that regional and local organizations are now becoming international actors.[3]

Fresh images of cartography are developing. For example, there is no longer a Soviet Union—but there is a loose Commonwealth of Independent States in which most former Soviet republics have membership. From Moscow's point of view, the administrative apparatus of the Soviet Union has been completely discarded, yet Russia's security frontiers are seen as extending to the old Soviet borders. Russia assumes a protector's role in this "near abroad," and has committed troops to Georgia, Tajikistan, and other areas.[4] In some ways, this "near abroad" concept may be compared to the Monroe Doctrine.

Pan-regions, often in the form of integrated economic zones, are now critical to our understanding of the world. Both NAFTA and ASEAN operate within a specific continent, but the Pacific Rim stretches across Asia, Australia (plus Oceania), North America, and South America. This geopolitical concept was spawned during the Vietnam War and was related to Japan's rapidly expanding economy.[5] Other pan-regions may be based on cultural affinity; witness the growth of the pan-Arab, pan-Turkic, pan-African, and pan-Islamic movements.

Inhabitants of Pulawat in the Caroline Islands are said to look at the ocean as "an assemblage of seaways," not a body of water. These "seaways" form a "thoroughfare" between islands and are routes of contact.[6] Contemporary geographers similarly describe the seas as transmission belts, not barriers or obstacles, a perspective evident in the April 1999 issue of *Geographical Review* entitled, "Oceans Connect." The land-based "Heartland" framework has lost some of its luster with the breakup of the Soviet Union and the end of the Cold War, and recent competition for mineral rights beneath the seas has contributed to the directing of greater attention there. Correspondingly, academic programs related to area studies of contiguous territories are being challenged by more dynamic approaches stressing cultural ties across saltwater. New fields thus include Mediterranean studies, Indian Ocean studies, and trans-Atlantic or African diaspora studies. So far, maps have lagged behind academia in acknowledging this cognitive phenomenon.

Territory has declined in importance as airborne weaponry has entered arsenals, and mental capital has become as crucial as natural resources in the development of technology. Despite their very limited sizes, Israel has been able to display a powerful military capability and Singapore has emerged as a high-tech leader. The territorial state, the keystone of diplomacy and international law, is in decline as sovereignty is being overridden by universal jurisdiction and humanitarian intervention. Continents too are losing their status. Particularly noteworthy during the "War on Terror" is the underlying cultural divide. Islam, with its concomitant concept of a community of believers (*umma*), is basically juxtaposed with a Christianity that is similarly transcontinental. Continental location is therefore diminished as a geographical determinant of identity and becomes secondary to an ethnic foundation for categorization.[7]

There have been several types of globalization during the past century. Communism aimed at the transformation of the entire world, and even ultranationalistic Nazism incorporated a global vision of *lebensraum*.[8] More recently, three variants of globalization have emerged. One may be considered globalization from above, which contains many democratic capitalist values. It is associated with the activities of the World Bank, International Monetary Fund, World Trade Organization, and major corporations. Another is globalization from below, which is anti-capitalist, frequently anti-American, and seeks to derive support from workers, women, environmentalists, and indigenous peoples.[9] Then there is militant Islamism, which aims at the establishment of a universal *dar al-Islam* ("abode of peace") after the defeat or conversion of the non-Islamic *dar al-harb* ("abode of war").

These three forms of globalization belie state sovereignty, reduce the salience of borders, and stress dynamic "flows and networks."[10] Forces and counter-forces evident in the globalization process are not territorially conscribed. They instead feature the movement of capital, weapons, personnel, ideologies, and commodities (sometimes including illegal drugs)—the post 9/11 atmosphere of rigid border security notwithstanding. Transnational, nongeographical terrorism has additionally surfaced as the prime threat to world peace, replacing state-centric armies.

Conventional world political maps, presenting state units and boundaries, are losing their relevance. They incorrectly imply constraint rather than fluidity, and are not attuned to the factuality of the "War on Terror."[11] Affiliation on the basis of cultural identity is partially supplanting that related to the state, and borders are becoming "softer." There is now free movement within the European Union for citizens of member states, and foreigners with a visa for a particular EU country enjoy the same privilege. No longer do European borders serve as military barriers with barbed wire and minefields, as constructed by communist-ruled states during the Cold War.[12] Yes, official borders still exist, but their "softness" is difficult to display on maps. Michael Klare, an expert on international relations, points to another problem with cartographical representation. He sees political boundaries as growingly inconsequential, with the locations of resources as the real foci of future conflicts. Klare thus imagines a map presenting oil, mineral, timber, water, and so forth in different colors—an approach that would accentuate equatorial regions, especially in Africa.[13]

There is even a "network civilization without a corresponding political form" that "has necessarily imprecise boundaries." It exists only in cyberspace, and it is based on the "information revolution" that has drawn together speakers of English. This so-called "Anglosphere" is a cultural community rooted in technological innovation, and is borderless.[14]

CULTURAL CONSTRUCTS

Although maps are political representations of the world order, it has been inherently understood that cultural factors underlie the visual composite of states and boundaries. British historian Arnold Toynbee recognized a linkage between cartography and civilizations, and it was readily apparent that some countries included noncontiguous regions incorporated due to their ethnicity.[15] This was the case with Germany and East Prussia, and Pakistan and East Bengal. Other countries, such as India and Cyprus, were ethnically partitioned—and there were states such as Israel, Germany, and Turkey that offered preferential citizenship to immigrants of a shared ethnicity.

During the early stages of the Cold War, culture was subordinated to a bipolar and ideological global image. Then emerged acknowledgment of a "Third World" and new economic perspectives on geography advanced by Wallerstein and Peters. Lastly, there has been the contemporary emphasis on ethnicity as a driving force behind what is generally called "globalization." Cultural distinctions have acquired political relevance, with rising ethnic identities contributing to the fragmentation of several countries—most notably the Soviet Union and Yugoslavia.[16] "Ethnic cleansing" has facilitated territorial control, and diasporas have come to be envisioned as affiliates of their homelands. Furthermore, Germans and Yemenis have both reunified into common states—and Hong Kong has reverted to China. Eventual integration of the two Koreas is a realistic possibility.

French historian Fernand Braudel wrote that "civilizations, vast or otherwise, can always be located on a map."[17] He saw a world divided into cultural zones, and believed that civilizations developed in response to their environments. Political scientist Samuel Huntington has adopted a similar cultural zone approach, but his concentration is more on a "clash of civilizations" than on interpreting the evolutionary processes within civilizations. Huntington, as had Toynbee, deemphasizes cultural connections. For him, the discordance between cultures now constitutes the predominant global phenomenon, superseding political, ideological, or economic agency. The end of the Cold War is cited as the event triggering this situation, with Huntington maintaining that "global politics began to be reconfigured along cultural lines."[18]

Huntington offers a limited treatment of civilizations that does not delve into their continuity, demise, or interaction.[19] He sees them as rather monolithic internally, and his selection and spatial delineation of cultural zones may easily be challenged. Notwithstanding, Huntington's depiction of cultures rather than states as the foundation of the world order (perhaps, "disorder") is highly insightful and a major contribution to our geographical comprehension.[20] The "War on Terror" does indeed have a cultural dimension that makes us reconsider the meanings of the Islamic *umma,* the "West," and "Europe"—and how they may be made consistent with cartographical presentation.

Militant Islamists operate in accordance with a mental map of a *dar al-Islam* and a *dar al-harb.* The *dar al-Islam* is to be based on the *Quran* and *sharia* (interpretations of Islamic law), and there is disagreement among Islamist factions as to its current expanse because this is dependent on whether certain governments are sufficiently Islamic. The *dar al-harb* is the territory of the *kuffar* ("nonbelievers" or "infidels") that is expected to come under Islam's sway in the future. The initial step is to reacquire land that was at one time part of the *dar al-Islam.* This would include Spain, Israel, and the Balkans. Then the *dar al-Islam* would spread out further. Abetting this transition would be Muslims living in the *dar al-harb,* who are considered to be on a *hijra* ("journey to sanctuary") similar to that made by Mohammed when he relocated from Mecca to Medina. It is claimed that Muslims in the *dar al-harb* will convert the *kuffar,* just as Mohammed won over the citizens of Medina after having been rebuffed by the Meccans.[21]

This interpretation is both geographical and cultural, and it should come as no surprise that the Central Asian Islamist movement *Hizb-ut-Tahrir* (Party of Liberation) produced a book entitled *The Inevitability of the Clash of Civilization.*[22] On one side of this "clash" is the *dar al-Islam;* on the other is a "Crusader" and "Zionist" alliance of Christians and Jews backed by the United States, and described sometimes as including Russia. The battle-lines in this "clash" are not delineated cartographically, but one Islamist cartoon depicts a three-headed dragon with its "Jewish" head cut off and a sword prepared to detach the "American" and "Russian" heads. Another cartoon sports a drawing of the map of Uzbekistan, and it is being attacked by four dogs. They are labeled "Jews," "Christians," "America," and "Russia."[23]

Many Islamists, notably Osama bin Laden and Zayman al-Zawahiri of al-Qaeda, advocate the reestablishment of the Caliphate, which was terminated in Istanbul in 1924 by Turkey's secular authorities. This Islamic territorial structure is expected to replace existing states, and to be supranational. It is additionally projected to be unitary, with no federal regions. The Caliphate is to serve as the spiritual center of Islam, the fount of Islamic law, and as the headquarters for spreading the Islamic message to the "nonbelievers." It is to be headed by a *Khalifah* (Caliph), a "successor" to the Prophet Mohammed, but actual rule is deemed to come from Allah (God). The guiding principles of the Caliphate, in terms of creating a worldwide system, are to be *dawa* and jihad. The former refers to the "calling," an obligation to disseminate the Islamic message. The latter, in the form of a "lesser jihad," applies to "struggle" against the *kuffar.*

Theoretically, the Caliphate will encompass the entire world. Practically, it could be founded anywhere in the *dar al-Islam*, but the *Hizb-ut-Tahrir* party suggests that its start could be in the Fergana Valley, which slices through Uzbekistan, Tajikistan, and Kyrgyzstan. From the Islamist point of view, failure by any Muslim to support the reestablishment of the Caliphate is a sin.[24]

Mirroring the Islamist image of the "clash of civilizations" is that of evangelical Christians, particularly advocates of the "10/40 Window." They aver that the fall of communism has opened new opportunities for proselytizing, but that Muslims have entered into competition with them. Furthermore, Muslims are viewed as the prime target group for the evangelical Christian mission. According to the "10/40" movement: "We must pray that just as eastern Europe recognized that the atheistic ideology of Communism could not stand the test of time, so also the 'eyes' and the 'hearts' of the Muslims will be opened to recognize that the Christ of the Koran is not only the highest prophet, but the Son of God, who died for the sins of man and rose again for our salvation and that millions of millions of Muslims over the next decade will be saved."

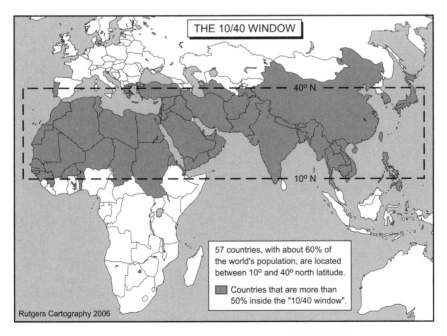

The 10/40 Window

In contrast to the Islamists, sponsors of the "10/40 Window" do offer a cartographical vision of their project. It is a world map accentuating in red the areas of Asia, Africa, and a small section of Europe that lie within the limits of 10 and 40 degrees north latitude. Although Cyprus, Gibraltar, Greece, and Portugal are within this zone, their inclusion is only incidental, as the commentary on the "10/40" mission does not refer to them. Essentially, areas of Asia and Africa have been selected for proselytizing and they appear very central visually because latitudes south of Cape Horn have been excised from the map's frame. The "10/40 Window" is said to contain two-thirds of the world's population and 97 percent of the inhabitants of the 55 least-evangelized countries. Ninety-five percent of these people have never been exposed to Christian missionaries as, due to the difficulties of operating in Muslim areas, only 1 1/4 percent of these missionaries work in the "Window."[25] Thus, one aspect of the Christian-Muslim "clash of civilizations" is a contest for souls. However, it should be noted that the evangelical Christians do not propose a theocracy nor consider violence to be an acceptable means of cultural confrontation, and they accept the existing system of states.

The core of the Christian world is the "West," but delineating this region is elusive. Greece is usually cited as the cradle of Western thought, yet it later turned to Orthodoxy, came under Ottoman rule, and basically was subsumed by the "East." A transition back to the "West" has taken place over the last century and a half. Turkey, the center of Byzantium, is moving toward membership in the "West." It belongs to NATO, and may ultimately join the European Union. At present, the "West" incorporates connotations of globalization from above and maintenance of "Judeo-Christian" traditions. Many Europeans are therefore dissociating from this identity due to perceived American hegemony, while multiculturally oriented Americans are doing likewise because of alleged Eurocentrism.[26]

Samuel Huntington challenges the notion that all of Europe should be identified with the "West." He provocatively remarks: "Europe ends where Western Christianity ends and Islam and Orthodoxy begin." Little of Europe is presently Islamic, but Orthodoxy is a significant factor and leads Huntington to draw a line east of Finland that cuts southward through Romania and the former Yugoslavia.[27] He implicitly endorses the vision of "European-ness" being defined by the "other," be it Russia or Turkey. Russia, the self-proclaimed protector of Orthodoxy after the fall of Constantinople, is beyond the European pale—an interpretation consistent with its lack of membership in the European Union.[28] Yet Orthodox Greece is already included in the EU, and Turkey is accepted at least institutionally as European.

The concept of Europe is still fluid and controversial. Whereas Huntington stresses the criticality of an East-West divide within

Christianity (reminiscent of the earlier North-South, Protestant-Catholic divide), some political figures in the European Union (plus the Vatican) have been attempting to use Christianity as a common denominator and have advocated that the preamble to the EU constitution include reference to Europe's Christian cultural heritage. Furthermore, the identity of *Mitteleuropa* is being reconstituted after the end of the Cold War and the reunification of Germany. It is a culturally Germanic construct, rather than a religious one, but it does downplay differences between Catholics and Protestants.

Mikhail Gorbachev referred to Europe as "our common European home," but current Russian President Vladimir Putin has a radically dissimilar perspective. He does not envision Russia as a future member of the EU, and he sees Europe conjoined with the United States. At a dinner in Brussels, Putin drew a map for his unidentified European eating companion and added connecting lines to demonstrate that Europe and the United States were conceptually linked, and so were Russia and China. Putin discoursed to the European on "your American cousins," and alluded (in the sense of "otherness") to the Africanization and Latin-Americanization of the United States and the Arabization of Europe.[29] This latter observation accords with that of non-Russians who have adopted the term "Eurabia."[30]

Putin's comments are consistent with recent Russian strategic analysis, which is focused on Russia as a component of the "Heartland." Mackinder and Slavophilism thus come together in an interpretation that is clearly cultural and bears overtones of a "clash of civilizations." Communists, nationalists, and many in between believe that Eurasia is the "Heartland," and that this region is confronted by the "Atlantic," a combination of the United States and the western portion of Europe. For them, Eurasia is oriented eastward, away from the "West." Russia, China, Iran, and Iraq are the key countries—with some geo-strategists including Japan as well. There are also analysts who, agreeing with Mackinder, consider Germany to be essential to the Eurasian "Heartland."[31]

There is surely a strategic territorial dimension to this type of geopolitical inquiry. Russia is portrayed as a land-based power threatened by sea-based "Atlanticists," particularly the United States and Britain. An alignment with Eurasian states is therefore needed to develop a security zone. However, cultural antagonisms are primary, with none other than Communist Party leader Gennadi Zyuganov expressing his accord with Huntington. Charles Clover, a journalist covering European affairs, cogently evaluates the transition in Russia away from dialectical materialist thinking as he writes: "Victory is now to be found in geography, rather than history; in space, rather than time." The battle is essentially about values, a juxtaposition of Russian uniqueness and the influence of American "bourgeois liberalism," which signifies moral decline. It is a return to the nineteenth-century Slavophiles vs. Westernizers controversy, with Russia encouraged to isolate itself from outside "pollution." Even a potential closing of ranks with militant Islamism is suggested as a way to combat the Western cultural menace.[32]

REEL TIME

Cartography is a form of mass communication, as in the European tradition of relating the globe to theatre. In *As You Like It,* Shakespeare wrote that "all the world's a stage." This observation was more than a catchy metaphor, since the noted playwright's Chamberlain's Men pointedly named their London venue the Globe Theatre and placed a sign outside featuring the Greek Titan Atlas supporting the world. The English had an image that combined performance and maps, a seemingly unusual amalgam linking projection from the stage to geometric cartography. Ortelius, a Fleming who saw maps as a means of reducing a divine world view to the limitations of human sight, notably entitled his 1570 atlas *Theatrum Orbis Terrarum* (known in English as *Theatre of the World*) as he too perceived geography in the context of theatre.[33] This organization of territory was connected to the division of plays into acts and scenes, but cartographical portrayal really went beyond attempted geographical rationalism and was indicative of psychologically projecting a desire to assert mortal constructs over space.[34]

The ancient Greeks first applied the metaphor of the world as a theater, and it later became common in European countries. Ann Blair, a specialist on the concept of nature within the history of science, has written in regard to the sixteenth century about "nature as a theater, in which the human is the spectator rather than the actor, looking out at the world as to a stage where God displays his skill and providence as author and producer." She also refers to the theater image as linked to the systematic organization of an "encyclopedic survey of all of nature." Blair therefore sheds light on the theater metaphor's relationship to both the globe and the publication of atlases.[35]

People seek to develop methodologies that enable them to "win." Such an art of manipulation (known as *heresthetic*) is reliant on selection, and has been incorporated into "social choice theory." Behavior is exhibited through games and strategy and is transmitted through language that comprises logic ("truth value"), grammar ("communications value"), and rhetoric ("persuasion value").[36] In this sense, mapmaking may embody objective "truths" regarding size, shape, distance, and direction but, simultaneously, may employ color, symbols, and framing in a subjective manner consonant with "persuasion." Cartography is a methodology for communicating knowledge of the world, so human agency is at work along with scientific procedures. Harrison and Peters strikingly exemplify this interpretation as they relied on basic mapmaking techniques, but added a great dose of their own creativity and imagination.

Human subjectivity, applied through cartographical manipulation, may be abetted by the apparently objective means of technological innovation. Satellite imagery, global positioning systems, and computer graphics contribute to mapmaking accuracy, but they obviously have no minds of their own and serve the purposes of the cartographer.[37] He can easily alter orientation, scale, angle, or altitudinal perspective so that cartographical representation becomes more like pictorial imagery or illustration. There is therefore a resemblance to journalism, with the attention of the viewer directed so that the mapmaker's subjective point is quickly grasped.[38] There are now thematic maps emphasizing the exhibition of statistical information in geographical form. Among them are cartograms that render countries unrecognizable in regard to size and shape, yet provide useful data on economic performance, military might, or demographics. They are educational, but are not authentic renderings of the earth's physical realities.

When a movie is projected onto a screen, the entire story is presented from a reel or cassette of film. However, this movie is really an assemblage of discrete frames employed by the director. He, or she, determines what is included or intentionally left out. Frames have fixed borders and are therefore similar to maps, which display only a section of the globe. An atlas may accordingly be compared to a movie—a compilation of frames.

Taking the movie analogy further, it is instructive to examine the growing symbiosis of cartography and journalism in terms of their framing. In essence, practitioners look through lenses to create frames expressing their psychological and ideological visions. They prioritize, arrange, and interpret in an effort to condition the consciousness of the viewer. "Facts" are selected based on their furtherance of a story's "line." Biases come into play regarding content and pertinence, and in controlling the discourse through language.[39] Journalists rely primarily on words, while cartographers utilize symbols, coloring, and labeling as their language. In both cases, information is transmitted through a process of communication whose objectivity is tempered by the projection outward of the transactor's persona. The frames that are produced then display a different type of projection, one of form. For journalists, placement, length, and the accompaniment of photos or charts are critical. For cartographers, it is the framework of Mercator, Peters, and so forth that predominates. Choices are made—with professional judgments, patronage, and the nature of one's audience affecting the degree of simplification and the mode of presentation.[40] Yes, a version of empirical existence emerges as the product—but projections influence what rendering of reality this constitutes. Maps are thus essential to the portrayal of international history and politics, yet they are just reflections. So don't focus only on these images. Consider as well the process, and the mastermind cartographer.

Notes

INTRODUCTION

1. For comments on such phenomena, see Miles Harvey, *The Island of Lost Maps* (New York: Broadway Books, 2000), p. 39, especially the observations by Robert Louis Stevenson.

2. James Cowan, *A Mapmaker's Dream* (Boston: Shambhala, 1996), pp. 6, 101, 111, 133, 147, and 151 and Joseph Conrad, "Heart of Darkness" in *Selected Stories of Joseph Conrad* (New York: Doubleday, Doran, 1930), Part I, p. 52. Dutch cartographers Louise Van Swaaij and Jean Klare interestingly provide fanciful maps of emotions, ideas, and experiences in geographical form. See *The Atlas of Experience* (New York: Bloomsbury, 2000).

3. Jonathan Swift, "Poetry, a Rhapsody" at The Literature Network, http://www.online-literature.com.

4. Lewis Carroll, *The Complete Illustrated Works* (New York: Gramercy Books, 1982), p. 727.

5. Jorge Luis Borges, "Of Exactitude in Science" in Borges, *A Universal History of Inquiry* (New York: E.P. Dutton, 1972), p. 141. Fellow Argentine author Adolfo Bioy Casares is credited with co-authoring Borges' essay. See also Peter Turchi, *Maps of the Imagination: The Writer as Cartographer* (San Antonio: Trinity University Press, 2004), p. 175.

6. Cowan, pp. 132 and 150.

7. Turchi, pp. 93, 166–67, 191, and 204. In the "Introduction" to the Swaaij and Klare atlas, the authors relate maps to poetry. Miles Harvey sees each map as a form of music: "It communicates in lines, hues, tones, coded symbols, and empty spaces, much like music. Nor does a map have its own voice. It is many-tongued, a chorus reciting centuries of accumulated knowledge in echoed chants." See Harvey, p. 38.

8. Meditation 17 (1624) in Anthony Raspa, ed., *Devotions Upon Emergent Occasions* (Montreal: McGill-Queen's University Press, 1975), p.87.

9. Aldous Huxley, *Heaven and Hell* (New York: Harper Brothers, 1955), p. 2.

10. In frontispiece to Graham Greene, *Journey Without Maps* (New York: Viking, 1961). Swaaij and Klare more whimsically declare on the rear of their book jacket: "Welcome to the Sea of Possibilities, the Ocean of Peace, the Stream of Inspiration, the Volcanoes of Passion."

11. Paul Bowles, *The Sheltering Sky* (New York: Vintage, 1990), p. 2 and Miguel de Cervantes, *Don Quixote de la Mancha* (New York: New American Library, 1957), p. 98.

12. Cited in Harvey, p. 20.

13. Huxley, p. 10.

14. See Cowan, pp. 59–60 and notes from the diary of German geographer Heinrich Barth in G. R. Crone, ed., *The Explorers* (New York: Thomas Y. Crowell, 1962), p. 98.

15. Greene, p. 222.

16. Humboldt's diary in Crone, pp. 233–34, and Thomson's in Crone, pp. 292–93.

17. Mark Twain, *Tom Sawyer Abroad* (New York: Oxford University Press, 1996), p. 2.

18. Jonathan Swift, *Gulliver's Travels* (New York: The Modern Library, 1969), pp. 330–31.

CHAPTER 1

1. In the nineteenth century, Chinese geographer Hsu Chi-yu lamented that canals planned for Suez and Panama would be "chiseled" by humans, thus destroying geographical boundaries established by "Heaven and Earth." See Fred Drake, *China Charts the World* (Cambridge: Harvard University Press, 1975), p. 142.

2. James Cowan, *A Mapmaker's Dream* (Boston: Shambala, 1996), p. 144. See also David N. Livingstone, *The Geographical Tradition* (Oxford: Blackwell, 1992), p. 3.

3. Cylindrical projections are rectangular and are well suited for printing on book pages. In practice, geometry now substitutes for the bulb-within-a-globe technique but it is still called a map "projection." For a discussion of this process, see American Cartographic Association, *Choosing a World Map* (Falls Church: American Congress on Surveying and Mapping, 1988), p. 8 and Ward Kaiser and Denis Wood, *Seeing Through Maps* (Amherst, MA: ODT, 2001), pp. 18–19. Note that Greek scholars such as Hipparchus and Strabo began during the first two centuries B.C. to work out the mathematics of transferring three-dimensional global features to two-dimensional maps.

4. James Halpern and Ilsa Halpern, *Projections* (New York: Seaview/Putnam, 1983), pp. 9–10; Maurice Apprey and Howard Stein, *Intersubjectivity, Projective Identification and Otherness* (Pittsburgh: Duquesne University Press, 1993), p. 258; Gardner Lindzey, *Projective Techniques and Cross-Cultural Research* (New York: Appleton-Century-Crofts, 1961), pp. 27 and 42; Bernard Heise, "Visions of the World: Geography and Maps During the Baroque Age, 1550–1750" (doctoral dissertation, Cornell University, 1998); and John O'Loughlin and Richard Grant, "The Political Geography of Presidential Speeches, 1946–87," *Annals of the Association*

of American Geographers, Vol. 80, No. 4 (1990):506. Cartographers were once generalists who had geometric knowledge, artistic ability, and engraving skills. With increased specialization, cartography has moved toward a step-by-step process incorporating many participants—thereby making the final product less representative of the subjectivity of an individual cartographer. See David Woodward, "Introduction," in Woodward, ed., *Art and Cartography: Six Historical Essays* (Chicago: University of Chicago Press, 1987), p. 8.

5. Cosmology, which includes astronomy, relates to the entire universe, whereas cartography is only concerned with the earth.

6. See Yi-Fu Tuan, *Topophilia* (Englewood Cliffs: Prentice-Hall, 1974), p. 30.

7. J. B. Harley, "The Map and the Development of the History of Cartography," in J. B. Harley and David Woodward, *The History of Cartography,* Vol. I (Chicago: University of Chicago Press, 1987), p. 1; Denis Wood, *The Power of Maps* (New York: Guilford Press, 1992), p. 17; Dan Baker and Cameron Stauth, *What Happy People Know* (Emmaus, PA: Rodale, 2003), p. 38; Oliver Morton, *Mapping Mars* (New York: Picador, 2002), p. 26 ; and Kaiser and Wood, p. 106. Inclusion on a map seems to provide the status of reality, but is really a distortion of it. Maps are actually "cultural products." See Geoff King, *Mapping Reality* (New York: St. Martin's, 1996), p. 18.

8. Howard Stein, "The Influence of Psychogeography Upon the Conduct of International Relations: Clinical and Metaphysical Considerations," in Howard Stein and William Niederland, eds., *Maps From the Mind: Readings in Psychogeography* (Norman: University of Oklahoma Press, 1989), pp. 184–186. Maps may be used to reshape the world, rather than represent it, by using territory as a means of power and as a spatial representation of a nation. See James Corner, "The Agency of Mapping: Speculation, Critique and Invention" in Denis Cosgrove, ed., *Mappings* (London: Reaktion Books, 1999), p. 213.

9. Phillip C. Muehrcke and Juliana O. Muehrcke, *Map Use: Reading, Analysis, and Interpretation,* 3rd ed. (Madison: JP Publications, 1992), p. 7.

10. See Leo Bagrow, *History of Cartography,* English edition (Cambridge: Harvard University Press, 1960), pp. 216–18 and Svetlana Alpers, "The Mapping Impulse in Dutch Art," in Woodward, pp. 51–54. European cartographers have usually put their names on maps, thus signifying artistic property. For a discussion of the relationship between European printing and cartography during the period 1420–1650, see David Buisseret, *The Mapmakers' Quest: Depicting New Worlds in Renaissance Europe* (Oxford: Oxford University Press, 2003), Chapter 2.

11. Colin Franklin, "A Western View of Japanese Mapmaking," *Mercator's World,* Vol. 2, No. 1 (January/February 1997): 28. Many Japanese maps were prepared by artists rather than by mathematically trained cartographers. See Hiroshi Nakamura, *East Asia in Old Maps* (Honolulu: East West Center Press, 1963), p. 77.

12. Maps have been described as a medium between humans who have not seen a place, and spatial reality. See Drake, p. 52. Japanese geographer Takahashi Kageyasu devised a useful method of separating the known from the unknown. His 1811 map of Japan used dotted lines to indicate areas of northern Japan that had not yet been explored. See Donald Keene, *The Japanese Discovery of Europe, 1720–1830* (Stanford: Stanford University Press, 1969), p. 147.

13. Donald S. Johnson, *Phantom Islands of the Atlantic* (New York: Walker and Company, 1994), p. 27. Maps are often based on preconceived notions (re: Columbus')

that persist despite visual observation. They therefore do not necessarily show where one has been, but where one thinks one has been. See J. H. Parry, *The Discovery of the Sea* (New York: Dial, 1974), p. 294.

14. Denis Cosgrove, "Introduction: Mapping Meaning" in Cosgrove, pp. 27–29.

15. Eratosthenes drew a "Parallel of Rhodes" that ran east-west through the Pillars of Hercules (Strait of Gibraltar) and the island of Rhodes, and a "Meridian of Alexandria" that extended north and south through the Egyptian city. He did not systematically identify locations because his spacing between parallels and meridians was not standardized, but his efforts led to the grid system of latitude and longitude. See A. G. Hodgkiss, *Understanding Maps* (Folkestone, UK: Dawson, 1981), p. 72.

16. Before location could be determined by precise measurements of latitude and longitude, navigators usually relied on "dead reckoning." They would combine their calculation of direction based on use of a sextant or compass with the delineation of distance derived from a sand-glass plus use of a wooden float tied to a line and pulled through the sea.

17. The Vikings, great seafarers from the ninth to the eleventh centuries, had neither drawn maps nor the compass.

18. John Pickles, *A History of Spaces* (London: Routledge, 2004), p. 35.

19. David Harvey, *Explanation in Geography* (New York: St. Martin's Press, 1969), pp. 376–77.

20. David Turnbull, *Maps are Territories: Science is an Atlas* (Chicago: University of Chicago Press, 1993), p. 15.

21. Heise, pp. 212–15 and 279.

22. George Demko, *Why in the World* (New York: Anchor, 1992), p. 5. The Aztecs viewed the world as impermanent, and feared that even the sun could die. See Ronald Wright, *Stolen Continents* (Boston: Houghton Mifflin, 1992), p. 33. Take into account that dynamic changes in the earth's physiography are difficult to display on static, paper maps. Edward Tufte, an expert on information processing, therefore discusses the need to "escape" from two-dimensional "flatland." See *Envisioning Information* (Cheshire, CT: Graphics Press, 1990), pp. 9 and 12. In the eleventh century, the interchangeability of land and sea was recognized in the Islamic classic *The Book of Curiosities of the Sciences and Marvels for the Eyes.* See Jeremy Johns and Emilie Savage-Smith, "The Book of Curiosities: A Newly Discovered Series of Islamic Maps," *Imago Mundi,* Vol. 55 (2003):12.

23. Tai Sung An, *The Sino-Soviet Territorial Dispute* (Philadelphia: Westminster, 1973), pp. 92–93.

24. Geographer Peter Vujakovic maintains that maps were used by the Western (particularly British) media during the Yugoslavia-Kosovo crisis to influence public opinion in a pro-interventionist direction. He writes that "cartography provides a critical visual metaphor of scientific accuracy" so maps were employed to stress the accuracy of targeting and the extent of damage. Afterward, when there were some "smart" weapons debacles such as in the Chinese embassy attack, maps were presented to explain what went wrong. See "Mapping the War Zone: Cartography, Geopolitics and Security Discourse in the UK Press," *Journalism Studies,* Vol. 3, No. 2 (2002):192 and 201.

CHAPTER 2

1. Norman J. W. Thrower, *Maps & Man* (Englewood Cliffs: Prentice-Hall, 1972), p. 1; J. B. Harley, "Deconstructing the Map" in Paul Laxton, ed., *The New Nature of Maps* (Baltimore: The Johns Hopkins University Press, 2001), p. 159; and Peter Whitfield, "Inner Worlds and Outer Worlds: Eight Centuries of World Maps," *Mercator's World*, Vol. 1, No. 5 (1996):14. Aztec maps emphasized humanistic values rather than accurate spatial representation, and they concentrated primarily on social relationships within the society. See Barbara Mundy, *The Mapping of New Spain* (Chicago: University of Chicago Press, 1996), p. xvi.

2. J. B. Harley, "Text and Context in the Interpretation of Early Maps," in Laxton, p. 44 and Donald S. Johnson, *Phantom Islands of the Atlantic* (New York: Walker, 1994), pp. 26–27.

3. Nathan Sivin and Gari Ledyard, "Introduction to East Asian Cartography," in J. B. Harley and David Woodward, eds., *The History of Cartography*, Vol. 2, Book 2, *Cartography in the Traditional East and Southeast Asian Societies* (Chicago: University of Chicago Press, 1994), p. 29 and Barbara Bartz Petchenik, "Cartography and the Making of an Historical Atlas: A Memoir," *The American Cartographer*, Vol. 4, No. 1 (1977): 23.

4. Alan Morantz, *Where is Here?: Canada's Maps and the Stories They Tell* (Toronto: Penguin, 2002), pp. 2 and 7; Susan Gole, *Indian Maps and Plans* (New Delhi: Manohar, 1989), p. 39; and Thomas Suarez, *Early Mapping of Southeast Asia* (Hong Kong: Periplus, 1999), pp. 32–33. Maps may also be displayed through clothing. Some people believe that Palestinian Authority President Yasser Arafat arranged his *keffiyeh* headwear to represent a map of Palestine. Maps may possibly have been incorporated into the quilts made by slaves in the Confederacy to guide travelers along the Underground Railroad. An exhibit of such quilts is located in the National Cryptologic Museum at Fort Meade, Maryland.

5. Bernard Heise, "Visions of the World: Geography and Maps During the Baroque Age, 1550–1750" (doctoral dissertation, Cornell University, 1998), pp. 146–47; Fred Drake, *China Charts the World* (Cambridge: Harvard University Press, 1975), pp. 31 and 33; and Suarez, pp. 32–33. Some cultures deemphasize distance and stress the location of hazards, plus spiritual and hunting sites. See Morantz, p. 29.

6. Ivor Wilks, "On Mentally Mapping Greater Asante: A Study of Time and Motion," *Journal of African History*, Vol. 33, No. 2 (1992):182–85.

7. Mary Helms, *Ulysses' Sail* (Princeton: Princeton University Press, 1988), p. 4; Robert David Sack, *Human Territoriality: Its Theory and History* (Cambridge: Cambridge University Press, 1986), p. 77; David Woodward, "Cartography in Indigenous Societies," *Mercator's World*, Vol. 3, No. 5 (September/October 1998): 33; Drake, p. 55; and David Woodward, Cordell D. K. Yee, and Joseph Schwartzberg, "Concluding Remarks," in Harley and Woodward, p. 846.

8. David Turnbull, *Maps are Territories: Science is an Atlas* (Chicago: University of Chicago Press, 1993), p. 52.

9. Turnbull, pp. 30–33, 36, and 42 and "Dreaming in Color: Aboriginal Art from Balgo," brochure published by the Kluge-Ruhe Aboriginal Art Collection, University of Virginia, 2003. Note that the Gumatj crocodile map resembles a

solar constellation. For completely different reasons, Dutch maps from the late sixteenth and early seventeenth centuries often shaped the Netherlands like a lion. This symbolized strength, provided a mnemonic tool for learning, and also was consistent with the lions depicted on the crests of several Dutch provinces. A good example of such a map is one made in 1607 by Petrus Montanus. See Heise, pp. 267–68 and Nigel Holmes, *Pictorial Maps* (New York: Watson-Guptill, 1991), p. 174.

10. It is easy to portray a central location on a flat map, but less so on a spherical globe. Globes were not generally in use until the late fifteenth century. Note that globes can sometimes have a centric bias, as evidenced by Roger Palmer's 1681 globe, which is in the Whipple Museum in Cambridge, England. It is tilted in a manner that places Britain at its top in the place customarily occupied by the North Pole. As for the southern orientation of many Islamic maps, it is significant that both of the world maps in the eleventh-century *Book of Curiosities* have such an orientation. It is also possible that al-Idrisi copied his 1154 map from one in the *Book of Curiosities*. See Jeremy Johns and Emilie Savage-Smith, "The Book of Curiosities: A Newly Discovered Series of Islamic Maps," *Imago Mundi*, Vol. 55 (2003):14.

11. Felipe Fernandez-Armesto, *Atlas of World Exploration* (New York: HarperCollins, 1991), p. 21. A Japanese temple houses a map brought from China in 858, but was drawn about 733. It has both Chinese and Tibetan inscriptions, and countries are represented in basically rectangular forms with relatively accurate placement but with no consideration given to size or shape. See Hiroshi Nakamura, *East Asia in Old Maps* (Honolulu: East West Center Press, 1963), p. 8, figure 1.

12. Yi-Fu Tuan, *Topophilia* (Englewood Cliffs: Prentice-Hall, 1974), p. 30.

13. Suarez, p. 20.

14. Cordell D. K. Yee, "Traditional Chinese Cartography and the Myth of Westernization," in Harley and Woodward, pp. 170–73; Daniel Kane, "Mapping 'All Under Heaven': Jesuit Cartography in China," *Mercator's World*, Vol. 4, No. 4 (July/August 1999):42–43; Derek Nelson, *Off the Map* (New York: Kodansha International, 1997), p. 9; Laura Hostetler, *Qing Colonial Enterprise* (Chicago: University of Chicago Press, 2001), pp. 54–55; and Richard J. Smith, *Chinese Maps* (Oxford: Oxford University Press, 1996), p. 78. A 1645 Chinese world map places a disproportionately large China at its center. See April Carlucci and Peter Barber, *Lie of the Land: The Secret Life of Maps* (London: The British Library, 2001), p. 39. Ricci's advocacy of the spherical earth concept failed to influence the Chinese, who continued to believe that the earth was flat. So too did the Japanese, who were also influenced by Ricci in other ways. It was not until the nineteenth century that Chinese and Japanese cartography started to represent sphericity. Note that Jesuit missionaries had made their first globe in China in 1623. See Carlucci and Barber, p. 9.

15. Drake, pp. 58–60.

16. For speculation that the Japanese started to center their maps in India because they resented Sinocentrism, see Nobuo Muroga and Kazutaka Unno, "The Buddhist World Map in Japan and Its Contact With European Maps," *Imago Mundi*, Vol. XVI (1962):52.

17. Kazutaka Unno, "Cartography in Japan," in Harley and Woodward, pp. 371 and 377–78 and map of Japan from Momoyama period (1573–1615) in Kobe City Museum and exhibited at "Turning Point: Oribe and the Arts of Sixteenth Century Japan," Metropolitan Museum of Art, New York, October 2003–January 2004.

18. "Turning Point." See also the 1779 map by Nagakubo Sekisui in Colin Franklin, "A Western View of Japanese Mapmaking," *Mercator's World*, Vol. 2, No. 1 (January/February 1997):30–31. Matteo Ricci placed America in the east on his world map, confusing the Japanese who considered it to be in the west and Japan to be the country furthest east. See Helen Wallis, "The Influence of Father Ricci on Far Eastern Cartography," *Imago Mundi*, Vol. XIX (1965):39.

19. Shintaro Ayusawa, "Two Types of World Map Made in Japan's Age of National Isolation," *Imago Mundi* (1953):124–25.

20. Norman Davies, *Europe: A History* (London: Oxford University Press, 1996) and *Heart of Europe: The Past in Poland's Present* (New York: Oxford University Press, 2001). American maps during the late eighteenth and nineteenth centuries usually featured the United States in the center, thereby stressing security in the protection provided by isolating seas. Globes were rarely used, perhaps because they could not present the United States in this context. The first American globe, constructed by the farmer and blacksmith John Wilson, did not even appear until 1810. Wilson's 1811 globe was exhibited in "Mapping the Republic," Osher Map Museum, University of Southern Maine, July 2004.

21. Simon Berthon, Andrew Robinson, and Patrick Stewart, *The Shape of the World* (Chicago: Rand McNally, 1991), p. 48.

22. Christian religious *mappaemundi* depicted Paradise, which was generally portrayed as separated from the rest of the world by mountains or a wall, or by depiction as an island. See Denis Cosgrove, *Mappings* (London: Reaktion Books, 1999), p. 60. Note that east was significant for Christians because of the following passage from Ezekiel 43:2: "Behold, the glory of the God of Israel came from the way of the east."

23. Despite Europe's gradual adoption of a northern orientation, there was not uniformity. Southern orientations were applied by Andreas Walsparger, a Salzburg monk, on his 1448 world map; by Erhard Etz of Nuremberg on his 1501 map of Europe; by Frenchman Pierre Desceliers on his 1550 world map presented to King Henri II; by Venetian Giacomo Gastaldi on his maps of Africa and Southeast Asia published during the 1560s; and by Francis Fletcher, the chaplain and journal keeper on the 1577–80 voyage of Britain's Francis Drake. There is also an interesting sixteenth-century tapestry in Seville's Alcazar palace that is oriented southward from Flanders. In Russia, there were maps from 1640 and 1670 with eastern orientations, and a 1699 map of Siberia by Ivashko Petlin that has a southern orientation. On the Russian maps, see Leo Bagrow, *A History of Russian Cartography up to 1800* (Wolfe Island, Ontario: Walker Press, 1975), pp. 9–10, 17, 38, and 41. Matthew Paris' map of Britain is notable for its accentuation of routes to Dover, the jumping-off point for the Crusades and journeys to continental Europe. It includes monasteries and guest houses along the way to Dover, especially en route from Newcastle. See Edward Lynam, *British Maps and Map-makers* (London: Collins, 1947), p. 8 and A. G. Hodgkiss, *Understanding Maps* (Folkestone, UK: Dawson, 1981), p. 120.

24. A. Gutkind Bulling, "Ancient Chinese Maps," *Expedition*, Vol. 20, No. 2 (Winter 1978):19. Qin maps dating from the third century B.C. were oriented northward, but Han maps produced approximately 150 years later were oriented southward. See Mei-Lind Hsu, "The Qin Maps: A Clue to Later Chinese Cartographic Development," *Imago Mundi*, Vol. 45 (1993):92.

25. See Ward Kaiser and Denis Wood, *Seeing Through Maps* (Amherst, MA: ODT, 2001), p. 130; Keith Hodgkinson, "Eurocentric World Views—The Hidden Curriculum of Humanities Maps and Atlases," *Multicultural Teaching to Combat Racism in School and Community*, Vol. 5, No. 2 (1987):30; and http://fga.freac.fsu.edu/academy/austral.htm.

26. Brinda Gill, "Pilgrim's Progress: Sacred Maps of India," *Mercator's World*, Vol. 4, No. 6 (November/December 1994): 26–28; Joseph Schwartzberg, "Conclusion," in J. B. Harley and David Woodward, eds., *The History of Cartography*, Vol. 2, Book 1, *Cartography in the Traditional Islamic and South Asian Societies* (Chicago: University of Chicago Press, 1992), p. 509; and Gole, p. 14. Inuit maps also represented significant sites as larger in scale. See Morantz, p. 10.

27. Natalia Lozovsky, *"The Earth is Our Book": Geographical Knowledge in the Latin West ca. 400–1000* (Ann Arbor: University of Michigan Press, 2000), p. 142.

28. For a comparison of theological and scientific approaches, see Charles Hummel, *The Galileo Connection* (Downers Grove, IL: InterVarsity Press, 1986), p. 257. Note that control over maps by the clergy was frequently paralleled by their control over calendars.

29. P.D.A. Harvey, "Medieval Maps: An Introduction," in J. B. Harley and David Woodward, eds., *A History of Cartography*, Vol. I (Chicago: University of Chicago Press, 1987), p. 284 and David Woodward, "Medieval Mappaemundi," in same volume, p. 310. Israel, as a holy land revered by several religions, still maintains a metaphysical dimension as the center of the world. Actual boundaries of the current state of Israel are not pertinent in this regard. See David Newman, "Citizenship, Identity and Location: The Changing Discourse on Israeli Geopolitics," in Klaus Dodds and David Atkinson, eds., *Geopolitical Traditions* (London: Routledge, 2000), pp. 325–26.

30. G. R. Tibbetts, *Arab Navigation in the Indian Ocean Before the Coming of the Portuguese* (London: The Royal Asiatic Society of Great Britain and Ireland, 1971), pp. 4 and 73. This volume is a translation of Ahmad bin Majid al-Najdi, *Kitab al-Fawa'id fi usul al-bahr wa'l-qawa'id*. The first citation is from the translator's introduction, and the second is from the text.

31. Cyrus Ala'i, "The Map of Mamun," *Mercator's World*, Vol. 3, No. 1 (January/February 1998):52.

32. David A. King, *World-Maps for Finding the Direction and Distance to Mecca* (Leiden: Brill, 1999), xiv and 23 and Tibbetts, p. 65.

33. Geoff King, *Mapping Reality* (New York: St. Martin's, 1996), p. 31 and Karl E. Meyer and Shareen Blair Brysac, *Tournament of Shadows* (Washington, D.C.: Counterpoint, 1999), p. 310. Christian *mappaemundi* have been described as "cartographical encyclopedias" of religious knowledge. See Cosgrove, p. 63. Evelyn Edson, a specialist on the history of cartography, maintains that Christian maps placed the earth "in both its cosmic and historical contexts." She also points out that these maps emphasize the significance of places, such as Jerusalem, rather

than their location. See *Mapping Time and Space: How Medieval Mapmakers Viewed Their World* (London: The British Library, 1997), pp. 163–65. Note also that the Christian clergy tried to change the identity of constellations away from paganism and toward Biblical imagery. See Peter Whitfield, *The Mapping of the Heavens* (San Francisco: Pomegranate Artbooks, 1995), p. 89.

34. Christians related the west to sunset and darkness.

35. Beginning in the third century, the Phison River cited in Genesis started to be interpreted as the Ganges. This viewpoint became common by the tenth century. See Steven Darian, *The Ganges in Myth and* History (Honolulu: University Press of Hawaii, 1978), p. 169. Mt. Meru and its four rivers also became conflated with Genesis' account of Paradise.

36. The three continents were sometimes associated with the Trinity and the wise men.

37. Christian ethnocentrism regarding the centrality of Jerusalem on maps was unusual in that Jerusalem was not in "Christendom" and was not under Christian control for most of the time period when Jerusalem was featured in this manner. See Samuel Edgerton, Jr., "From Mental Matrix to *Mappamundi* to Christian Empire: The heritage of Ptolemaic Cartography in the Renaissance," in David Woodward, ed., *Art and Cartography: Six Historical Essays* (Chicago: University of Chicago Press, 1987), p. 27.

38. Jeffrey Burton Russell, *Inventing the Flat Earth* (New York: Praeger, 1991), p. 21.

39. Jonathan Lanman, "The Religious Symbolism of the T in T-O Maps," *Cartographica*, Vol. 18, No. 4 (1981):18.

CHAPTER 3

1. Cordell D. K. Yee, "Chinese Maps in Political Culture," in J. B. Harley and David Woodward, eds., *The History of Cartography*, Vol. 2, Book 2, *Cartography in the Traditional East and Southeast Asian* Societies (Chicago: University of Chicago Press, 1994), pp. 73, 76, and 77; Thomas Suarez, *Early Mapping of Southeast Asia* (Hong Kong: Periplus, 1999), p. 39; and Susan Gole, *Indian Maps and Plans* (New Delhi: Manohar, 1989), p. 27. The Greeks demonstrated their power in the third century B.C. by assembling a huge map collection in the Alexandria Library. See Denis Cosgrove, ed., *Mappings* (London: Reaktion Books, 1999), p. 27. In eighteenth-century Saxony, the prestige of the ruler was enhanced by his possession of the best maps available. See Bernard Heise, "Visions of the World: Geography and Maps During the Baroque Age, 1550–1750," (doctoral dissertation, Cornell University, 1998), pp. 408–410.

2. www.kb.nl/infolev/liber/2002.html; Karl Meyer and Shareen Blair Brysac, *Tournament of Shadows* (Washington, D.C.: Counterpoint, 1999), p. 527.

3. Jonathan Crush, "Post-colonialism, De-colonization, and Geography," in Anne Godlewska and Neil Smith, *Geography and Empire* (Oxford: Blackwell, 1994), p. 337; Jeremy Black, *Maps and Politics* (Chicago: University of Chicago Press, 1997), p. 20; Robert David Sack, *Human Territoriality: Its Theory and History* (Cambridge: Cambridge University Press, 1986), p. 5; and Peter Perdue, "Boundaries, Maps and Movement: Chinese, Russian, and Mongolian Empires in Early Modern

Central Eurasia," *The International History Review,* Vol. XX, No. 2 (June 1998):272; and Barbara Mundy, *The Mapping of New Spain* (Chicago: University of Chicago Press, 1996), pp. 11–12. During the late sixteenth century, Pope Gregory XIII established the Vatican's map gallery to demonstrate the Church's power.

4. Mark Monmonier, *Drawing the Line* (New York: Henry Holt, 1995), p. 106.

5. J. B. Harley, "Deconstructing the Map," in Paul Laxton, ed., *The New Nature of Maps* (Baltimore: The Johns Hopkins University Press, 2001), p. 165. King Louis XIV of France rued that his country had lost more land due to the inadequacies of his surveyors than to any military battle. Noted by map collector Joel Kovarsky, Virginia Festival of the Book, Charlottesville, March 17, 2005.

6. Suarez, p. 31.

7. Robert Rundstrom, "A Cultural Interpretation of Inuit Map Accuracy," *The Geographical Review,* Vol. 80, No. 2 (April 1990):165–66.

8. Alan Morantz, *Where is Here? Canada's Maps and Stories They Tell* (Toronto: Penguin, 2002), pp. 100–101 and Peter Nabokov, "Orientations from Their Side: Dimensions of Native American Cartographic Discourse," in G. Malcolm Lewis, ed., *Cartographic Encounters: Perspectives on Native American Mapmaking and Map Use* (Chicago: University of Chicago Press, 1998), pp. 242–43.

9. T. J. Ferguson and E. Richard Hart, *A Zuni Atlas* (Norman: University of Oklahoma Press, 1985), pp. 37–51 and 56–57.

10. Kazutaka Unno, "Cartography in Japan," in Harley and Woodward, p. 445. Beginning in 1791, most mapping of boundaries in France was carried out by the army. See Josef Konvitz, *Cartography in France, 1660–1848* (Chicago: University of Chicago Press, 1987), p. 38. Note as well that the end of the Cold War may slow down the mapping of space because it is less essential militarily. See Oliver Morton, *Mapping Mars* (New York: Picador, 2002), p. 268.

11. Peter Barber, "England II: Monarchs, Ministers, and Maps, 1550–1625," in David Buisseret, ed., *Monarchs, Ministers, and Maps* (Chicago: University of Chicago Press, 1992), pp. 77–78; Gole, p. 26; and John Rennie Short, *Making Space: Revisioning the World, 1475–1600* (Syracuse: Syracuse University Press, 2004), p. 147.

12. Marcia Yonemoto, *Mapping Early Modern Japan* (Berkeley: University of California Press, 2003), p. 13; Kobe City Museum maps exhibited at "Turning Point: Oribe and the Arts of Sixteenth Century Japan," Metropolitan Museum of Art, New York, October 2003-January 2004; Richard J. Smith, *Chinese Maps* (Oxford: Oxford University Press, 1996), p. 5; A. G. Hodgkiss, *Understanding Maps* (Folkestone, UK: Dawson, 1981), p. 121; and Robert Mayhew, *Enlightenment Geography: The Political Languages of British Geography, 1650–1850* (London: Macmillan, 2000), p. 75..

13. Miles Harvey, *The Island of Lost Maps* (New York: Broadway Books, 2000), p. 337. The Inuit were more generous with their cartographic knowledge and gave information to European explorers later used to relocate the nomadic Inuit to fixed settlements. See Robert Rundstrom, "A Cultural Interpretation of Inuit Map Accuracy," *The Geographical Review,* Vol. 80, No. 2 (April 1990):161 and Rundstrom, "Mapping, Postmodernism, Indigenous People and the Changing Direction of North American Cartography," *Cartographica,* Vol. 28, No. 2 (Summer 1991):9. When the author of this book visited Liberia's capital city of Monrovia in 1971, he

was unable to find any local map and was told that they were not published for fear of their use in preparing a coup.

14. Harvey, p. xii and Joel Kovarsky, "Maps in a Time of War," *Mercator's World,* Vol. 7, No. 3 (May/June 2992):33 and George D. Winius, ed., *Portugal the Pathfinder: Journeys from the Medieval toward the Modern World 1300-ca.1600* (Madison: Hispanic Seminary of Medieval Studies, 1995), p. 153. Jeffrey Stone, a specialist on African cartography, questions the degree of secrecy practiced by the Portuguese. See *Norwich's Maps of Africa,* 2nd ed. (Norwich: Terra Nova Press, 1997), p. xxi.

15. Samuel Bawlf, *The Secret Voyage of Sir Francis Drake, 1577–1580* (Vancouver: Douglas & McIntyre, 2003), p. 46 and Buisseret, pp. 77 and 86.

16. Bawlf, pp. 160–61.

17. April Carlucci and Peter Barber, *Lie of the Land* (London: The British Library, 2001), p. 12.

18. F.J. Ormeling, Jr., "Cartographic Consequences of a Planned Economy—50 Years of Soviet Cartography," *The American Cartographer.* Vol. 1, No. 1 (April 1974):43.

19. Perdue, p. 284.

20. Colin Franklin, "A Western View of Japanese Mapmaking," *Mercator's World,* Vol. 2, No. 1 (January/February 1997): 28; Donald Keene, *The Japanese Discovery of Europe* (Stanford: Stanford University Press, 1969), pp. 149–52; Shintaro Ayusawa, "Two Types of World Map Made in Japan's Age of National Isolation," *Imago Mundi* (1953):126–28; Lutz Walter, "Philipp Franz von Siebold," in Walter, ed., *Japan: A Cartographic Vision* (Munich: Prestel, 1994), pp. 69 and 72–74; and Ulrich Pauly, "From Marco Polo to Siebold: An Overview," in Walter, p. 29.

21. F. J. Ormeling, "Soviet Cartographic Falsification," *Military Engineer,* Vol. 62 (1970):389–90 and the *New York Times,* September 3, 1988, pp. 1 and 4. The reference to "rotational and linear displacement" comes from Ormeling.

22. Many places in the Crimea had Tatar names, and additional Turkic names were imposed by the Ottomans. However, Russian maps refused to recognize them, so they designated locations with the older Greek and Latin names. Even after the Crimea was annexed to Russia in 1783, Russian maps continued to conform to this usage as there was aversion to place names reminiscent of Islam. Maps based on these concepts were exhibited at "Russia Engages the World, 1453–1825," New York Public Library (42nd Street), January 2004. Also note that space may be defined by movement as well as naming. Communities in Mexico often walked their boundaries collectively as a means of reinforcing identity and laying claim. See Mundy, p. 111.

23. When the National Geographic Society started to use the term "Arabian Gulf" on its maps, Iran barred its magazine and would not let its reporters into the country. See Davood Rahni, "Persian Gulf Eternally Remains Iranian," http:// www.iranian.us/iran_news/publish/printer_4989shtml.

24. According to linguistic anthropologist Daniel Lefkowitz, a street in Haifa was renamed "U.N. Boulevard" following passage of the partition plan for Palestine that called for the establishment of an independent Jewish state. Then, when the U.N. General Assembly adopted a resolution in 1975 that

labeled Zionism a form of racism, "U.N. Boulevard" was turned into "Zionism Boulevard." Presented at Virginia Festival of the Book, Charlottesville, March 17, 2005.

25. Lee Ki-suk, *East Sea in World Maps* (Seoul: The Society for East Sea, 2002), foreword and pp. 16–19, 46, and 53. The South Korean government is now in the process of establishing a commission to investigate historical disputes over territory and labeling. Included is the issue of the "East Sea." See *The Korea Times,* August 18, 2005, at http://times.hankooki.com.

26. Robert Shannon Peckham, "Map Mania: Nationalism and the Politics of Place in Greece, 1870–1922," *Political Geography,* Vol. 19, No. 1 (January 2000):81.

27. Jack Child, *Antarctica and South American Geopolitics* (New York: Praeger, 1988), pp. 118–19.

28. Child, pp. 66 and 107; Bruce Davis, "Maps on Postage Stamps as Propaganda," *Cartographic Journal,* Vol. 22, No 2 (1985):125 and 130; Hans Speier, "Magic Geography," *Social Research,* Vol. 8, No. 3 (September 1941):321; and Jayseth Guberman, "Postage Stamps and Politics," *Mercator's World,* Vol. 1, No. 3 (1996):29–31. In January 2004, South Korea issued a series of stamps depicting birds and flowers on the contested Tokto Island group—known by the Japanese as Takeshima. Japan quickly protested. See the *New York Times,* January 17, 2004, p. A4.

CHAPTER 4

1. Ward Kaiser and Denis Wood, *Seeing Through Maps* (Amherst, MA: ODT, 2001), p. 124.

2. Walter Ristow, "Journalistic Cartography," *Surveying and Mapping,* Vol. 17, No. 4 (October-December 1957): 389 and Keith Hodginson, "Eurocentric World Views—the Hidden Curriculum of Humanities Maps and Atlases," *Multicultural Teaching to Combat Racism in School and Community,* Vol. 5, No. 2 (1987):27. Note that some maps produced by journalistic cartographers employed a "bird's eye" approach in which the image was from the perspective of the viewer and did not follow basic cartographical guidelines such as scale, projection, or measurements of latitude and longitude.

3. Phillip C. Muehrcke and Juliana O. Muehrcke, *Map Use: Reading, Analysis, and Interpretation,* 3rd ed. (Madison: JP Publications, 1992), p. 499. Ladis Kristof, a political scientist specializing in geopolitics, wrote: "Men have already learned to distrust words and figures but they have not yet learned to distrust maps." See "The Origins and Evolution of Geopolitics," *The Journal of Conflict Resolution,* Vol. 4, No.1 (March 1960):45.

4. Jeffrey Murray, "Going for Gold: Misleading Maps Lured Prospectors to the Klondike," *Mercator's World,* Vol. 2, No. 4 (July/August 1997):38–40; Derek Hayes, *Historical Atlas of Canada* (Vancouver: Douglas & McIntyre, 2002), pp. 244–45; and Allan Morantz, *Where is Here?: Canada's Maps and the Stories They Tell* (Toronto: Penguin, 2002), pp. 160–63. During Australia's gold rush in the mid-nineteenth century, maps frequently falsified the proximity of towns to the gold fields. One map depicted Melbourne as closer to the gold fields than Geelong even though the reverse was true. See David Turnbull, *Maps are Territories: Science*

is an Atlas (Chicago: University of Chicago Press, 1993), pp. 46–47 and Kaiser and Wood, p. 90.

5. J. B. Harley, "Text and Contexts in the Interpretation of Early Maps," in Paul Laxton, ed., *The New Nature of Maps* (Baltimore: The Johns Hopkins University Press, 2001), p. 45 and Harley, "Silence and Secrecy," in Laxton, p. 85. On exclusions from maps, see Robert Rundstrom, "Mapping, Postmodernism, Indigenous People and the Changing Direction of North American Cartography," *Cartographica*, Vol. 28, No. 2 (Summer 1991):6.

6. Denis Cosgrove, *Apollo's Eye* (Baltimore: The Johns Hopkins University Press, 2001), p. 13 and Cosgrove, ed., *Mappings* (London: Reaktion Books, 1999), p. 10.

7. H. R. Wilkinson, *Maps and Politics* (Liverpool: University Press of Liverpool, 1951), p. 316. A scale of 1/250,000 is a smaller scale than 1/25,000. Scale was generally not listed on maps until the early thirteenth century. See A. G. Hodgkiss, *Understanding Maps* (Folkestone, UK: Dawson, 1981), p. 25.

8. Jeremy Black, *Maps and Politics* (Chicago: University of Chicago Press, 1997), p. 29.

9. Louis B. Thomas, "Maps as Instruments of Propaganda," *Surveying and Mapping*, Vol. 9 (1949):80; Alan Burnett, "Propaganda Cartography," in David Pepper and Alan Jenkins, eds., *The Geography of Peace and War* (Oxford: Basil Blackwell, 1985), p. 65; and John Ager, "Maps and Propaganda," *Bulletin of the Society of University Cartographers* (1977):4. Symbols may be difficult to understand for those of other cultures. For example, background on religious texts was critical to comprehending many Hindu and Jain maps. See Susan Gole, *Indian Maps and Plans* (New Delhi: Manohar, 1989), p. 25. Knowledge of languages used for labeling is also important, and has political implications. An eighteenth-century map of the Manchu-controlled Qing Empire is labeled in Manchu except for the names of Chinese provinces that are labeled in Chinese. See Laura Hostetler, *Qing Colonial Enterprise* (Chicago: University of Chicago Press, 2001), p. 75.

10. Wilkinson, especially pages 6 and 326.

11. See Black, p. 40. A nineteenth-century Chinese atlas devoted a great amount of space to the United States because it was admired for its defeats of Britain and for balancing European power, which had the effect of reducing European pressure on China. See Fred Drake, *China Charts the World* (Cambridge: Harvard University Press, 1975), p. 150. James Akerman has written about atlases: "In general, people read an atlas narratively because someone has consciously or unconsciously *produced* within its structure a narrative or, preferably, an 'exposition,' because most atlases illustrate and argue geographical ideas rather than tell tales." See "From Books With Maps to Books as Maps: The Editor in the Creation of the Atlas Idea," in Joan Winearls, ed., *Editing Early and Historical Atlases* (Toronto: University of Toronto Press, 1993), p. 4.

12. Bernard Heise, "Visions of the World: Geography and Maps During the Baroque Age, 1550–1750" (doctoral dissertation, Cornell University, 1998), pp. 38–39; A. E. Moodie, *Geography Behind Politics* (London: Hutchinson's University Library, 1947), p. 81; Malcolm Anderson, *Frontiers: Territory and State Formation in the Modern World* (Cambridge: Polity, 1996), p. 21; Josef Konvitz, *Cartography in France, 1660–1848* (Chicago: University of Chicago Press, 1987), p. 33; April

Carlucci and Peter Barber, *Lie of the Land: The Secret Life of Maps* (London: The British Library, 2001), p. 48; and Ladis Kristof, "The Nature of Frontiers and Boundaries," in W. A. Douglas Jackson, ed., *Politics and Geographical Relationships* (Englewood Cliffs: Prentice-Hall, 1964), pp. 136–37. For a classification of boundaries into four categories, see Saul Cohen, *The Geopolitics of Israel's Border Question* (Boulder: Westview, 1986), p. 19. Also note that the absence of a state boundary does not necessarily promote integration. Serbia and Montenegro represent an unusual case where the two regions are officially unified into one country, but there are nevertheless "customs posts" between them.

13. K. A. Sinnhuber, "The Representation of Disputed Political Boundaries," *Cartographic Journal,* Vol. 1, No. 2 (1964): 28; Dick Wilson, *Zhou Enlai* (New York: Viking, 1984), pp. 222–23; Karl Meyer and Shareen Blair Brysac, *Tournament of Shadows* (Washington, D.C.: Counterpoint, 1999), pp. 437 and 559; and Anderson, p. 91.

14. Barbara Bartz Petchenik, "Cartography and the Making of an Historical Atlas: A Memoir," *The American Cartographer,* Vol. 4, No. 1 (1977):24.

15. Dennis Doolin, *Territorial Claims in the Sino-Soviet Conflict* (Stanford: Hoover Institution, 1965), pp. 16 and 18.

16. Sinnhuber, pp. 26 and 28.

17. Sinnhuber, p. 27.

18. For an interesting commentary on the China-India boundary issue, see "No Order on the Border," *The Economist,* Vol. 368, No. 8335 (August 2, 2002):41. In reference to the "line of control" within Kashmir, it is not surprising that stamps issued by India have included the Indian zone as part of their country but a Pakistani stamp labels Kashmir as a territory with its "final status not yet determined." See Hodgkiss, p. 12.

19. The U.S. Department of State uses the term "separation barrier," as in a January 12, 2004, address at a Department of State conference by Assistant Secretary of the Bureau of Near Eastern Affairs David Satterfield. Ahmed Qurei, Prime Minister of the Palestinian Authority, refers to a "racist separation wall." On Qurei, see the *New York Times,* January 12, 2004, p. 1.

CHAPTER 5

1. David Woodward and G. Malcolm Lewis, eds., *The History of Cartography,* Vol. 2, Book 3, *Cartography in the Traditional African, Arctic, Australian and Pacific Societies* (Chicago: University of Chicago Press, 1998), p. 40.

2. Lee Ki-suk, *East Sea in World Maps* (Seoul: The Society for East Sea, 2002), p. 31.

3. Fred Drake, *China Charts the World* (Cambridge: Harvard University Press, 1975), pp. 65–66 and 112.

4. Kuei-sheng Chang, "Africa and the Indian Ocean in Chinese Maps of the Fourteenth and Fifteenth Centuries," *Imago Mundi,* Vol. 24 (1970):26; Halford Mackinder, *Democratic Ideals and Reality* (New York: W. W. Norton, 1962), p. 62—original edition in 1919; and Francois Bellec, *Unknown Lands* (Woodstock and New York: Overlook Press, 2001), p. 119. The word "continent" derives from the Latin for "held together," and refers to the concept that all land surfaces are

linked. See James Enterline, *Erikson, Eskimos & Columbus* (Baltimore: The Johns Hopkins University Press, 2002), p. 18.

5. Bellec, p. 94. For interpretations pertaining to the term "Europe," see Peter Gommers, *Europe–What's in a Name?* (Leuven: Leuven University Press, 2001). Note that the Greeks identified three continents, but it was the Hebrews who related these continents to the sons of Noah.

6. "Turkey and Europe: Looking to the Future from a Historical Perspective," http://www.mfa.gov.tr(grupb/bf)01.htm.

7. Michael Heffernan, *The Meaning of Europe: Geography and Geopolitics* (London: Arnold, 1998), pp. 9–13; Gerard Delanty, *Inventing Europe: Idea, Identity, Reality* (New York: St. Martin's, 1995), pp. 23–28; and Heikki Mikkeli, *Europe as an Idea and an Identity* (New York: St. Martin's, 1998), p. 30.

8. "Turkey and Europe."

9. David Woodward, "Medieval Mappaemundi," in J. B. Harley and David Woodward, eds., *The History of Cartography*, Vol. I (Chicago: University of Chicago Press, 1987), p. 333.

10. John Noble Wilford, *The Mapmakers* (New York: Knopf, 1981), p. 41; Simon Berthon, Andrew Robinson, and Patrick Stewart, *The Shape of the World* (Chicago: Rand McNally, 1991), pp. 63–64; and Robert Silverberg, *The Realm of Prester John* (Athens: Ohio University Press, 1972), pp. 6–7. For a discussion of the historical background of the Prester John story, see Charles Nowel, "The Historical Prester John," *Speculum* Vol. 28, No. 3 (July 1953):435–45 and Charles Beckingham and Bernard Hamilton, eds., *Prester John, the Mongols and the Ten Lost Tribes* (Aldershot, UK: Variorum, 1996).

11. Silverberg, pp. 8–9.

12. Silverberg, pp. 58 and 61 and Paolo Novaresio, *The Explorers: From the Ancient World to the Present* (New York: Stewart, Tabori and Chang, 1996), p. 33.

13. Delanty, pp. 27, 44, and 65; Heffernan, pp. 14 and 17; and Yi-Fu Tuan, *Topophilia* (Englewood Cliffs: Prentice-Hall, 1974), p. 42.

14. Mark Bassin, "Russia Between Europe and Asia: The Ideological Construction of Geographical Space," *Slavic Review*, Vol. 50, No. 1 (Spring 1991):2–3 and 7; Denis Shaw, "Geographical Practice and its Significance in Peter the Great's Russia," *Journal of Historical Geography*, Vol. 22, No. 2 (1996):160–76; Laura Hostetler, *Qing Colonial Enterprise* (Chicago: University of Chicago Press, 2001), p. 75; Leo Bagrow, *A History of Russian Cartography Up to 1800* (Wolfe Island, Ontario: Walker Press, 1975), p. 133; James Cracraft, *The Petrine Revolution in Russian Imagery* (Chicago: University of Chicago Press, 1997), pp. 1, 274, and 276; and Peter Perdue, "Boundaries, Maps and Movement: Chinese, Russian, and Mongolian Empires in Early Modern Central Eurasia," *The International History Review*, Vol. 20, No. 2 (June 1998):281–82. The Swedish officer was Philipp Johann von Strahlenberg, who was captured during the battle of Poltava and exiled to Siberia for 13 years. Recognize that many Russians see even a Ural continental divide as too restrictive, believing that the highly Russified areas of Siberia and the Far East are legitimately parts of Europe. See Dmitri Trenin, *The End of Eurasia* (Washington, D.C.: Carnegie Endowment for International Peace, 2002), p. 34.

15. Anomalously, the U.S. Department of State established a Bureau of Near Eastern Affairs in 1949, and it is still in existence. Note that Sudanese in the late

nineteenth century referred to undesirable northerners in their midst as "Turks" no matter what their ethnicity. This epithet encompassed southern European businessmen, Christian missionaries, and Egyptian administrators and soldiers. See Gianni Guadalupi and Antony Shugaar, *Latitude Zero* (New York: Carroll and Graf, 2001), pp. 166–67.

16. Tuan, p. 42 and Wang Hui, "An Asia that isn't the East," *Le Monde Diplomatique*, February 2005, pp. 1–3.

17. Derek Howse, *Greenwich Time and the Longitude* (London: Philip Wilson, 1997), p. 125; David A. King, *World Maps for Finding the Direction and Distance to Mecca* (Leiden: Brill, 1999), p. 27; and John Kirtland Wright, *The Geographical Lore of the Time of the Crusades* (New York: Dover Publications, 1965), p. 86.

18. Howse, pp. 127–30 and 133.

19. Peter Galison, *Einstein's Clocks, Poincare's Maps* (New York: W.W. Norton, 2003), p. 144; Lawrence Reed, "It Wasn't Government that Fixed Your Clock," www.mackinac.org/article; The National Watch and Clock Museum, "Running the Trains," www. nawcc.org/museum/nwcm/galleries/depot/depot.htm; and George Warnock, "The Forgotten Man of the Hour," www.seniorscan.ca/crm/sw/forgotten.html.

20. Howse, pp. 134–36 and 145, and the *New York Times*, October 3, 1884, p. 5.

21. Editorial in the *New York Times*, October 2, 1884, p. 4.

22. Jeremy Black, *Maps and Politics* (Chicago: University of Chicago Press, 1997), pp. 37–38 and Arno Peters, *The New Cartography* (New York: Friendship Press, 1983), p. 96.

CHAPTER 6

1. W.G.L. Randles, *Geography, Cartography and Nautical Science in the Renaissance* (Aldershot, UK: Ashgate, 2000), p. V, 1; Svat Soucek, *Piri Reis & Turkish Mapmaking After Columbus* (London: Nour Foundation, 1996), p. 68. A 1427 Latin edition was the first to include maps. See James Enterline, *Erikson, Eskimos & Columbus* (Baltimore: The Johns Hopkins University Press, 2002), p. 31.

2. Portolan charts did not display latitude and longitude, and were not reliable for long distances because they failed to take the curvature of the earth into account. They were oriented northward, probably due to reliance on the compass. See Gregory McIntosh, *The Piri Reis Map of 1513* (Athens: University of Georgia Press, 2000), p. 9; Jerry Brotton, *Trading Territories* (Ithaca: Cornell University Press, 1998), p. 162; and Geoffrey Martin, *All Possible Worlds: A History of Geographical Ideas*, 4th ed. (New York: Oxford University Press, 2005), p. 46.

3. The decline of *mappaemundi* may have been related to the fact that Paradise had not been discovered in the East. The concept of Paradise therefore ceased to be contemporary about 1500, and became historical and archaeological. See Alessandro Scafi, "Mapping Eden: Cartographies of the Earthly Paradise," in Denis Cosgrove, ed., *Mappings* (London: Reaktion Books, 1999): 66–70. The transition away from Christian cartography was influenced by Abraham Cresques, a Jewish Majorcan who issued the "Catalan Atlas" in 1375 under a commission provided by the King of Aragon. It represented an important step in the development of accurate world maps, and it covered an extensive geographical

range including Asia. See A. G. Hodgkiss, *Understanding Maps* (Folkestone, UK: Dawson, 1981), p. 106.

4. Louis Arthur Norton, "The Legacy of Prince Henry," *Mercator's World*, Vol. 6, No. 3 (May/June 2001): 47–48. Note that the Muslims were not constrained by the Esdras II image of land and sea. Ahmad bin Majid al-Najdi, the famous navigator, commented that "the sea is greater than the land." See *Kitab al-Fawa'id fi usul al-bahr wa'l-qawa'id* as translated by G. R. Tibbetts, *Arab Navigation in the Indian Ocean Before the Coming of the Portuguese* (London: The Royal Asiatic Society of Great Britain and Ireland, 1971), p. 66. On Jewish contributions to Portuguese cartography during the fifteenth and sixteenth centuries, see David N. Livingstone, *The Geographical Tradition* (Oxford: Blackwell, 1992), pp. 60–61.

5. Frank Sherry, *Pacific Passions* (New York: William Morrow, 1994), p. 17; Donald S. Johnson, "Charting Neptune's Realm: From Classical Mythology to Satellite Imagery," *Occasional Publication No. 2* (Portland, ME: Osher Library Associates, 2000), p. 29; and J. H. Parry, *The Discovery of the Sea* (New York: Dial, 1974), pp. 131 and 214–16. The Dias journey proved that the eastward route to the Orient was feasible. However, Portugal had considered a westward route and had agreed to fund Flemish navigator Ferdinand van Olmen for a 1487 expedition. Approval for this voyage preceded Dias' return from the southern tip of Africa, but it is unclear if van Olmen's venture was ever initiated. See Franco Cardini, *Europe 1492* (New York: Facts on File, 2000), p. 217 and Ronald Fritze, *New Worlds: The Great Voyages of Discovery, 1400–1600* (Phoenix Mill: Sutton, 2002), pp. 78–79. Dias called the southern extremity of Africa the "Cape of Storms," but King Joao II renamed it the "Cape of Good Hope."

6. Fritze, p. 17.

7. Gerald Tibbetts, "The Beginnings of a Cartographic Tradition," in J. B. Harley and David Woodward, eds., *The History of Cartography*, Vol. 2, Book 1, *Cartography in the Traditional Islamic and South Asian Societies* (Chicago: University of Chicago Press, 1992), p. 101 and Hugh Kennedy, ed., *An Historical Atlas of Islam*, 2nd rev. ed. (Leiden, the Netherlands: Brill, 2002), p. xiii. The Islamic Mamun map in the ninth century had a 52-degree Mediterranean Sea. See Cyrus Ala'i, "The Map of Mamun," *Mercator's World*, Vol. 3, No. 1 (January/February 1998):55.

8. Jeffrey Stone, *A Short History of the Cartography of Africa* (Lewiston, N.Y.: Edwin Mellen Press, 1995), p. 11; J. Spencer Trimingham, "The Arab Geographers and the East African Coast," in H. Neville Chitlick and Robert Rotberg, eds., *East Africa and the Orient* (New York: Africana: 1975), p. 118; and Randles, p. III, 10.

9. Martin, p. 22. Indonesians had sailed to Madagascar and the Cape of Good Hope since about the first century. See Thomas Suarez, *Early Mapping of Southeast Asia* (Hong Kong: Periplus, 1999), p. 29.

10. Dias' voyage around the Cape of Good Hope influenced later maps by Henricus Martellus, Francesco Rosselli, and Giovanni Contarini. Also impacting on Contarini was Vasco da Gama's expedition to India in 1497–98. See Francesc Relano, *The Shaping of Africa* (Aldershot, UK: Ashgate, 2002), p. 165 and Ernest Ravenstein, *Martin Behaim: His Life and Globe* (London: George Philip and Son, 1908), p. 67. Fra Mauro's map marked a radical departure from Christian cartography as it was oriented southward rather than eastward and was not centered on Jerusalem. See Hodgkiss, pp. 78–79.

11. Kuei-sheng Chang, "Africa and the Indian Ocean in Chinese Maps of the Fourteenth and Fifteenth Centuries," *Imago Mundi*, Vol. 24 (1970):22–23 and http://news.bbc.co.uk/2/hi/africa/2446907.stm. Retired British naval officer Gavin Menzies discusses a 1402 Korean map reportedly presented to Chinese Emperor Zhu Di by the Korean ambassador in 1403. It portrays the sea route around Africa, but Menzies claims that it was based on the voyages of ships from Zheng He's fleet, which didn't go to the African coast until 1421. Either the map's date is incorrect or it wasn't based on information gleaned by Zheng He's fleet. Part of the problem is that the original map no longer exists, and Menzies relies on a 1470 copy that may possibly have been altered once data was received from the Chinese fleet. See Menzies, *1421: The Year China Discovered the World* (London: Bantam, 2002), pp. 94–97. For an analysis of Korean reliance on Chinese maps, see Hirosi Nakamura, "Old Chinese World Maps Preserved by the Koreans," *Imago Mundi*, Vol. IV (1965):3–22. Note that Chinese maps correctly had the tip of Africa pointing southward, whereas European and Arab maps had it extending eastward. See Joseph Needham, *Science and Civilisation in China* (Cambridge: Cambridge University Press, 1959), p. 552. The al-Idrisi world map of 1154 even had Africa extending further east than Malaya.

12. Lecture by historian of science Henrique Leitao, June 12, 2005, and lecture by Admiral Antonio Canas, June 10, 2005, at a seminar in Lisbon on "The Portuguese Discoveries and Their Scientific, Political, Religious, and Artistic Impact."

13. See Jeanne Hein, "Portuguese Communication with Africans on the Searoute to India," in Ursula Lamb, ed., *The Globe Encircled and the World Revealed* (Aldershot, UK: Variorum, 1995), pp. 6–7.

14. In his copy of Pierre d'Ailly's cartographical treatise *Imago Mundi* (1410), Columbus had written: "The end of Spain and the beginning of India are not far distant, but close, and it is evident that this sea is navigable in a few days with a fair wind." See Cardini, p. 213.

15. Francois Bellec, *Unknown Lands* (Woodstock and New York: Overlook, 2001), pp. 28 and 59–60; Samuel Eliot Morison, *The European Discovery of America: The Southern Voyages of* A.D. *1492–1616* (New York: Oxford University Press, 1974), p. 40; Edmundo O'Gorman, *The Invention of America* (Westport, CT: Greenwood, 1972), p. 75; and Jeffrey Burton Russell, *Inventing the Flat Earth* (New York: Praeger, 1991), p. 8. In 1488–89, Christopher's brother Bartolomeo unsuccessfully attempted to secure British financial support for Christopher's voyage westward. See Derek Hayes, *Historical Atlas of Canada* (Vancouver: Douglas & McIntyre, 2002), p. 15.

16. J. Kr. Tornoe, *Columbus in the Arctic?* (Oslo: A.W. Broggers Boktrykkeri, 1965), pp. 73–74; Enterline, pp. xviii-xix and 205; and Always Ruddock, "Columbus and Iceland: New Light on an Old Problem," *The Geographical Journal*, Vol. 136, Part 2 (June 1970):180, 183–84, and 188. The Vikings did not prepare maps. Had they done so, perhaps they would have been credited with the discovery of America.

17. Among the alleged expeditions to "America" were those led jointly by Didrik Pining and Hans Pothorst, and one by Johannes Scolvus (Skolp). Although they supposedly took place between 1471 and 1481, there was no written record of them until a reference to Pining and Pothorst in 1548 and one to Scolvus in 1575. See Morison, pp. 37–38; Tornoe, pp. 41–42, 58, and 75; and Samuel Eliot

Morison, *The European Discovery of America: The Northern Voyages* A.D. *500–1600* (New York: Oxford University Press, 1971), pp. 89 and 93. Skepticism about early Portuguese knowledge of Newfoundland arises in part from the fact that German cartographer Martin Behaim lived in the Portuguese-controlled Azores in the 1480s, but did not display any knowledge about Newfoundland on his maps. See Samuel Eliot Morison, *Portuguese Voyages to America in the Fifteenth Century* (Cambridge: Harvard University Press, 1940), p. 36. The Portuguese certainly reached Newfoundland with the 1500 Gaspar Corte-Real expedition, as reflected in Pedro Reinel's 1504 map. See Hayes, p. 21.

18. Enterline, p. 299. For allegations that a Scandinavian-Portuguese expedition had reached the West Indies, and that Columbus had a map of that area before departing Spain in 1492, see Tornoe, pp. 58 and 66. In 1959, a Soviet historian claimed that Columbus had indicated in a letter to Isabella that he knew where the New World was located. See Tornoe, pp. 41–42.

19. George Nunn, *The Geographical Conceptions of Columbus* (New York: American Geographical Society, 1924), p. 71; Derek Nelson, *Off the Map* (New York: Kodansha International, 1997), p. 54; Denis Cosgrove, *Apollo's Eye* (Baltimore: The Johns Hopkins University Press, 2001), p. 83; Valery Flint, *The Imaginative Landscape of Christopher Columbus* (Princeton: Princeton University Press, 1992), p. 39; and Ravenstein, pp. 58–59, 62, and 95. Behaim lived in Nuremberg during the period 1490–93, and his globe (influenced by Ptolemy and the accounts of Marco Polo) was exhibited in Nuremberg's town hall for over one hundred years upon its completion. It is the world's oldest surviving terrestrial globe. From 1484 to 1490, Behaim lived in Lisbon, so it is possible that he and Columbus met each other there.

20. Mauricio Obregon, *The Columbus Papers* (New York: Macmillan, 1991), p. 5; Daniel Boorstin, *The Discoverers* (New York: Vintage, 1983), p. 243; Nunn, pp. 11 and 27–28; and Erroll Stevens, "The Asian-American Connection: The Rise and Fall of a Cartographic Idea," *Terrae Incognitae,* Vol. 21 (1989):31. Columbus thought that Hispaniola was really Japan, thus confusing cartographer Johannes Ruysch, who eliminated Japan from his 1508 world map. See Hiroshi Nakamura, *East Asia in Old Maps* (Honolulu: East West Center Press, 1963), p. 25. Note that Columbus underestimated the earth's circumference, and overestimated the longitudinal extent of Asia.

21. Bellec, pp. 88 and 92; Flint, pp. xiii and 116; and Pauline Moffitt Watts, "Prophesy and Discovery: On the Spiritual Origins of Christopher Columbus' 'Enterprise of the Indies'," *The American Historical Review,* Vol. 90, No. 1 (February 1985):74 and 93.

22. Ursula Lamb, *Cosmographers and Pilots of the Spanish Maritime Empire* (Aldershot, UK: Variorum, 1995), XIV-5 and 6.

23. Robert Schoch, *Voyages of the Pyramid Builders* (New York: Jeremy P. Tarcher/Putnam, 2003), p. 84. In 1537, a bull issued by Pope Paul III also recognized the humanity of the "Indians."

24. Luc Cuyvers, *Into the Rising Sun* (New York: TV Books, 1999), p. 80; Obregon, pp. 4 and 33; and Morison, *Portuguese Voyages,* p. 83.

25. See Alfredo Pinheiro Marques, "Epilogue: Triumph and Disgrace," in George Winius, ed., *Portugal the Pathfinder: Journeys from the Medieval toward*

the Modern World 1300–ca. 1600 (Madison, WI: Hispanic Seminary of Medieval Studies, 1995), pp. 364–65. Vasco da Gama's 1499 return to Portugal from a successful voyage to India contributed to the decline of Columbus' image.

26. Mark Monmonier, *Drawing the Line* (New York: Henry Holt, 1995), p. 107; Philip Steinberg, "Lines of Division, Lines of Connection: Stewardship in the World Ocean," *The Geographical Review,* Vol. 89, No. 2 (April 1999):255; and Morison, *Portuguese Voyages,* p. 129. Newfoundland lay west of the Tordesillas line, so any historical claims there by the Portuguese could not be legalized. Those in West Africa could.

27. Derek Wilson, *The Circumnavigators: A History* (New York: Carroll & Graf, 2003), p. 5 and Cuyvers, pp. 81–82. Gaspar Corte-Real's 1502 map moved the New World eastward, thus attempting to legitimize more extensive Portuguese claims under the Treaty of Tordesillas, but the "Cantino map" of that year made it clear that Newfoundland lay to the west of the Tordesillas line. See Alan Morantz, *Where is Here? Canada's Maps and the Stories They Tell* (Toronto: Penguin, 2002), p. 82. Note also that Spain, on an expedition led by Vicente Yanez Pinzon, may have "discovered" the eastern tip of Brazil four months earlier than Cabral, but couldn't claim it because it was in the Portuguese zone. See N.P. Macdonald, *The Making of Brazil* (Sussex: The Book Guild, 1996), p. 31. The "Cantino map" provides detailed information about the Brazilian coast, leading some historians to conclude that so much data could not have been gathered since Cabral's landfall. Previous Portuguese knowledge is therefore conjectured. This interpretation was discussed in the lecture by Henrique Leitao.

28. Francis Rogers, *The Quest for Eastern Christians* (Minneapolis: University of Minnesota Press, 1962), p. 137. Father Francisco Alvares, who went to Ethiopia in the early sixteenth century, published about 1540 an account of his sojourn entitled "The Prester John of the Indies." For additional information about Prester John in Africa, see George Hourani, *Seafaring in the Indian Ocean in Ancient and Early Medieval Times* (Princeton: Princeton University Press, 1951), p. 39 and Francesc Relano, *The Shaping of Africa* (Aldershot, UK: Ashgate, 2002), pp. 53–56. Gerardus Mercator's 1569 world map labels the southern Atlantic as the "Ethiopian Ocean." Abraham Ortelius' 1573 map entitled "The Empire of Prester John" locates his kingdom in East Africa.

29. Henri Baudet, *Paradise on Earth* (New Haven: Yale University Press, 1965), pp. 14–15 and Benjamin Braude, "The Sons of Noah and the Construction of Ethnic and Geographical Identities in the Medieval and Early Modern Periods," *The William and Mary Quarterly,* Vol. 54, No. 1 (January 1997):126. Alexander the Great, as well as the sixth-century Byzantine historian Procopius, thought that the Nile originated in India. See Steven Darian, *The Ganges in Myth and History* (Honolulu: University Press of Hawaii, 1978), p. 170. Prester John was first cited as the King of Ethiopia in 1324 by Jordan Catalani, a Catholic bishop in India. Early maps locating Prester John in Ethiopia include one by Gulielmus Filiastrus (Guillaume Filastre) in 1417, by Andrea Bianco in 1436, and another by Fra Mauro in 1459. Previously, a 1339 map by Angelino Dulcert (Angelino da Dalorto, a Genoese based in Majorca) had depicted Prester John there, and he may have appeared on a destroyed 1306 map by a Venetian, Giovanni da Carignano. See Bernard Hamilton, "Continental Drift: Prester John's Progress

Through the Indies," in Charles Beckingham and Bernard Hamilton, eds., *Prester John, the Mongols and the Ten Lost Tribes* (Aldershot, UK: Variorum, 1996), p. 252; Charles Beckingham, "Prester John in West Africa," in Beckingham and Hamilton, pp. 207–208; Charles Beckingham, "The Quest for Prester John," in Beckingham and Hamilton, pp. 272–73; and John Larner, *Marco Polo and the Discovery of the World* (New Haven: Yale University Press, 1999), pp. 191 and 193.

30. Boorstin, p. 171 and Robert Silverberg, *The Realm of Prester John* (Athens: Ohio University Press, 1972), pp. 200–204.

31. Baudet, p. 18 and Bellec, p. 43. The "Cantino map" was prepared after da Gama's voyage to India, so it corrected Ptolemy on the inland sea issue and on the longitudinal extent of Asia. See Donald Lach, *Asia in the Making of Europa: A Century of Wonder,* Volume II, Book Three (Chicago: University of Chicago Press, 1977), p. 451.

32. There was a legend that Prester John drank from a fountain of life within his kingdom. See Tahir Shah, *In Search of King Solomon's Mines* (New York: Arcade, 2002), p. 168.

33. Silverberg, pp. 220 and 323. Once Portugal had extended its influence around the African continent and into Asia, it had less of a need to find a Christian ally against the Muslims, so the quest for Prester John was ended. See Hamilton, pp. 256–57.

34. Bellec, p. 146; Arthur Davies, "Magellan and His Grand Design," *Geographical Magazine,* Vol. LII, No. 1 (October 1979):31; and Jerry Brotton, "Terrestrial Globalism: Mapping the Globe in Early Modern Europe," in Cosgrove, p. 82. A 1514 bull issued by Pope Leo X stipulated that Portugal would have the rights to all heathen lands reached by sailing eastward. This implied support for Portuguese claims to the Moluccas, but Spain's effort to get to the Moluccas by sailing westward undercut the bull. See Parry, p. 264.

35. It wasn't until 1979–82 that there was a north-south circumnavigation of the earth (with some portions overland) completed by British adventurer Sir Ranulph Fiennes.

36. Henry Kamen, *Empire: How Spain Became a World Power, 1492–1763* (New York: HarperCollins, 2003), pp. 199–200; Suarez, p. 162; Peter Whitfield, *New Found Lands* (New York: Routledge, 1998), p. 94; and lecture by Henrique Leitao.

CHAPTER 7

1. Derek Hayes, *Historical Atlas of Canada* (Vancouver: Douglas & McIntyre, 2002), p. 15. Cabot made a globe in 1497, but no copy of it exists.

2. Loren Baritz, "The Idea of the West," *The American Historical Review,* Vol. LXVI, No. 3 (April 1961): 629.

3. Hayes, p. 18. The "Cantino map" of 1502 recognized the New World as distinct from Asia, but it was ambiguous as to whether there was a land connection between them. See Alfredo Pinheiro Marques, "Epilogue: Triumph and Disgrace," in George Winius, ed., *Portugal the Pathfinder: Journeys from the Medieval toward the Modern World 1300–ca.1600* (Madison, WI: Hispanic Seminary of Medieval Studies), p. 369.

4. Waldseemuller was a German cartographer at St. Die sponsored by the Duke of Lorraine. He was very knowledgeable about Portuguese expeditions, and he corrected many errors made by Ptolemy. See Donald Lach, *Asia in the Making of Europe: A Century of Wonder,* Vol. II, Book Three (Chicago: University of Chicago Press, 1977), p. 455.

5. Many eighteenth-century Spanish maps portrayed a land link between Asia and North America, possibly to enhance claims under the Treaty of Tordesillas, which unintentionally placed North America in the Spanish zone of influence. See Helga Gemagah, "Two 16th Century Jesuits & the 'Asian' Origin of all First Americans," http://iias.leiden.univ.nl/iiasn/26/general/26G3.html. A land bridge connecting Asia and North America would also buttress the argument that native Americans were of Asian origin, and were therefore human.

6. Hayes, pp. 11 and 16–17; Samuel Eliot Morison, *Portuguese Voyages to America in the Fifteenth Century* (Cambridge: Harvard University Press, 1940), p. 38; and Donald S. Johnson, *Phantom Islands of the Atlantic* (New York: Walker and Company, 1994), p. 35. Russians explored the Svalbard Archipelago (Spitsbergen) in 1435, and named it "Greenland," but this area is geographically distinct from what we know as Greenland further west. The term "Greenland" was also applied on some maps to Labrador and parts of Scandinavia. See James Enterline, *Erikson, Eskimos & Columbus* (Baltimore: The Johns Hopkins University Press, 2002), p. 217. A map prepared about 1700 by Englishmen John and Samuel Thornton showed Greenland connected to North America. See Donald S. Johnson, "Charting Neptune's Realm: From Classical Mythology to Satellite Imagery," *Occasional Paper No. 2* (Portland, ME: Osher Library Associates, 2000), p. 8.

7. Alan Morantz, *Where is Here? Canada's Maps and the Stories They Tell* (Toronto: Penguin, 2002), p. 63; Leo Bagrow, *A History of Russian Cartography Up to 1800* (Wolfe Island, Ontario: Walker Press, 1975), pp. 22 and 157–58; Basil Dmytryshyn, E.A.P. Crownhart-Vaughan, and Thomas Vaughan, eds., *Russian Penetration of the North Pacific Ocean, 1700–1797,* Volume 2 (Portland: Oregon Historical Society Press, 1988), pp. 69 and 85–86; and Derek Hayes, *Historical Atlas of the North Pacific Ocean* (Vancouver: Douglas & McIntyre, 2001), p. 65. A 1764 map prepared by Swiss geographer Samuel Engel took Bering's expeditions into account and depicted the Bering Strait.

8. Hayes, *Historical Atlas of Canada,* pp. 156–57.

9. Johnson, p. 8 and Hayes, *Historical Atlas of Canada,* p. 13.

10. Erroll Stevens, "The Asian-American Connection: The Rise and Fall of a Cartographic Idea," *Terrae Incognitae,* Vol. 21 (1989):31–33 and 37.

11. Hayes, p. 25.

12. For a conceptual interpretation of this issue, see Gunther Barth, "Strategies for Finding the Northwest Passage: The Roles of Alexander Mackenzie and Meriwether Lewis," in Edward C. Carter II, ed., *Surveying the Record: North American Scientific Exploration to 1930* (Philadelphia: American Philosophical Society, 1999), pp. 253–66.

13. Note that Hudson, who was British, had sailed on behalf of the Netherlands in 1609 and had journeyed up the Hudson River as far as Albany.

14. Glynn Williams, *Voyages of Delusion* (New Haven: Yale University Press, 2002), p. 407 and Seymour Schwartz, *The Mismapping of America* (Rochester: The University of Rochester Press, 2003), Chapter Three.

15. Samuel Bawlf, *The Secret Voyage of Sir Francis Drake, 1577–1580* (Vancouver: Douglas & McIntyre, 2003), pp. 210–11, 237–38, and 267. Bawlf believes that a map produced by British geographer Richard Hakluyt in 1587, after Drake's return, depicts the American coast up toward Alaska. For a refutation of Bawlf's claims by Oliver Seeler (written on October 6, 2000—prior to the publication of Bawlf's book), see www.mcn.org/2/oseeler/bc.htm. See also Hayes, *Historical Atlas of the North Pacific Ocean*, pp. 26–29.

16. According to one tale, the Dutch found a stranded whale on the Korean coast sometime in the sixteenth century. It was pierced by a weapon that came from Spitsbergen, so they theorized that the whale must have transited a strait between Asia and America. See Barry Lopez, *Arctic Dreams* (New York: Charles Scribner's Sons, 1986), pp. 324–25.

17. For speculation that the French effort to locate a Northwest Passage was part of a program to reach a southern continent, see Frank Sherry, *Pacific Passions* (New York: William Morrow, 1994), p. 82. There is also a French chart from the late sixteenth century that includes a detailed portrayal of an irregular coast, along with place names. This reputedly is part of the southern continent. See April Carlucci and Peter Barber, *Lie of the Land: The Secret Life of Maps* (London: The British Library, 2001), p. 44.

18. Patricia Gilmartin, "The Austral Continent in 16th Century Maps," *Cartographica*, Vol. 21, No. 4 (1984): 41 and 49; P. L. Madan, *Indian Cartography: A Historical Perspective* (New Delhi: Manohar, 1997), p. 23; and A. G. Hodgkiss, *Understanding Maps* (Folkestone, UK: Dawson, 1981), p. 72. Despite being influenced by Ptolemy, Arab geographers did not maintain the existence of a southern continent and believed that the Southern Hemisphere was mostly a sea. See Charles Issawi, "Arab Geography and the Circumnavigation of Africa," *Osiris*, Vol. 10 (1952):121. For a comparison of discovery and deduction, see Dennis Skocz, "Herodotus and the Origins of Geography: The Strange, the Familiar, and the Earthbound," in Gary Backhaus and John Murungi, eds., *Earthways: Framing Geographical Meanings* (Lanham, MD: Lexington, 2004), p. 4.

19. James Roman, *The Edges of the Earth in Ancient Thought* (Princeton: Princeton University Press, 1992), pp. 130–31 and J. Kr. Tornoe, *Columbus in the Arctic?* (Oslo: A.W. Broggers Boktrykker, 1965), p. 72. Many Chinese, even as late as the nineteenth century, believed that the temperature increased in the direction of the South Pole. See Fred Drake, *China Charts the World* (Cambridge: Harvard University Press, 1975), p. 62. Of course, the Portuguese voyages southward along the West African coast dispelled the European notion that the torrid zone was impassable.

20. Simon Ryan, *The Cartographic Eye: How Explorers Saw Australia* (Cambridge: Cambridge University Press, 1996), pp. 105–106 and 117; Laura Hostetler, *Qing Colonial Enterprise* (Chicago: University of Chicago Press, 2001), pp. 13–16; and Gabriel de Foigny, "A New Discovery of Terra Australis Encognita or the Southern World," in Glenn Negley and J. Max Patrick, eds., *The Quest for Utopia* (College Park: McGrath, 1971), p. 403.

21. Gilmartin, p. 49 and Sherry, pp. 21, 162, 164, and 169.

22. Derek Nelson, *Off the Map* (New York: Kodansha International, 1997), p. 57; Thomas Suarez, *Early Mapping of Southeast Asia* (Hong Kong: Periplus, 1999), p. 160; W.A.R. Richardson, "Mercator's Southern Continent: Its Origins, Influence and Gradual Demise," *Terrae Incognitae,* Vol. 25 (1993):70; and Gregory McIntosh, *The Piri Reis Map of 1513* (Athens: University of Georgia Press, 2000), p. 50. Piri Reis' map, which is basically a portolan, relies on a map prepared by Columbus (of which no copies now exist) for its information about the New World. Reis' map was almost lost to posterity as well. It was deposited in the Topkapi Palace library, but was used occasionally by the staff as a tablecloth. In 1929, it was recognized as a major work of cartography and referred to frequently by Turkish president Mustafa Kemal Ataturk as a significant achievement of the Turks. See Svat Soucek, *Piri Reis & Turkish Mapmaking After Columbus* (London: Nour Foundation, 1996), pp. 50, 54, and 105.

23. Gilmartin, p. 45 and Richardson, pp. 89 and 94.

24. Eric Whitehouse, *Australia in Old Maps, 820 to 1770* (Brisbane: Boolarong Press, 1994), pp. 5, 14, and 48–49; "Mapping New Worlds: The Cartography of European Exploration and Colonization, 1450–1750," exhibition at Canaday Library, Bryn Mawr College, February 2005; and Peter Whitfield, *New Found Lands* (New York: Routledge, 1998), pp. 47–48. Whitehouse claims that Spanish expeditions to Australia date back to the early sixteenth century. See p. 89. There is also an assertion by Australian social scientist David Turnbull that the Portuguese knew about Australia prior to the 1529 Treaty of Saragossa, in which they acquired rights to most of that continent. See *Maps are Territories: Science is an Atlas* (Chicago: University of Chicago Press, 1993), p. 58.

25. Jeffrey Stone, ed., *Norwich's Maps of Africa*, 2nd ed. (Norwich: Terra Nova, 1997), p. 176 and Whitehouse, pp. 52–53. European cartography of Australia first focused on its western region, and then gradually extended eastward. Especially significant are the 1680 sea chart by Dutch cartographer Johannes van Keulen and the 1687 map by French-Italian cartographer Vicenzo Maria Coronelli. See Stone, pp. 63 and 304.

26. Sherry, pp. 339–40 and Richardson, pp. 95–97. Australia has been described as an inversion of Europe, lacking its own identity. See Ryan, p. 105.

27. Kenneth Bertrand, *Americans in Antarctica, 1775–1948* (New York: American Geographical Society, 1971), pp. 4 and 189; R. T. Gould, "The First Sighting of the Antarctic Continent," *The Geographical Journal,* Vol. 65 (1925):200; Whitfield, p. 178; William Stanton, *The Great United States Exploring Expedition of 1838–1842* (Berkeley: University of Chicago Press, 1975), p. 311; and Derek Wilson, *The Circumnavigators: A History,* rev. ed. (New York: Carroll & Graf, 2003), pp. 231–33. In January 1821, a Russian expedition commanded by Fabian Gottlieb von Bellingshausen landed on two Antarctic islands, but not on the mainland of Antarctica. Note that Antarctica is fixed to the earth's crust and may therefore be considered a continent. There is no similar Arctic continent, only a frozen sea that drifts.

28. Hayes, *Historical Atlas of the North Pacific Ocean,* pp. 40 and 51; John Fairbank, *China: A New History* (Cambridge: Harvard University Press, 1992), pp. 138–39; and Ma Huan, *Ying-Yai Sheng-Lan* ("The Overall Survey of the Ocean's Shores") (London: Cambridge University Press, 1970). Ma Huan served as an

interpreter on three of Zheng He's voyages, and his account was originally published in 1451.

CHAPTER 8

1. Ricardo Padron, a specialist on the relationship between literature and cartography, at Virginia Festival of the Book, Charlottesville, March 16, 2005; Luis Adao da Fonseca, "Prologue: The Discovery of Atlantic Space," in George Winius, ed., *Portugal the Pathfinder: Journeys from the Medieval toward the Modern World 1300–ca.1600* (Madison, WI: Hispanic Seminary of Medieval Studies, 1995), p. 16; Samuel Edgerton, Jr., "From Mental Matrix to *Mappamundi* to Christian Empire: the Heritage of Ptolemaic Cartography in the Renaissance," in David Woodward, ed., *Art and Cartography: Six Historical Essays* (Chicago: University of Chicago Press, 1987), p. 13; and John Rennie Short, *Making Space: Revisioning the World, 1475–1600* (Syracuse: University Press, 2004), pp. 29 and 61.

2. Australian geographer Louise Johnson argues that geographers contributed to colonization by constructing "othered" places and prepared maps to dispossess those "others" by showing their areas of settlement as empty spaces. See *Placebound: Australian Feminist Geographies* (South Melbourne: Oxford University Press, 2000), pp. 163 and 170.

3. G. Malcolm Lewis, "Introduction," in Lewis, ed., *Cartographic Encounters: Perspectives on Native American Mapmaking and Map Use* (Chicago: University of Chicago Press, 1998), p. 2 and Lewis, "Frontier Encounters in the Field: 1511–1925," in Lewis, pp. 19–22.

4. Peter J. Taylor, "Full Circle, or New Meaning for the Global?" in R. J. Johnston, ed., *The Challenge for Geography: A Changing World: A Changing Discipline* (Oxford: Blackwell, 1993), p. 183. See also David Turnbull, *Mapping the World in the Mind* (Victoria, AU: Deakin University, 1991), p. 11.

5. For an analysis of the feminist interpretation of female imagery, see Joe Painter, *Politics, Geography & 'Political Geography'* (London: Arnold, 1995), p. 117.

6. See James Cameron, "Agents and Agencies in Geography and Empire: The Case of George Grey," in Morag Bell, Robin Butlin, and Michael Heffernan, eds., *Geography and Imperialism, 1820–1940* (Manchester: Manchester University Press, 1995), p. 14. Astronomers "discover" features of planets through telescopic observation, obviously not through direct contact. Nevertheless, they impose their imprint on these "discoveries" by naming locations after themselves.

7. Mercator, in common with some European Christians, did perceive an earth-centric rather than solar-centric universe.

8. For a discussion of new projections produced in Europe during the sixteenth century, see Rudiger Finsterwalder, "The Round Earth on a Flat Surface," in Hans Wolff, ed., *America: Early Maps of the New World* (Munich: Prestel, 1992), pp. 161–73.

9. Donald S. Johnson, *Phantom Islands of the Atlantic* (New York: Walker, 1994), p. 23; Bjorn Axelson and Michael Jones, "Are All Maps Mental Maps?" *GeoJournal,* Vol. 14, No. 4 (1987):450; and "Maps: Global War Teaches Global Cartography," *Life,* Vol. 13, No. 5 (August 3, 1942):61. If a flat map displays parallels as equidistant, there is distortion as the rhumb line cannot be presented as

straight. Mercator solved this problem by increasing the spacing of parallels the closer they were to the poles, thereby compensating for the distortion caused by the narrowing of meridians. See Arthur Robinson, "Straightening a Rhumb," in American Cartographic Association, *Matching the Map Projection to the Need* (Bethesda: American Congress on Surveying and Mapping, 1991), pp. 20–21. Note that if navigators in the Northern Hemisphere adhere to an east-west course along a parallel of latitude, they could maintain course by referring to the North Star. The star's number of degrees above the horizon corresponds to the degree of latitude.

10. Mercator overestimated the width of the Mediterranean, and correspondingly underestimated the breadth of the Pacific. However, he gradually reduced the range of his error. His world map of 1538 portrayed a 62-degree Mediterranean; his globe of 1541 made it 58 1/2 degrees; while his European map of 1554 set it at 53 degrees. Note that Mercator's maps were useful for navigators seeking "true" north. The compass pointed to magnetic north, so there was geomagnetic distraction—especially at northern latitudes. See Mark Monmonier, *Rhumb Lines and Map Wars* (Chicago: University of Chicago Press, 2004), p. 10.

11. "Maps: Global War," p. 63; Arno Peters, *The New Cartography* (New York: Friendship Press, 1983), p. 62; Axelson and Jones, p. 450; and Monmonier, p. 138. Mercator's exaggerated land areas approaching the poles were due to the use of parallel meridians (causing east-west stretching) plus the increasing distances between parallels in polar areas (causing north-south stretching).

12. Nicholas Crane, *Mercator: The Man Who Mapped the Planet* (New York: Henry Holt, 2002), p. 207. For details on Mercator's map publication rights, see Jerry Brotton, *Trading Territories* (Ithaca: Cornell University Press, 1998), p. 163.

13. Mercator's 1569 world map was on eighteen separate sheets with a combined area of 80 x 49 inches. See Monmonier, p. 47.

14. Thomas Saarinen, Michael Parton, and Roy Billberg, "Relative Size of Continents on World Sketch Maps," *Cartographica*, Vol. 33, No. 2 (Summer 1996):37–38 and 46.

15. Cornelis Koeman, *The History of Abraham Ortelius and his Theatrum Orbis Terrarum* (New York: American Elsevier, 1964), pp. 13 and 36; Donald Lach, *Asia in the Making of Europe: A Century of Wonder*, Vol. II, Book Three (Chicago: University of Chicago Press, 1977), p. 471; Short, p. 60; Monmonier, pp. 2 and 6; lecture by Nuno Crato, an expert on Portuguese mathematics and science at a seminar in Lisbon on "Portuguese Discoveries and Their Scientific, Political, Religious, and Artistic Impact," June 12, 2005; and A. G. Hodgkiss, *Understanding Maps* (Folkestone, UK: Dawson, 1981), p. 108.

16. Thomas Bassett, "Cartography and Empire Building in Nineteenth-Century West Africa," *The Geographical Review*, Vol. 84, No. 3 (July 1994):317 and 326; Peter Barber, "England II: Monarchs, Ministers, and Maps, 1550–1625," in David Buisseret, ed., *Monarchs, Ministers, and Maps* (Chicago: University of Chicago Press, 1992), p. 66; and Linda Colley, *Captives* (New York: Pantheon, 2002), p. 4.

17. Sophie Crossfield, "A Study of a Nineteenth Century Jigsaw Globe From the Whipple Collection," *Case Studies at the Whipple Museum*, (Cambridge, UK: n.d.), pp. 13–16.

18. Terry Cook, "A Reconstruction of the World / George R. Parkin's British Empire Map of 1893," *Cartographica*, Vol. 21, No. 4 (1984):53–62. Parkin participated in a "New Imperialism" movement linking Anglophone countries such as Canada and Britain. See Alan Morantz, *Where is Here? Canada's Maps and the Stories They Tell* (Toronto: Penguin, 2002), p. 92.

19. Peter Perdue, "Boundaries, Maps and Movement: Chinese, Russian, and Mongolian Empires in Early Modern Central Eurasia," *The International History Review*, Vol. 20, No. 2 (June 1998): 272 and Morantz, pp. 32, 41, and 45–46. For an evaluation of the motivations behind French cartography, see Josef Konvitz, *Cartography in France, 1660–1848* (Chicago: University of Chicago Press, 1987), pp. 158–59.

20. Colley, pp. 6, 346, and 371. American geographer Mark Monmonier refers to the manipulation of maps to demonstrate superiority as "mapism," and deems it akin to racism. See *Drawing the Line* (New York: Henry Holt and Company, 1995), p. 3.

21. Simon Katzenellenbogen, "It Didn't Happen at Berlin," in Paul Nugent and A. I. Asiwaju, eds., *African Boundaries* (London: Pinter, 1996), p. 22 and Jeffrey Stone, *A Short History of the Cartography of Africa* (Lewiston, NY: Edwin Mellen, 1995), p. 77. Sub-Saharan Africa, despite its historical contacts with Islamic Arabs, did not produce its own drawn maps, so the application of Eurocentric cartography was thus facilitated. See Jeffrey Stone, ed., *Norwich's Maps of Africa*, 2nd ed. (Norwich: Terra Nova, 1997), pp. xi–xiii.

22. Fred Drake, *China Charts the World* (Cambridge: Harvard University Press, 1975), pp. 56 and 130–31 and Robert Solomon, "Boundary Concepts and Practices in Southeast Asia," *World Politics*, Vol. 23, No. 1 (October 1970):6.

23. Thomas Suarez, *Early Mapping of Southeast Asia* (Hong Kong: Periplus, 1999), pp. 261–63. For a conceptual analysis of Siam's boundary development, see Thongchai Winichakul, *Siam Mapped: A History of the Geo-Body of a Nation* (Honolulu: University of Hawaii Press, 1994).

24. Matthew Edney, *Mapping an Empire: The Geographical Construction of British India, 1765–1843* (Chicago: University of Chicago Press, 1997), pp. 2–3, 15, 325, 333, and 335. Edney interestingly points out that the word "surveyor" means one who watches from above, and it implies separation from the actual environment. See pp. 339–40.

25. Susan Schulten, *The Geographical Imagination in America, 1880–1950* (Chicago: University of Chicago Press, 2001), pp. 6, 53–57, and 89; Neil Smith, *American Empire: Roosevelt's Geographer and the Prelude to Globalization* (Berkeley: University of California Press, 2003), pp. xx, 146–47, 174, and 177; and Geoffrey Martin, *All Possible Worlds: A History of Geographical Ideas* (New York: Oxford University Press, 2005), p. 451.

26. There were many theories of imperialism, which basically means the establishment of empires. Some stressed access to raw materials, some Christian proselytization, and some slavery. Best known, however, is the Marxist interpretation according to which capitalism expands overseas in the quest for markets to absorb surplus industrial production. Lenin later divided this expansion into two stages, the first based on the export of "industrial capital" and the second on "finance capital."

27. See Painter, pp. 107–108; Jeremy Black, *Maps and History* (New Haven: Yale University Press, 1997), pp. 81–82; Lach, p. 488; and Martin, p. xiii. In Britain, many maps were issued by an organization called the Society for the Diffusion of Useful Knowledge. See Stone, *Norwich's Maps,* p. 157. All geography in the nineteenth century did not fit the biased and nationalistic stereotype. See Margarita Bowen, *Empiricism and Geographical Thought* (Cambridge: Cambridge University Press, 1981), Chapter 7 and G. R. Crone, *Modern Geographers: An Outline of Progress in Geography Since* 1800 A.D. (London: The Royal Geographical Society, 1951), pp. 11–12.

28. Brian Hudson, "The New Geography and the New Imperialism: 1870–1918," *Antipode,* Vol. 9, No. 2 (1977):13–18; Karl Meyer and Shareen Blair Brysac, *Tournament of Shadows* (Washington, D.C.: Counterpoint, 1999), p. 227; Martin van Creveld, *The Art of War* (London: Cassell, 2000), pp. 100 and 104; John MacKenzie, *Propaganda and Empire: The Manipulation of British Public Opinion, 1880–1960* (Manchester: Manchester University Press, 1984), p. 7; Rex Walford, *Geography in British Schools, 1850-2000* (London: Woburn, 2001), pp. 52–53 and 82; and Simon Ryan, *The Cartographic Eye: How Explorers Saw Australia* (Cambridge: Cambridge University Press, 1996), p. 33. The Stanley quote appears in Hudson, p. 15. Note that the Royal Geographical Society published advice on surveying, and sold surveying instruments. See Stone, *Norwich's Maps,* p. xxvi.

29. Felix Driver, *Geography Militant: Cultures of Exploration and Empire* (Oxford: Blackwell, 2001), pp. 41, 120, 126, and 203; Stone, *Norwich's Maps,* p. xxvi; and David N. Livingstone, *The Geographical Tradition* (Oxford: Blackwell, 1992), pp. 160 and 168.

30. Milan Hauner, *What is Asia to Us?* (Boston: Unwin Hyman, 1990), p. 41.

31. Hudson, p. 14. The initial meeting of the International Geographical Congress was in Antwerp in 1871. Most delegates were Europeans, and Japan was the only Asian founding member. Nine of the first ten congresses were held in European cities. See Smith, p. 279.

32. Crossfield, p. 4.

CHAPTER 9

1. G. R. Sloan, *Geopolitics in the United States Strategic Policy, 1890–1987* (New York: St. Martin's, 1988), p. viii; Robert Strausz-Hupe, *Geopolitics* (New York: G.P. Putnam's Sons, 1942), p. 102; and Geoffrey Parker, *Western Geopolitical Thought in the Twentieth Century* (New York: St. Martin's, 1985), p. 63.

2. Colin Gray, "Inescapable Geography," in Colin Gray and Geoffrey Sloan, eds., *Geopolitics, Geography and Strategy* (London: Frank Cass, 1999), pp. 162 and 169; Russell Fifield and G. Etzel Pearcy, *Geopolitics in Principle and Practice* (Boston: Ginn and Company, 1944), pp. 5–6; John O'Loughlin and Herman van der Wusten, "Political Geography of Panregions," *The Geographical Review,* Vol. 80, No. 1 (January 1990):1; Richard Hartshorne, "Recent Developments in Political Geography II," *American Political Science Review,* Vol. 29, No. 6 (December 1935):961; Ladis Kristof, "The Origin and Evolution of Geopolitics," *The Journal of Conflict Resolution,* Vol. 4, No. 1 (March 1960):34; and Hans Weigert, *Generals*

and Geographers (New York: Oxford University Press, 1942), p. 79. Weigert was a German-born American political scientist.

3. William Livezey, *Mahan on Sea Power* (Norman: University of Oklahoma Press, 1981), pp. 60–62, 67–68, 316, and 349 and Stephen B. Jones, "Global Strategic Views," *The Geographical Review,* Vol. 45, No. 4 (October 1955):494.

4. Weigert, p. 95; Holger Herwig, "*Geopolitik:* Haushofer, Hitler and Lebensraum," in Gray and Sloan, p. 220; Parker, pp. 8 and 11; Saul Cohen, *Geography and Politics in a Divided World,* 2nd ed. (New York: Oxford University Press, 1973), p. 40; W. H. Parker, *Mackinder: Geography as an Aid to Statecraft* (Oxford: Clarendon Press, 1982), p. 235; Fifield and Pearcy, p. 8; A. G. Hodgkiss, *Understanding Maps* (Folkestone, UK: Dawson, 1981), p. 61; G. R. Crone, *Modern Geographers: An Outline of Progress in Geography Since 1800* A.D.. (London: The Royal Geographical Society, 1951), p. 38; and Geoffrey Martin, *All Possible Worlds: A History of Geographical Ideas,* 4th ed. (New York: Oxford University Press, 2005), p. 168. Recognize that the views of Ratzel had some commonality with those of Frederick Jackson Turner, who expounded upon his "frontier thesis" in the eighteen nineties.

5. G. Parker, p. 55; Andreas Dorpalen, *The World of General Haushofer: Geopolitics in Action* (Port Washington, NY: Kennikat, 1942), p. 24; and James Tyner, "The Geopolitics of Eugenics and the Incarceration of Japanese Americans," *Antipode,* Vol. 30, No. 3 (1998):252–57. Kjellen added the *volk* concept, later used by the Nazis, to Ratzel's analysis of state expansionism. See Edmund Walsh, "Geopolitics and International Morals," in Hans Weigert and Vilhjalmur Stefansson, eds., *Compass of the World* (New York: Macmillan, 1944), pp. 16–17.

6. W. H. Parker, p. 242.

7. Robert Mayhew, *Enlightenment Geography: The Political Languages of British Geography, 1650–1850* (London: Macmillan, 2000), pp. 230 and 242–43 and Mark Polelle, *Raising Cartographic Consciousness* (Lanham, MD: Lexington, 1999), p. 63.

8. Milan Hauner, *What is Asia to Us?* (Boston: Unwin Hyman, 1990), pp. 141–42.

9. Livezey, p. 318. Mackinder's views on Russian railroads were influenced by those of George (Lord) Curzon. See Karl Meyer and Shareen Blair Brysac, *Tournament of Shadows* (Washington, D.C.: Counterpoint, 1999), pp. 565–66.

10. Arthur Hall, "Mackinder and the Course of Events," *Annals of the Association of American Geographers,* Vol. 45, No. 2 (June 1955):110–13.

11. Brian Blouet, *Halford Mackinder: A Biography* (College Station: Texas A&M University Press, 1987), pp. 108–109 and 142–43 and Halford Mackinder, "The Geographical Pivot of History," *The Geographical Journal,* Vol. 23, No. 4 (April 1904):423, 434, and 436. The "pivot area's" threat to Europe from the north may possibly be compared to earlier religious imagery concerning Gog and Magog.

12. Hall, pp. 114–15; Hauner, p. 141; and Halford Mackinder, *Democratic Ideals and Reality* (New York: W.W. Norton, 1962), p. 11. The Mackinder book is a reprint of the original 1919 edition.

13. Hall, pp. 113–14; W. H. Parker, pp. 164 and 171; and Polelle, pp. 77–78. In the March 1918 Treaty of Brest-Litovsk, Germany was allotted a considerable amount of Russian territory.

14. See Hauner, p. 147.

15. Halford Mackinder, "The Round World and the Winning of the Peace," *Foreign Affairs,* Vol. 21, No. 4 (July 1943):601; Hall, p. 120; and Fifield and Pearcy, pp. 14–15.

16. Nicholas Spykman, *America's Strategy in World Politics* (New York: Harcourt, Brace, 1942), p. 8 and Spykman, *The Geography of the Peace* (New York: Harcourt, Brace, 1944), pp. 41, 43, and 50.

17. John Ager, "Maps and Propaganda," *Bulletin of the Society of University Cartographers* (1977):2; Guntram Herb, "Maps as Weapons in German Nationalist Propaganda," *Mercator's World,* Vol. 4, No. 3 (May/June 1999):27; Louis B. Thomas, "Maps as Instruments of Propaganda," *Surveying and Mapping* Vol. 9 (1949):76; and Louis Quam, "The Use of Maps in Propaganda," *The Journal of Geography,* Vol. 42, No. 1 (January 1943):28.

18. Dorpalen, p. 16. Hitler was intrigued by maps and used them to justify his policies. This proclivity was parodied by Charlie Chaplin in "The Great Dictator," which portrayed Hitler playing with an inflated world globe.

19. Livezey, pp. 320–23 and Charles Kruszewski, "The Pivot of History," *Foreign Affairs,* Vol. 32, No. 3 (April 1954):397. Haushofer emphasized land power as the key to counteracting Germany's weakness in sea power, but he additionally called for the strengthening of the German navy.

20. Dorpalen, p. 208.

21. Dorpalen, pp. 64–65.

22. Fifield and Pearcy, p. 15 and Dorpalen, pp. 23 and 38.

23. Dorpalen, pp. 23, 27, and 38 and Polelle, p. 103.

24. Richard Edes Harrison, *Look at the World* (New York: Knopf, 1944), p. 33.

25. Dorpalen, pp. 3, 8, 11–12, and 36–38.

26. Spykman, *The Geography of the Peace,* p. 37 and Michael Heffernan, *The Meaning of Europe: Geography and Geopolitics* (London: Arnold, 1998), pp. 135–37 and 144. Note that Germans during the thirties generally considered the United States to be marginal, and not a threat to their country. Hitler viewed the United States as weak, and eventually subject to German conquest in the course of extending *lebensraum.* These views were expressed by Gerhard Weinberg, CUNY Graduate Center, November 11, 2003 (Book TV, C-Span 2).

27. O'Loughlin and van der Wusten, p. 9.

28. David Atkinson, "Geopolitical Imagination in Modern Italy," in Klaus Dodds and David Atkinson, eds., *Geopolitical Traditions* (London: Routledge, 2000), pp. 104–105 and Polelle, pp. 103–104.

29. Spykman, *The Geography of the Peace,* p. 7.

30. Colin Gray, *The Geopolitics of Super Power* (Lexington: University of Kentucky Press, 1988), p. 43; Gray and Sloan, p. 2; Kristof, p. 31; and C. Troll, "Geographic Science in Germany during the Period 1933–1945: A Critique and Justification," *Annals of the Association of American Geographers,* Vol. 39, No. 2 (June 1949):135. After World War II, geopolitics fell into some disrepute because Haushofer and Spykman had used their avowedly scientific discipline for partisan purposes.

31. Heffernan, pp. 140–41; Lucio Gambi, "Geography and Imperialism in Italy," in Anne Godlewska and Neil Smith, eds., *Geography and Empire* (Oxford: Blackwell, 1994), pp. 89–90; Heather Hyde Minor, "Mapping Mussolini: Ritual and Cartography in Public Art during the Second Roman Empire," *Imago*

Mundi, Vol. 51 (1999):158–59; Atkinson, pp. 97–99; Denis Cosgrove, *Apollo's Eye* (Baltimore: The Johns Hopkins University Press, 2001), p. 224; and David Atkinson, "Geopolitics, Cartography and Geographical Knowledge: Envisioning Africa From Fascist Italy," in Morag Bell, Robin Butlin, and Michael Heffernan, eds., *Geography and Imperialism, 1820–1940* (Manchester: Manchester University Press, 1995), pp. 280–81, 283, 286–87, and 296–97. When *Geopolitica* started publishing, Mussolini wrote to the editor: "Geopolitics is much more than mere geography. I myself will be the most attentive and assiduous reader of your magazine." See Fifield and Pearcy, p. 9.

32. Keiichi Takeuchi, "The Japanese Imperial Tradition, Western Imperialism and Modern Japanese Geography," in Godlewska and Smith, pp. 195 and 198; Martin, pp. 328 and 330; Keiichi Takeuchi, "Japanese Geopolitics in the 1930s and 1940s," in Dodds and Atkinson, pp. 75 and 88; and George Blakeslee, "The Japanese Monroe Doctrine," *Foreign Affairs,* Vol. 11, No. 4 (July 1933):675.

CHAPTER 10

1. Nicholas Spykman, *America's Strategy in World Politics* (New York: Harcourt, Brace, 1942), pp. 4–6; Francis Pickens Miller, "The Atlantic Area," *Foreign Affairs,* Vol. 19, No. 4 (July 1941):727; and John Logan, Jr., *No Transfer: An American Security Principle* (New Haven: Yale University Press, 1961), p. 389. During World War II, the United States discarded some of its Wilsonian idealism and adopted a geopolitical interpretation of world affairs based on a competitive model. See Neil Smith, *American Empire: Roosevelt's Geographer and the Prelude to Globalization* (Berkeley: University of California Press, 2003), p. 282.

2. Note that German Foreign Minister Joachim von Ribbentrop warned that the Monroe Doctrine could only be valid if the United States refrained from intervention in Europe. See Gaddis Smith, *The Last Years of the Monroe Doctrine* (New York: Hill and Wang, 1994), p. 36.

3. Arthur Whitaker, *The Western Hemisphere Idea: Its Rise and Decline* (Ithaca: Cornell University Press, 1954), pp. 159–60.

4. According to the Monroe Doctrine, hemispheric defense included U.S. protection of independent American states from any European extension of power. Such a policy was considered vital to U.S. peace and security.

5. Canada was obviously within the Western Hemisphere geographically, but there had always been ambiguity as to whether its defense fell within the confines of the Monroe Doctrine. The United States had been reluctant to clarify this issue because Canada was part of the Commonwealth and the United States did not want to antagonize Britain by claiming to be Canada's protector. Eventually, President Franklin Roosevelt, on a visit to Kingston, Ontario, in August 1938, declared that Canada was indeed covered by the Monroe Doctrine. See Russell Fifield and G. Etzel Pearcy, *Geopolitics in Principle and Practice* (Boston: Ginn and Company, 1944), p. 161.

6. Logan, pp. 324–25. S.W. Boggs, the chief State Department cartographer, indicated that the government considered the Western Hemisphere to stretch from 20 degrees west longitude to 160 degrees east, but he believed that there was no logic in this depiction. He pointed out that an infinite number of hemi-

spheres may be drawn, depending upon their central point. See S. W. Boggs, "This Hemisphere," *The Department of State Bulletin*, Vol. 12, No. 306 (May 6, 1945):846.

7. Logan, pp. 5 and 248.

8. Richard Showman and Lyman Judson, *The Monroe Doctrine and the Growth of Western Hemispheric Solidarity* (New York: H. W. Wilson, 1941), p. 73.

9. http://www.state.gov/documents/organization/14541.

10. Eviatar Zerubavel, *Terra Cognita: The Mental Discovery of America* (New Brunswick: Rutgers University Press, 1992), p. 27.

11. Dexter Perkins, "Bringing the Monroe Doctrine Up to Date," *Foreign Affairs*, Vol. 20, No. 2 (January 1942):257.

12. Logan, p. 299 and Isaiah Bowman, "The Strategy of Territorial Decisions," *Foreign Affairs*, Vol. 24, No. 2 (January 1946):181 and 186.

13. Logan, pp. 300–301 and Jean-Baptiste Duroselle, *From Wilson to Roosevelt* (Cambridge: Harvard University Press, 1963), p. 263.

14. Gaddis Smith, *The Last Years of the Monroe Doctrine* (New York: Hill and Wang, 1994), p. 35.

15. George Blakeslee, "The Japanese Monroe Doctrine," *Foreign Affairs*, Vol. 11, No. 4 (July 1933):671 and 680.

16. Bernt Balchen, Corey Ford and Oliver La Farge, *War Below Zero* (Boston: Houghton Mifflin, 1944), p. 5 and Vilhjalmur Stefansson, *Greenland* (Garden City: Doubleday, 1947), p. 295.

17. *New York Times*, April 11, 1941, pp. 1 and 4 and April 17, 1941, p. 12.

18. Vilhjalmur Stefansson, *Iceland: The First American Republic* (New York: Doubleday, Doran, 1939) and Stefansson, "What is the Western Hemisphere?" *Foreign Affairs*, Vol. 19, No. 2 (January 1941):343–46.

19. Vilhjalmur Stefansson, *Discovery* (New York: McGraw-Hill, 1964), pp. 310–12.

20. For an analysis of this period, see Donald Nuechterlein, *Iceland: Reluctant Ally* (Westport, CT: Greenwood, 1961).

21. Robert Sherwood, *Roosevelt and Hopkins: An Intimate History* (New York: Harper & Brothers, 1948), p. 290; Nuechterlein, pp. 27 and 31; and *New York Times*, July 8, 1941, p. 3.

22. *New York Times*, July 8, 1941, p. 1; Logan, pp. 370–71; and Sherwood, p. 290.

23. Sherwood, p. 291 and Logan, p. 371.

24. Roosevelt had promised Iceland that U.S. troops would be withdrawn at the end of "the present emergency." However, once the war was over, the United States asked for a continuance of bases there as they were needed as a stepping stone to occupied Germany. Icelandic protests then led to a 1946 agreement that the United States could maintain the Keflavik air base as a transit point for planes related to the occupation of Germany, but that the United States would withdraw militarily from the rest of Iceland within 180 days. See Hans Weigert, "U.S. Strategic Bases and Collective Security," *Foreign Affairs*, Vol. 25, No. 2 (January 1947):259.

25. Richard Dunlop, *Donovan: America's Master Spy* (Chicago: Rand McNally, 1982), pp. 305 and 324–25. The position of Coordinator of Information was abolished in June 1942 when the Office of Strategic Services was established. Donovan was then appointed as director of the OSS.

26. John B. Garver, Jr., "The President's Map Cabinet," *Imago Mundi,* Vol. 49 (1997):153. The "Map Room" later became a depository for presidential gifts and trophies, and a hideaway for national security advisor Henry Kissinger when he met with Soviet ambassador Anatoly Dobrynin and representatives of the Chinese liaison office. Kissinger remarked: "I use this room for meetings when I do not want them to be known." See William Burr, ed., *The Kissinger Transcripts* (New York: The New Press, 1998), pp. 43 and 128–29.

27. Admiral Mahan and President Theodore Roosevelt had recognized early in the twentieth century that U.S. security was linked to that of Britain, and that Germany and Japan would emerge as the most likely enemies. They did not believe that oceans provided protection, and instead cited the rise of foreign naval power and the threat to the U.S. mainland posed by overseas conflicts. See Serge Ricard, "America is Our Sphere: Alfred Thayer Mahan, the Monroe Doctrine, and the Isthmian Canal," Annual Meeting of the Society for Historians of American Foreign Relations, Austin, Texas, June 2004, pp. 2, 5, and 9–10. The cartographical image of Mahan and Theodore Roosevelt was based on Mercator projections, not on polar projections that would have buttressed their position.

28. Harold and Margaret Sprout, "Geography and International Relations in an Era of Revolutionary Change," in W. A. Douglas Jackson, ed., *Politics and Geographical Relationships* (Englewood Cliffs: Prentice-Hall, 1964), p. 40; Richard E. Harrison and Hans Weigert, "World View and Strategy," in Hans Weigert and Vilhjalmur Stefansson, eds., *Compass of the World* (New York: Macmillan, 1944), pp. 84–88; Alan Henrikson, "The Map as an 'Idea': The Role of Cartographic Imagery During the Second World War," *The American Cartographer,* Vol. 2, No. 1 (April 1975):19–20 and 24; Stephen B. Jones, "Views of the Political World," *The Geographical Review,* Vol. 45, No. 3 (July 1955):313; and Richard Edes Harrison, *Look at the World* (New York: Knopf, 1944), p. 23.

29. Harrison and Weigert, pp. 82–83 and Harrison, p. 12. In the United States the Mercator projection was predominant, but under siege. *Goode's School Atlas* of 1923 advocated the use of multiple projections, and the 38 map supplements issued by *National Geographic* during the period 1936–47 included only two Mercator projections. See Susan Schulten, *The Geographical Imagination in America, 1880–1950* (Chicago: University of Chicago Press, 2001), p. 209.

30. "Maps: Global War Teaches Global Cartography," *Life,* Vol. 13, No. 5 (August 3, 1942):57; Henrikson, p. 36; Ward Kaiser and Denis Wood, *Seeing Through Maps* (Amherst, MA: ODT, 2001), p. 125; Schulten, pp. 139–41; and Richard Edes Harrison in *Saturday Review of Literature,* Vol. 26 (August 7, 1943):24.

31. David Greenhood, *Mapping* (Chicago: University of Chicago Press, 1964), pp. 150–51.

32. American geographers Russell Fifield and G. Etzel Pearcy called the Arctic "a future aerial Mediterranean," and their map centered on the North Pole was labeled "The Arctic Mediterranean." See Fifield and Pearcy, pp. 84 and 161.

33. Henrikson, p. 35; Greenhood, p. 31; "Maps: Global War," p. 54; and *New York Times,* February 21, 1943, p. 8E.

34. Exhibit at Maritime Museum, Halifax, Nova Scotia. Sea convoys were unprotected from the air within a zone south of Greenland known as the "black pit."

35. Alan Henrikson, "America's Changing Place in the World: From 'Periphery' to 'Center'?" in Jean Gottmann, *Center and Periphery* (Beverly Hills: Sage Publications, 1980), p. 83 and Nicholas Spykman, *The Geography of the Peace* (New York: Harcourt, Brace, 1944), pp. 17–18 and 57.

36. George Renner, "Air Age Geography," *Harper's Magazine*, Vol. 187, No. 1117 (June 1943):38. Renner, a pro-interventionist, maintained that the United States had not joined the League of Nations because Mercator projections had created a false sense of isolated security. See Schulten, p. 138.

37. Harrison, *Saturday Review of Literature*, p. 26; Wilbur Zelinsky, "In Memorium: Richard Edes Harrison, 1901–1994," *Annals of the Association of American Geographers*, Vol. 85, No. 1 (1995):189; Schulten, p. 223; and *New York Times*, January 7, 1994, p. A22. Bird's-eye views were common in the Netherlands in the sixteenth and seventeenth centuries.

38. Richard Edes Harrison, "The Face of One World," *Saturday Review of Literature*, Vol. 27 (July 1, 1944):5–6 and March 8, 2004, e-mail from Pennsylvania State University map librarian Joanne Perry.

39. www3.newberry.org/k12maps/module_15/curator.html.

40. Harrison, *Look at the World*. This atlas includes an interesting gnomonic projection of the world featuring true great circle direction. Scale, shape, and area are distorted, but any straight line on this map represents the shortest possible distance on a great circle route. Certainly, this projection was critical to an understanding of aviation. See p. 54. The map labeled "Argentina: a dagger pointed at the heart of Antarctica," is a good example of Harrison's emotive cartography. See p. 52. On Mitchell, see Ladis Kristof, "The Origins and Evolution of Geopolitics," *The Journal of Conflict Resolution*, Vol. 4, No. 1 (March 1960):37.

CHAPTER 11

1. Arthur Whitaker, *The Western Hemisphere Idea: Its Rise and Decline* (Ithaca: Cornell University Press, 1954), p. 175. The "East" vs. "West" emphasis on American maps gradually came to be misleading as ideological similarities between communist-ruled states did not prevent political cleavages within their cartographical sphere. See Geoff King, *Mapping Reality* (New York: St. Martin's, 1996), p. 97.

2. Douglas Fleming, "Cartographic Strategies for Airline Advertising," *The Geographical Review*, Vol. 74, No. 1 (January 1984):90.

3. James Burnham, *The Struggle for the World* (New York: The John Day Company, 1947), pp. 100, 104, and 114–15. See also Karl Meyer and Shareen Blair Brysac, *Tournament of Shadows* (Washington, D.C.: Counterpoint, 1999), pp. 568–69. Soviet invulnerability had been undermined by the advent of air power, but the Soviet "Heartland" did have important assets in its natural resources and industrial development. See Arthur Hall, "Mackinder and the Course of Events," *Annals of the Association of American Geographers*, Vol. 45, No. 2 (June 1955):125.

4. Stephen B. Jones, "Global Strategic Views," *The Geographical Review*, Vol. 45, No. 4 (October 1955): 497.

5. "United States Assistance to Other Countries from the Standpoint of National Security," April 29, 1947 (JCS 1769/1) in Thomas Etzold and John Lewis

Gaddis, eds., *Containment: Documents on American Policy and Strategy, 1945–1950* (New York: Columbia University Press, 1978), p. 72. Next in order on the list were Canada, Turkey, Greece, Latin America, Spain, Japan, China, Korea, and the Philippines. Note that the "containment doctrine" was formulated after Spykman's death in 1943 and that he had never mentioned "containment." However, his stress on the "Rimland" contributed to the "containment doctrine" and the establishment of U.S. military facilities around the periphery of the Soviet Union.

6. "Washington's Exploratory Conversations on Security," September 9, 1948, in Etzold and Gaddis, p. 145.

7. "NSC 68," April 7, 1950, in Etzold and Gaddis, p. 387.

8. Hal Friedman, *Creating an American Lake* (Westport, CT: Greenwood, 2001), pp. 46–47.

9. "Resume of World Situation," November 6, 1947 (PPS 13), in Etzold and Gaddis, p. 96.

10. "The Position of the United States With Respect to Asia," December 23, 1949 (NSC 48/1), in Etzold and Gaddis, pp. 257–58.

11. Alexander De Seversky, *Air Power: Key to Survival* (New York: Simon and Schuster, 1950), p. 307. South America and Africa were geographical obstacles on the European routes to Asia, but were therefore important as way stations. Once the Suez and Panama Canals were built, these waterways served as sea passages to Asia. South America and Africa then waned in importance geopolitically. See Richard Edes Harrison, *Look at the World* (New York: Knopf, 1944), p. 21.

12. See Whitaker, p. 173.

13. Robert Ferrell. ed., *America in a Divided World, 1945–1972* (Columbia: University of South Carolina Press, 1975), pp. 212–17.

14. Eugene Rostow, "Containment, Peace and the Charter," in Terry Deibel and John Lewis Gaddis, eds., *Containment: Concept and Policy*, Vol. 2 (Washington, D.C.: National Defense University Press, 1986), p. 696 and Mark Polelle, *Raising Cartographic Consciousness* (Lanham, MD: Lexington, 1999), pp. 132 and 134.

15. Daniel Yergin, *Shattered Peace* (Boston: Houghton Mifflin, 1977), pp. 210–11. The first non-stop polar flight from Moscow to the United States took place in 1937.

16. Jones, p. 503 and De Seversky, pp. xxii–xxiii, 297, and 307. Isolation was not a logical option for the United States after World War II, since changes in transport and communications had created greater global interdependence. See Albert Wohlstetter, "Illusions of Distance," *Foreign Affairs*, Vol. 46, No. 2 (January 1968): 250. Note that polar projections distort the sizes of countries as one proceeds away from the North Pole or South Pole, but are accurate in regard to distances from a pole to any given point.

17. See Nicholas Spykman, *The Geography of the Peace* (New York: Harcourt, Brace, 1944), p. 46.

18. Fleming, pp. 76–93. Note that polar projections don't accurately reflect the contiguity of Africa and South America. See Saul Cohen, *Geography and Politics in a Divided World*, 2nd ed. (New York: Oxford University Press, 1973), p. 53. Great circle routes are segments of circumference lines, such as meridians, but latitudinal lines other than the equator are shorter than the earth's circumference.

19. John Ager, "Maps and Propaganda," *Bulletin of the Society of University Cartographers* (1977):5. The National Geographic Society, an American organization, used (Alphons) Van der Grinten projections from 1922 to 1988 that made the Soviet Union 223 percent larger than its actual size. In 1988, as the Cold War was ending along with the Soviet threat to the United States, the maps were changed to (Arthur) Robinson projections so that the Soviet Union was only 18 percent too large. In 1998, the National Geographic Society adopted the Winkel Tripel projections (developed in the early nineteen twenties by German cartographer Oswald Winkel), which have even less size distortion toward the poles than the Robinson projections.

20. See W. H. Parker, *Mackinder: Geography as an Aid to Statecraft* (Oxford: Clarendon, 1982), p. 195. Marshal Vasilii Sokolovskii, chief of the Soviet general staff from 1952 to 1960, asserted: "During the first postwar years, American ruling circles attempted to encircle the socialist countries with a system of hostile military-political groups and blocs of capitalist states and to unite the latter into a single anti-Communist coalition." See *Soviet Military Strategy* (Englewood Cliffs: Prentice-Hall, 1963), p. 150. This book was first published in Russian in 1962. In reference to encirclement, Canadian political scientist Albert Legault has observed: "Land space can, in fact, be broken down into a series of successive concentric points without it actually being known who encircles whom and what is encircled by what." See "Geopolitics and the Conduct of Modern Warfare," in Ciro Zoppo and Charles Zorgbibe, eds., *On Geopolitics: Classical and Nuclear* (Dordrecht, NL: Martinus Nijhoff, 1985), p. 203.

21. See Ciro Zoppo, "The Geopolitics of Nuclear Deterrence," in Zoppo and Zorgbibe, pp. 144–46 and 153.

22. See Carl Pletsch, "The Three Worlds, or the Division of Social Scientific Labor, circa 1950–1975," *Comparative Studies in Society and History,* Vol. 23, No. 4 (October 1981):568 and 573 and Stuart Corbridge, "Colonialism, Post-colonialism and the Political Geography of the Third World," in Peter J. Taylor, ed., *Political Geography of the Twentieth Century: A Global Analysis* (London: Belhaven, 1993), pp. 189–90.

23. Martin Lewis and Karen Wigen, *The Myth of Continents* (Berkeley: University of California Press, 1997), pp. 3 and 6.

24. Pletsch, pp. 568, 573, 577, 582, and 584–85.

25. Arthur Jay Klinghoffer, *Soviet Perspectives on African Socialism* (Cranbury, NJ: Associated University Presses, 1969), pp. 44–49 and 53. During the early stages of the Cold War, the Soviet image of Africa was as a component of the "East." Then, in 1961, the journal *Sovremennyi Vostok* (Contemporary East) was renamed *Aziia i Afrika Segodnia* (Asia and Africa Today), and the journal *Problemy Vostokovedeniia* (Problems of Oriental Studies) was changed to *Narody Azii i Afriki* (Peoples of Asia and Africa).

26. The Report of the Independent Commission on International Development Issues, *North-South: A Programme for Survival* (London: Pan Books, 1980) and The Report of the South Commission, *The Challenge to the South* (New York: Oxford University Press, 1990).

27. The end of the Cold War tore asunder the distinction between the "First World" and "Second World," and therefore rendered the concept of a "Third World" rather superfluous. Nevertheless, the journal *Third World Quarterly* continues to publish.

CHAPTER 12

1. J. B. Harley, "Silence and Secrecy," in Paul Laxton, ed., *The New Nature of Maps* (Baltimore: The Johns Hopkins University Press, 2001), p. 99; Harley, "Deconstructing the Map," in Laxton, p. 163; and Jeremy Black, *Maps and Politics* (Chicago: University of Chicago Press, 1997), p. 19. British geographer Robert Mayhew saw the leftist critique as questioning the rational, empirical and intellectual basis of geographical knowledge deriving from the Enlightenment. See *Enlightenment Geography: The Political Languages of British Geography, 1650–1850* (London: Macmillan, 2000), p. 13.

2. David N. Livingstone, *The Geographical Tradition* (Oxford: Blackwell, 1992), p. 351.

3. Russell Jacoby, "Marginal Returns: The Trouble with Post-Colonial Theory," *Lingua Franca*, Vol. 5, No. 6 (September/October 1995):31; Richard Peet, "The Development of Radical Geography in the United States," in Peet, ed., *Radical Geography: Alternative Viewpoints on Contemporary Social Issues* (Chicago: Maaroufa, 1977), pp. 10–11 and 15; James Peck and Jane Wills, "Geography and Its Discontents," *Antipode*, Vol. 32, No. 1 (2000):3; and Richard Peet, *Modern Geographical Thought* (Oxford: Blackwell, 1998), p. 109. Central to the dissemination of radical geographical concepts was the founding of the journal *Antipode* in 1969. Note that there was a specific movement labeled "radical geography," but the interpretation presented in this chapter as "radical" extends to other critics of traditional geography as well.

4. Peet, "The Development," p. 17.

5. Simon Ryan, *The Cartographic Eye: How Explorers Saw Australia* (Cambridge: Cambridge University Press, 1996), p. 104

6. See J. B. Harley, "Maps, Knowledge and Power," in Laxton, pp. 77 and 79 and Simon Dalby, "Geopolitical Discourse: The Soviet Union as Other," *Alternatives*, Vol. 13 (1988):416 and 421. Although Harley was surely critical of traditional cartography, he was attacked by a specialist on literature for being too conservative because he deemed maps to be visual images of the world. He therefore did not take the deconstructionism of Derrida and Foucault as far as she believed appropriate. See Barbara Belyea, "Images of Power: Derrida/Foucault/Harley," *Cartographica*, Vol. 29, No. 2 (Summer 1992):1.

7. Joe Painter, *Politics, Geography & 'Political Geography'* (London: Arnold, 1995), pp. 31–32; Anne Godlewska and Neil Smith, "Introduction," in Godlewska and Smith, eds., *Geography and Empire* (Oxford: Blackwell, 1994), p. 13; and Peter J. Taylor, "Full Circle, or New Meaning for the Global?" in R. J. Johnston, ed., *The Challenge for Geography* (Oxford: Blackwell, 1993), pp. 189–90.

8. See Jonathan Crush, "Post-colonialism, De-colonization, and Geography," in Godlewska and Smith, p. 337 and J. B. Harley, "The Map and the Development of the History of Cartography," in J. B. Harley and David Woodward, *The History of Cartography*, Vol. I (Chicago: University of Chicago Press, 1987), p. 34.

9. Arno Peters, *The New Cartography* (New York: Friendship Press, 1983), p. 7.

10. Gillian Rose, *Feminism and Geography* (Minneapolis: University of Minnesota Press, 1993), p. 11 and Ryan, pp. 196 and 294. From a different perspective, female imagery had been used historically to symbolize emancipation. Cuban nationalist

Jose Marti's 1891 essay "Nuestra America" referred to "Madre America" as representative of independence from European colonization. See Ofelia Schutte, "Latin America and Postmodernity," in Pedro Lange-Churion and Eduardo Mendieta, eds., *Latin America & Postmodernity* (Amherst, NY: Humanity Books, 2001), p. 171.

11. Richard Peet, "Introduction," in Peet, ed., *Radical Geography*, p. 1; Peet, "The Development," p. 21; and Jack Hitt, "Atlas Shrugged: The New Face of Maps," *Lingua Franca*, Vol. 5, No. 5 (July/August 1995):31. In a similar vein, later ecological interpretations included references to "environmental despoliation" and to colonial mapping as "estrangement from the physical landscape." See Geoff King, *Mapping Reality* (New York: St. Martin's, 1996), p. 145.

12. Mona Domosh and Joni Seager, *Putting Women in Place: Feminist Geographers Make Sense of the World* (New York: Guilford, 2001), pp. 174–76.

13. Louise Johnson, *Placebound: Australian Feminist Geographies* (South Melbourne: Oxford University Press, 2000), pp. 2–4, 35, and 159.

14. Emmanuel Wallerstein, "The Rise and Future Demise of the World Capitalist System: Concepts for Comparative Analysis," *Comparative Studies in Society and History*, Vol. 16, No. 4 (September 1974):387–415. Karl Haushofer had earlier applied the concepts of "core" and "periphery." but Wallerstein's ideological context was far removed from that of Haushofer.

15. Painter, pp. 107–109 and Richard Rieser, "The Territorial Illusion and Behavioural Sink," in Peet, *Radical Geography*, p. 207. In addition to the closure of geography departments, there was also a slowdown in establishing new departments. Only eight started to operate during the period 1970–79, and two during the years 1980–89. Such figures contrast starkly with those for 1960–69, when 33 were created. See Malcolm Douglass, *The History, Psychology, and Pedagogy of Geographic Literacy* (Westport, CT: Praeger, 1998), p. 57.

16. See J. M. Blaut, *The Colonizer's Model of the World* (New York: Guilford, 1993); Peter J. Taylor, "Geopolitical World Orders," in Taylor, ed., *Political Geography of the Twentieth Century* (London: Belhaven, 1993); and Dalby, pp. 435–37. During the 1980s, geopolitics made a comeback in conjunction with President Reagan's realist world view. After 9/11, area studies regained some prestige—especially in regard to primarily Islamic regions.

17. David Landes, *The Wealth and Poverty of Nations* (New York: W. W. Norton, 1998), pp. 4–5, 513, and 516.

18. Ricardo Hausmann, "Prisoners of Geography," *Foreign Policy*, No. 122 (January/February 2001):45–46 and 51.

19. James Corner, "The Agency of Mapping: Speculation, Critique and Invention," in Denis Cosgrove, ed., *Mappings* (London: Reaktion Books, 1999), p. 213.

20. John Loxton, "The Peters Phenomenon," *The Cartographic Journal*, Vol. 22 (December 1985):106; Mark Monmonier, *Drawing the Line* (New York: Henry Holt, 1995), p. 25; obituary by Anthea Milner, *The Independent*, December 2002, http://www.carelpress.co.uk/adobe/arno.pdf; and Ward Kaiser and Denis Wood, "Arno Peters—The Man, The Map, the Message," *The Cartographic Journal*, Vol. 40, No. 1 (June 2003):54.

21. Peters, pp. 128 and 145. J. B. Harley referred to Mercator's "unconscious distortions." See Harley, "Maps, Knowledge, and Power," p. 66. Peters was

especially critical of cartographers who based their projections on Mercator's and thus perpetuated his distortions for centuries. See Peter Vujakovic, "Damn or be Damned: Arno Peters and the Struggle for the 'New Cartography'," *The Cartographic Journal*, Vol. 40, No. 1 (June 2003):63. Note that the Peters projection was also distorted the closer the proximity to the poles because Peters decreased the distances between parallels of latitude. The aim was to maintain accurate size for land masses, but a consequence was horizontal shape distortion. Mercator had increased the distances between parallels as one approached the poles.

22. Arno Peters, *Peters Atlas of the World* (New York: Harper and Row, 1990), foreword and Peters, *The New Cartography*, pp. 144 and 147.

23. Black, p. 37. It is possible that Peters retained the Greenwich prime meridian so as to accentuate Africa. According to this interpretation, he was greatly influenced by concepts of black liberation expressed by William Pickens in his book *Breaking Bonds*. Pickens was a friend of his mother, Lucy, and had given a copy of his tome to her that was then read avidly by a youthful Arno. See africanfront.com (AUF). Also recognize that Africa had traditionally been treated dismissively. Even its European imposed name meaning "without frigidity" was based on what it was lacking rather than on its attributes. See Seymour Schwartz, *The Mismapping of America* (Rochester: The University of Rochester Press, 2003), p. 2. In regard to Peters' use of Mercator's graticule, the intent was to maintain Mercator's fidelity of axis pertaining to the accurate direction of north.

24. Peters, *The New Cartography*, pp. 134–35 and Terry Hardaker's introduction to *Peters Atlas of the World*.

25. *Peters Atlas of the World*.

26. D. H. Maling, "Personal Projections," *Geographical Magazine*, Vol. 46 (August 1974):600.

27. Scott Minerbrook, "'Mental Maps': The Politics of Cartography," *US News & World Report*, Vol. 110, No. 14 (April 15, 1991):60; Arthur Robinson, "Arno Peters and His New Cartography," *The American Cartographer*, Vol. 12, No. 2 (1985):103; and *North-South: A Programme for Survival* (London: Pan Books, 1980).

28. Gall started to discuss his projection publicly in 1855, but didn't publish it until 1885. See Mark Monmonier, *Rhumb Lines and Map Wars* (Chicago: University of Chicago Press, 2004), pp. 16 and 149. See also John Snyder, "Social Consciousness and World Maps," *The Christian Century*, Vol. 105, No. 6 (February 24, 1988):191–92; Ward Kaiser and Denis Wood, *Seeing Through Maps* (Amherst, MA: ODT, 2001), pp. 22–24; and Mark Monmonier, "Faith-Based Cartography," *Mercator's World*, Vol. 7, No. 2 (March/April 2002):52. Note that the popular *State of the World Atlas* (numerous editions published by Penguin) uses the Winkel Tripel equal-area projection on its maps.

29. Monmonier, "Faith-Based Cartography," p. 54; Ward Kaiser, "An Explanation of the Peters World Map" (Amherst, MA: ODT, 2001); and Vujakovic, p. 61.

30. Robinson and Winkel Tripel projections are very close to being equal area representations, and they are more faithful than the Peters projection in presenting the accuracy of shape. Robinson projections have their greatest size and shape accuracy at 38 degrees north or south latitude.

31. Kaiser and Wood, *Seeing Through Maps*, pp. 11, 22, 28 and 90.

CHAPTER 13

1. Dmitri Trenin, *The End of Eurasia* (Washington, D.C.: Carnegie Endowment for International Peace, 2002), p. 5. In the case of the former Soviet Union, internal borders have now become external borders. See p. 107.

2. David Newman, "Geopolitics Renaissant: Territory, Sovereignty and the World Political Map," in Newman, ed., *Boundaries, Territory and Postmodernity* (London: Frank Cass, 1999), p. 5 and Trenin, p. 9.

3. Christer Jonsson, Sven Tagil, and Gunnar Tornqvist, *Organizing European Space* (London: Sage, 2000), p. 188.

4. Some newly independent states emerging from the Soviet Union have their own equivalents of the "near abroad." Armenia assumes the right to protect the interests of ethnic Armenians in Azerbaijan's Nagorno-Karabakh region, and several Central Asian states assert some authority within neighboring countries on the ground of ethnic affinity. The former Soviet Union had established enclaves within Central Asian republics for ethnic minorities, and some of these areas still adhere to the time zone of their ethnically related independent territories rather than to that of their country of residence. Kyrgyzstan incorporates five Uzbek enclaves, and two Tajik ones. See Charles William Maynes, "America Discovers Central Asia," *Foreign Affairs*, Vol. 82, No. 2 (March/April 2003):127–28.

5. Arif Dirlik, "Introduction: Pacific Connections," in Dirlik, ed., *What is in a Rim?: Critical Perspectives on the Pacific Region Idea*, 2nd ed. (Lanham, MD: Rowman and Littlefield, 1998), p. 8 and Bruce Cumings, "Rimspeak; or, The Discourse of the 'Pacific Rim'," in Dirlik, p. 54.

6. Thomas Gladwin, "The Way of the Voyager," in David Turnbull, *Mapping the World in the Mind* (Victoria, AU: Deakin University, 1991), p. 49.

7. Americans filling out government forms are instructed not to select "Asian-American" as their identity if their ancestry is in territory from Iran westward, nor should they denote "African-American" if their ancestry is in North Africa. Perceived racial distinctions trump continental origin, as people from Western Asia and North Africa are classified together with those of European origin.

8. Eminent historian Gerhard Weinberg maintains that Hitler's main concern was not to recover territories lost in World War I, but to extend *lebensraum* into colonization of the whole world. Expressed at CUNY Graduate Center, November 11, 2003 (Book TV, C-Span 2).

9. Geographer David Slater has written: "Globalization from above can be thought of as another name for neo-liberal globalization, a process that is founded on privatization, competitiveness, deregulation, standardization and more profoundly the commodification of social life." Globalization from below "is associated with heterogeneity, diversity and bottom-up participatory politics" and it is "counter-hegemonic." See *Geopolitics and the Post-colonial: Rethinking North-South Relations* (Malden, MA: Blackwell, 2004), pp. 219 and 221.

10. On "flows and networks," see Colin Flint, "Geographies of Inclusion/ Exclusion," in Susan Cutter, Douglas Richardson, and Thomas Wilbanks, eds., *The Geographical Dimensions of Terrorism* (New York: Routledge, 2003), p. 55.

11. Peter Perdue, "Boundaries, Maps and Movement: Chinese, Russian, and Mongolian Empires in Early Modern Central Eurasia," *The International History*

Review, Vol. 20, No. 2 (June 1998):265 and Alexander Murphy, "The Space of Terror," in Cutter, et al., p. 47. A "revolution in military affairs" has reduced the importance of distance and topography. Geographer Peter Vujakovic refers specifically to the impact of long-range bombers, "smart" missiles, helicopters, and computer-based command-and-control functions, and his comments on such technological innovations may logically be related to the declining pertinence of borders as well. See "Mapping the War Zone: Cartography, Geopolitics and Security Discourse in the UK Press," *Journalism Studies,* Vol. 3, No. 2 (2002):191.

12. Trenin, pp. 104–105.

13. Michael Klare, *Resource Wars* (New York: Metropolitan/Owl Book, 2002), pp. 213–17.

14. James C. Bennett, *The Anglosphere Challenge* (Lanham, MD: Rowman and Littlefield, 2004), pp. 68, 75, 80, and 288.

15. On Toynbee, see Martin Lewis and Karen Wigen, *The Myth of Continents* (Berkeley: University of California Press, 1997), pp. 126–29.

16. See Newman, "Geopolitics Renaissant," p. 5; Gearoid O Tuathail, "De-Territorialised Threats and Global Dangers: Geopolitics and Risk Society," in Newman, p. 147; and Samuel Huntington, *The Clash of Civilizations* (New York: Touchstone, 1997), p. 28.

17. Fernand Braudel, *A History of Civilizations* (New York: Penguin, 1993), p. 9. This book was originally published in French in 1963.

18. Lewis and Wigen, p. 130 and Huntington, pp. 19 and 21. Huntington's initial article on a "clash of civilizations" appeared in the summer 1993 issue of *Foreign Affairs.*

19. For essays on cultural fluidity, see Matthew Melko and Leighton Scott, eds., *The Boundaries of Civilizations in Space and Time* (Lanham, MD: University Press of America, 1987).

20. Huntington's emphasis on cultural "fault lines" was strongly influenced by William Wallace's *The Transformation of Western Europe* (London: Pinter, 1990).

21. On the Medina analogy, see Graham Fuller, *The Future of Political Islam* (New York: Palgrave/Macmillan, 2003), p. 185.

22. *The Inevitability of the Clash of Civilisation* (London: Al-Khilafah, 2002).

23. Martha Brill Olcott and Bakhtiyar Babajanov, "The Terrorist Notebooks," *Foreign Policy,* No. 135 (March/April 2003):37 and 39.

24. International Crisis Group, "Central Asia: Islamist Mobilisation and Regional Security," http://iicas.org; http://www.hizb-ut-tahrir.org; and Khilafah. com. French scholar of Islamism Olivier Roy writes: "More than ever, al-Qaida militants have a global, non-territorial vision of jihad. Their goal is not to liberate the Middle East but to combat the world order as they see it." According to Roy, al-Qaida (al-Qaeda) is "deliberately out to provoke a clash of cultures." See *Le Monde Diplomatique,* August 2005, p. 5.

25. Luis Bush, "10/40 Window" April 1996, http://www.gmi.org/products/1040_g.pdf.

26. David Gress, *From Plato to NATO* (New York: The Free Press, 1998), pp. 121, 127 and 499. As East European states become members of NATO, they are identifying with the "West" and are abandoning their connection to

"Eastern Europe" and opting for one to "Central Europe." See Jason Dittmer, "NATO, the EU and Central Europe: Differing Symbolic Shapes in Newspaper Accounts of Enlargement," *Geopolitics*, Vol. 10, No. 1 (2005):93.

27. Huntington, pp. 158–59.

28. William Wallace, "Where does Europe end?" in Jan Zielonka, ed., *Europe Unbound* (London: Routledge, 2002), pp. 82, 89, and 93.

29. Robert M. Cutler, "Emerging Triangles: Russia-Kazakhstan-China," *Asia Times*, January 14, 2004. Russian geopolitical analysis, largely in remission under the communists, started to resurface during the eighties when Gorbachev emphasized "new thinking." It was the subject of a closed conference at the Ministry of Foreign Affairs in July 1988. See Milan Hauner, *What is Asia to Us?* (Boston: Unwin Hyman, 1990), p. 249.

30. Bat Yeor, "Eurabia: The Road to Munich," *The Israel Report*, October 2002 and James Pinkerton, "The Credible Hulks," http://www.techcentralstation.com/102303A.html.

31. Karl Meyer and Shareen Blair Brysac, *Tournament of Shadows* (Washington, D.C.: Counterpoint, 1999), p. 570; Charles Clover, "Dreams of the Eurasian Heartland," *Foreign Affairs*, Vol. 78, No. 2 (March/April 1999):10; and Andrei Tsygankov, "Mastering Space in Eurasia," http://bss.sfsu.edu/tsygankov/Research/RusEurasPap.htm. It is ironic that the "Heartland" concept has been revived in Russia at just the time that Russia has lost influence over neighboring areas due to the breakup of the Soviet Union.

32. Clover, pp. 9, 11, and 13 and Tsygankov.

33. John Gillies, *Shakespeare and the Geography of Difference* (Cambridge: Cambridge University Press, 1994), pp. 70–71 and 91–92; John Russell Brown, *Shakespeare and His Theatre* (Harmondsworth, UK: Kestrel, 1982), pp. 9–12; and John Rennie Short, *Making Space: Revisioning the World, 1475–1600* (Syracuse: Syracuse University Press, 2004), p. 154. Ortelius published the first atlas in 1570, but some collections of maps had appeared as early as 1550 under the editorship of a Frenchman, Antoine Lafrere. He had moved to Rome and adopted the name Antonio Lafreri. Lafrere, or Lafreri, was not a cartographer, but he assembled maps into volumes. Books of this type are often not recognized as atlases because the maps are not standardized in size or scale. It is possible that Lafrere originated the symbol of Atlas holding a globe, but confirmed credit goes to Mercator, who definitely placed the Atlas on the frontispiece of the initial volume of his "atlas" published in 1585. We therefore have come to know a map collection as an "atlas." Note, however, that Mercator's Atlas was not the Greek Titan, but rather a mythological King of Mauretania associated with the region around Morocco. See Peter Barber, *The Map Book* (New York: Walker, 2005), p.154 and Paul Binding, *Imagined Corners* (London: Headline Book Publishing, 2003), p. 85. Ortelius' *Theatrum Orbis Terrarum* was not referred to as an "atlas" when originally issued. An interesting sidelight to Ortelius' *Theatrum* is that he sent a copy to King Philip II of Spain. Diego Cardinal Espinosa y Arevalo then became upset that his hometown of Martin Munoz de las Posadas did not appear, so Ortelius apologized in a letter to the Cardinal. When a new edition was published in 1573, Martin Munoz de las Posadas was included. See Cornelis Koeman, *The History of Abraham Ortelius and his Theatrum Orbis Terrarum* (New York: American Elsevier, 1964), pp. 36–37.

34. See Barry Lopez, *Arctic Dreams* (New York: Charles Scribner's Sons, 1986), p. 279.

35. Ann Blair, *The Theater of Nature: Jean Bodin and Renaissance Science* (Princeton: Princeton University Press, 1997), p. 153.

36. William Riker, *The Art of Political Manipulation* (New Haven: Yale University Press, 1986), ix-xi and 142.

37. U.S. satellite photographs from the 1960–62 Corona program significantly aided American military cartography as information from the photographs of Soviet installations could be incorporated into maps. See Philip Taubman, *Secret Empire* (New York: Simon and Schuster, 2003), p. 326.

38. Nigel Holmes, *Pictorial Maps* (New York: Watson-Guptill, 1991), pp. 13, 129, 141, 160, and 163. Satellites have been described as the "new explorers," using remote sensing rather than direct observation. See Malcolm Douglass, *The History, Psychology, and Pedagogy of Geographic Literacy* (Westport, CT Praeger, 1998), pp. 106–107.

39. Kathleen Hall Jamieson and Paul Waldman, *The Press Effect* (Oxford: Oxford University Press, 2003), xii, xiv, and 197 and Robert Entman, "Framing: Toward Clarification of a Fractured Paradigm," *Journal of Communication*, Vol. 43, No. 4 (Autumn 1993):51–53.

40. For a discussion of professional choices made by journalists, see Jamieson and Waldman, p. 170.

Index

About the Author

ARTHUR JAY KLINGHOFFER is Professor of Political Science at Rutgers University in Camden, New Jersey. He is the author of numerous books on a variety of subjects, among them, human rights, genocide, Soviet Communism, South African apartheid, and the politics of oil and gold.